GW01271872

PRAISE FOR *THE CATH*

"In this new and compelling book, Fr. Lane makes it clear from the witness of the Scriptures that Jesus, himself High Priest of a New Covenant, intended to form a priestly people and to establish a priesthood in accord with that New Covenant. This book will assist both the baptized in understanding more deeply their royal priesthood and the ordained in appropriating the full richness of their call to serve the Body of Christ *in persona Christi capitis.*"

—Most Rev. Kevin C. Rhoades,
Bishop of Fort Wayne-South Bend

"For years I have wanted an up-to-date and robustly *biblical* analysis of the priesthood that I could assign to seminarians. Fr. Lane's *The Catholic Priesthood: Biblical Foundations* fills a major lacuna. It covers an impressively wide range of topics and incorporates fresh insights from recent exegesis in a faithful and illuminating way."

—Brant Pitre,
Professor of Sacred Scripture,
Notre Dame Seminary

"Fr. Lane unveils through his study the superabundance of the biblical record for Christological, liturgical, sacramental, and spiritual theology. In short, he has answered the call of Pope Emeritus Benedict XVI to make biblical study properly theological, and theology return to the Bible as its 'soul.'"

—John D. Love,
Associate Professor of Systematic and Moral Theology,
Department Chair of Moral Theology,
Mount St. Mary's Seminary

THE CATHOLIC PRIESTHOOD

BIBLICAL FOUNDATIONS

THE CATHOLIC PRIESTHOOD

BIBLICAL FOUNDATIONS

FR. THOMAS J. LANE

EMMAUS ROAD
PUBLISHING

Steubenville, Ohio
www.emmausroad.org

Emmaus Road Publishing
1468 Parkview Circle
Steubenville, Ohio 43952

Library of Congress Control Number: 2016945832
ISBN: 978-1-941447-93-2

Cover images: Christ washes His disciples' feet, Basilica
Cattedrale di Santa Maria Nuova di Monreale in Sicily,
12th century.

Jesus Christ Pancreator, Hagia Sofia

Cover design and layout by Margaret Ryland

To all priests of Jesus Christ

TABLE OF CONTENTS

ABBREVIATIONS xv

INTRODUCTION xvii

CHAPTER 1: OLD TESTAMENT PRIESTHOOD 1

Worship of God before the Institution of
the Levitical Priesthood 3

Establishment of the Levitical Priesthood 5

Ordination of the High Priest and the Priests 5

Levites Set Apart for Service of the Lord 8

Holiness Demanded of the Priests 10

God was the Levites' Portion and Cup 11

Duties of Levitical Priests 12

The Levitical Priests' Duty to Keep the People
Conscious of Being a Priestly People 12

The Priests' Duty to Discern God's Will 14

The Priests' Duty to Teach the Torah 15

The Priests' Duty to Offer Sacrifice 15

Priests' Other Sacred Duties 16

Discontent with the Levitical Priesthood and Hopes for
Renewal 18

Prophetic Critique of the Levitical Priesthood 18

Hopes for a Renewed Priesthood 20

Some Echoes in Catholic Liturgy 25

CHAPTER 2: THE PRIESTHOOD OF CHRIST 29

Indications of Christ's Priesthood in the Gospels 31

The Temple and Its Liturgies Are Transfigured
in Jesus 31

Jesus Understands Psalms Fulfilled in Himself 35

Jesus Prays as High Priest in John 17 37

Sacrificial Language during the Last Supper........................38

Jesus' Seamless Robe 40

Jesus' Priestly Death...42

Jesus' Priestly Blessing 43

The Priesthood of Christ in the Letter to the
Hebrews 44

Hebrews 1–2 45

Christ a Merciful and Trustworthy High Priest
Like His Brothers in Every Respect (2:17–18)........................46

Jesus Our Trustworthy High Priest (3:1–4:14)......................48

Jesus Our Merciful High Priest (4:15–5:10) 49

Christ a Priest after the Order of Melchizedek
(Hebrews 7) 55

Superiority of Christ's Sacrifice, the New Covenant,
and Christ's Priestly Ministry in Heaven
(Hebrews 8–9) 60

Salvific Effects of Christ's Priestly
Sacrifice (Hebrews 10)..66

Jewish Tradition and Yom Kippur................................68

Christ's Priesthood 69

Theology of Hebrews in Catholic Liturgy 70

CHAPTER 3: JESUS CALLED TWELVE APOSTLES OUT
OF HIS MANY DISCIPLES AND CONSECRATED
THEM..73

Jesus Called Twelve Apostles out of the Many
Disciples 75

Mark 3:13–19...75

Luke 6:12–16..78

Matthew 10:1–4...79

John 6:66–71..81

The Twelve and the Restoration of Israel............................82

The Lists of the Twelve...83

The Twelve Apostles as Agents of Jesus 83

The Primacy of Saint Peter 86

   Peter the Rock, on whom Jesus builds his Church,
   is given the keys (Matt 16:18–19) 86

   Simon, strengthen your brothers (Luke 22:32) 91

   Simon, do you love me? (John 21:15–17) 93

   Succession 95

First Experimental Mission of the Twelve 98

   Mark 6:7–13, 30–31 99

   Luke 9:1–6 100

   Matthew 10:5–15 100

The Seventy(-Two) (Luke 10:1–20) 101

Consecration of the Twelve During
the Last Supper 107

   Washing of the Feet (John 13) 108

   The Apostles Are Consecrated in Truth as Priests
   of the New Covenant (John 17:17–19) 109

   Do This in Memory of Me 114

The Authority to Forgive Sins (John 20:19–23) 115

Commissioned to Preach, Teach, and Baptize 116

The Apostles Continue Jesus' Ministry after
Pentecost 119

   Reconstitution of the Twelve Apostles
   before Pentecost 119

   The Twelve Receive the Holy Spirit at Pentecost 120

   The Apostles' Ministry after Pentecost 120

Christ's Intention to Form a New Priesthood of
the New Covenant 122

Resonances in Catholic Liturgy 123

CHAPTER 4: APOSTLES, OVERSEERS, PRESBYTERS,
AND DEACONS IN THE EARLY CHURCH 127

The Apostles Are Assisted by Presbyters,
Overseers, and Deacons 130

Presbyters 130

Overseers 135

Deacons 137

Earlier Fluidity in the Designations of
Church Leaders 141

PAUL CALLED TO BE AN APOSTLE 143

Is Acts 13:1–3 Paul's Consecration for Ministry? 146

PAUL A NEW COVENANT MINISTER 152

Paul's Consciousness of His Vocation—
An Apostle 152

Paul's Consciousness of His Vocation—
Priestly Consciousness 153

Applying Priestly Language to the Apostles
and Paul 160

LEADERS IN THE CHURCHES FOUNDED BY PAUL 162

Overseers and Deacons in Philippi (Phil 1:1) 163

Caring Leaders in Thessalonica over Them in the
Lord (1 Thes 5:12) 163

Stephanas and Others in Corinth 164

Presbyters/Overseers in Ephesus 165

Leaders in Churches not Founded by Paul 165

Paul Regards Church Leadership to Be
Divinely Planned 165

PASTORAL EPISTLES—REQUIREMENTS FOR OVERSEERS,
PRESBYTERS, AND DEACONS 166

Overseers (1 Tim 3:1–7) 167

Presbyters (1 Tim 5:17–22; Tit 1:5–9) 168

Deacons (1 Tim 3:8–13) 169

Developing Church Governance 170

LAYING ON OF HANDS 172

Old Testament 172

New Testament 173

Succession.. 176

Ministry Received from Christ.............................. 179

POST NEW TESTAMENT.. 180

CATHOLIC LITURGICAL TEXTS 183

A Bishop, Priests, and Deacons 183

Enquiry among the People of God and
Recommendation... 183

The Presbyterate 184

Laying on of Hands during Ordination.............. 185

Prayer of Ordination 186

CHAPTER 5: PRIESTLY PEOPLE 189

LIVING STONES IN A PRIESTLY HOUSE (1 PET 2:5)...... 190

ROYAL PRIESTHOOD UNDER JESUS THE
KING (1 PET 2:9)... 192

MADE PRIESTS BY CHRIST (REV 1:4–6)........................ 192

MADE PRIESTS BY CHRIST'S BLOOD (REV 5:9–10) 194

MARTYRS SHALL BE PRIESTS (REV 20:6) 194

OTHER TEXTS INTIMATING THE PRIESTHOOD OF
CHRISTIANS.. 195

PRIESTHOOD OF THE FAITHFUL IN THE LITURGY........ 196

CONCLUSION 199

APPENDIX 1: MELCHIZEDEK AND SHEM.................... 205

APPENDIX 2: OLD TESTAMENT ORDINATION
LITURGY... 207

APPENDIX 3: QUMRAN ON THE RENEWED
PRIESTHOOD... 211

APPENDIX 4: BROTHERS AND SISTERS OF JESUS........ 213

APPENDIX 5: THE TWELVE APOSTLES......................... 217

GLOSSARY 223

WORKS CITED... 227

BIBLICAL INDEX.. 241

ABBREVIATIONS

AThr	*Anglican Theological Review*
Bib	*Biblica*
CBQ	*Catholic Biblical Quarterly*
JBL	*Journal of Biblical Literature*
JPS	Jewish Publication Society
JSHJ	*Journal for the Study of the Historical Jesus*
JSJ	*Journal for the Study of Judaism in the Persian, Hellenistic and Roman Period*
JSOTSup	Journal for the Study of the Old Testament Supplement Series
JSPSS	Journal for the Study of the Pseudepigrapha Supplement Series
NRTh	*La nouvelle revue théologique*
NTS	*New Testament Studies*
RB	*Revue biblique*
ScEccl	*Sciences ecclésiastiques*
WUNT	Wissenschaftliche Untersuchungen zum Neuen Testament

INTRODUCTION

CHRIST CALLED MANY DISCIPLES and chose twelve of those disciples to be apostles. Christ consecrated them during the Last Supper (John 17:17). Christ is the truth (John 14:6), and by their consecration in truth (John 17:17) they received everything from Christ. They would not offer anything of their own during their ministry because everything they gave in ministry came from their consecration by Christ. Their ministry would be an extension of Christ's ministry. They would be joined by overseers (later called bishops) and presbyters (later called priests) to assist them in ministering, and also by deacons. Around the end of the first century a hierarchical structure as we have today is visible; one overseer leading a college of presbyters in a local church assisted by deacons. It would be about another century before we have documentation of priestly language being applied to overseers by Tertullian. The first extant account of a liturgy that we have from the early Church for the ordination of bishops, priests, and deacons is in *The Apostolic Tradition* attributed to St. Hippolytus, dated to the early third century.

What took place during the first two centuries of the Church, the application of priestly language to its ministers and the development of a hierarchical structure, was making explicit what was already there from the beginning. The word "development" is used with a caveat: it is development in the sense of maturation of what was already implicit. Christ had given the apostles everything they had for ministry. The beginning of the Church is something living that matures. Joseph Ratzinger puts it this way: "The purification of Christianity, the search for its original essence, is carried on today, in the era of historical consciousness, almost entirely by seeking its oldest forms and establishing them as normative. The original is confused with the primitive. By contrast, the faith of the Church sees in these beginnings something living that conforms to its own constitution only insofar as it *develops*."[1] It is not only in the priesthood that we see something living maturing. We see this also, for example, in the great Christological councils that, in reaction to heresies, had to use non-biblical terminology to define the Incarnation ever more precisely—for example, the Council of Nicaea in AD 325 used the Greek word *homoousios* in response to the Arian heresy denying the divinity of Christ to state that Christ was of the same substance of the Father. The synthesis of doctrine that arose during that council is known as the Nicene Creed. The Council of Chalcedon in AD 451 used the terminology "hypostatic union" to explain the two natures of Christ, human and divine, in one person, each retaining their own characteristics. This is the last council accepted by all the main Protestant churches. Centuries had to pass, until this council, to see the full implications of Christ and what the Sacred Scriptures contained.[2] But the development of a priestly hierarchy, and the application to it of priestly language, had taken place three and a half and two and a half centuries beforehand, respectively. Much less time was needed—only until the end of the second century—to see that Christ established New Covenant priests when calling and consecrating the twelve apostles, and that it was legitimate to designate as "priests" those who ministered in the name of Christ in succession to those chosen by Christ and those who ministered in collaboration with them.

No one would apply the term "priest" either to Christ or his apostles at the time of Christ because priesthood meant belonging to the

---

[1]   Joseph Ratzinger, *Daughter Zion: Meditations on the Church's Marian Belief,* trans. John M. McDermott (San Francisco: Ignatius Press, 1983), 38.

[2]   For more on the unfolding of the implications of Christ in later doctrine, see Jared Wicks, *Doing Theology* (Mahwah, NJ: Paulist Press, 2009), 69–76.

tribe of Levi and offering sacrificed animals on the altar in the temple. Clearly neither Christ nor his apostles were from the priestly tribe of Levi, and they were unrelated to the temple sacrificial liturgies. A new understanding of priesthood had to grow, the understanding that Christ's death on the Cross was his own priestly self-sacrifice, the one priestly sacrifice of the New Covenant, and that he shared his priesthood with the apostles. This study is an examination of the Scriptural evidence showing that it was indeed Christ's intention to establish the New Covenant priesthood. The objective is to show that the Catholic priesthood has biblical foundations and was intended by Christ, even though apostles, overseers, and presbyters are not called priests in the New Testament, but approximately two centuries later. As Cardinal Donald Wuerl states, "a gradual development or clarification of priestly functions does not mean that such functions came into being later in the life of the Church. When we state that the designation by name of a particular office required time, we are not necessarily saying that the office and work do not exist from the beginning of the life of the Church."[3]

Chapter 1 examines Israelite priesthood for the context necessary to understand the priesthood of Christ. Initially, firstborn sons functioned as priests. But from the time of the covenant at Sinai, the Old Testament depicts God bestowing the priesthood on and confining it to men in the tribe of Levi descended from Aaron. This Levitical priesthood had a hierarchy; the high priest descended from Aaron, the other priests, and the remainder of the tribe of Levi. The ordination of the high priest and priests climaxed in their anointing with oil. The high priesthood was to be passed on in a direct line of succession from father to son. Priests had three main duties—to discern God's will, teach the Torah, and offer sacrifice—that could perhaps be summarized as reminding all God's people of their priestly dignity according to Exodus 19:6. As the centuries passed, discontent with the priesthood grew, evident above all in the prophets' critiques of the priesthood. Biblical texts and non-biblical texts alike looked forward to a renewed priesthood. These hopes were fulfilled in Christ, whom the second chapter will show is the high priest of the New Covenant.

Chapter 2 shows that Jesus was a high priest, though of a different kind from the Levitical high priest. Some Gospel passages could

---

3   Donald W. Wuerl, *The Catholic Priesthood Today* (Chicago: Franciscan Herald Press, 1976), 161.

be taken to imply that Jesus is a priest, though not of the tribe of Levi. When Christ preaches in the temple and suggests the temple liturgies—for example, Tabernacles and Dedication/Hanukah will be fulfilled, or better, transfigured in him—this has implications for the Levitical priesthood and suggests its days of service in the temple are numbered because God has something much better in store. When Jesus cleanses the temple, driving out the animal sellers and money-changers, he alludes to his resurrected body replacing the temple (John 2:19, 21). During the Last Supper Jesus prays as high priest in John 17. A case can be made that Jesus goes to Calvary wearing a seamless robe because it symbolizes Jesus' priesthood, since the temple high priest wore a seamless robe. Jesus ascends to heaven, in Luke, raising his hands in blessing just like a priest.

The second part of chapter 2 examines the Letter to the Hebrews, the only New Testament document to describe Jesus as high priest. The Letter describes Jesus' death in a novel way, like no other New Testament book, as a liturgy, the Yom Kippur/Day of Atonement liturgy. Yom Kippur was the only day in the year when the Jewish high priest entered the Holy of Holies sprinkling blood to atone for sins. When Christ the high priest of the New Covenant died, he took his blood not into the Holy of Holies in the temple in Jerusalem like the high priest once a year, but into the heavenly sanctuary to gain salvation for us. Christ's death was his self-sacrifice that brought his priesthood to its perfect realization. Christ's sacrifice was effective once for all time, and the superiority of his sacrifice made him the mediator of the New Covenant. Christ's death opened the way for us to enter God's sanctuary, and Hebrews invites us to enter through the flesh and blood of Jesus. The Eucharist is the way for us to enter the heavenly sanctuary, the true Holy of Holies. Hebrews describes Christ as a priest many times. This is not metaphorical. For Hebrews, it is the Levitical priesthood that is a metaphor/shadow of Christ's priesthood.

Following on from chapter 2 showing Jesus is the high priest of the New Covenant, chapter 3 shows Jesus sharing his priesthood with the apostles. Christ specially prepared the twelve apostles to continue his ministry. Jesus called the twelve apostles out of the disciples (Luke 6:13). Mark tells us Jesus "created" twelve (Mark 3:14). It is depicted as a second calling following their first calling to be disciples. The Twelve can be understood in terms of the Jewish idea of agency whereby the agent acted with the authority of the one who sent him and was his representative. Christ gave Peter primacy over the Twelve symbolized by the language of keys and binding and loosing. Jesus sent the Twelve on a mission with his same powers, and they preached, worked miracles, and exorcised as Jesus did. Their ministry was an extension of Jesus' ministry. The seventy(-two) disciples sent out in Luke 10 anticipate the presbyters who will assist the apostles in Acts. Jesus consecrated the apostles during the Last Supper (John 17:17) and gave them the authority to offer the Eucharist ("Do this in memory of me" in Luke 22:19 and 1 Cor 11:24), and after his Resurrection, he also gave them the authority to forgive sins in the name of God and commissioned them to preach, teach, and baptize. Christ had a specific intention when choosing the Twelve: to empower them to lead the new worship in spirit and truth (John 4:23) of the New Covenant. The apostles continued the ministry of Jesus after Pentecost.

Chapter 4 examines many others also ministering in the name of Jesus, assisting the apostles. The New Testament designates the assistants in Jerusalem "presbyters," corresponding to the Hebrew word for "elders" in Judaism. Clement of Rome tells us the apostles appointed presbyters and he gives the impression some of them were still alive as he wrote. The apostles also chose deacons to assist them. The word *episkopos* (ἐπίσκοπος), "overseer," (from which our word "bishop" is indirectly derived) began to be used in Gentile Christianity for its leaders, but "overseer" and "presbyter" continued to be used interchangeably for some time without indicating different rank. Paul, who termed himself an apostle, became the apostle to the Gentiles. Acts 13:1–3 is at least a blessing bestowed on Paul and Barnabas for ministry and much more likely to be their consecration for ministry. Every new mission in the early Church preserved its link with the apostles in Jerusalem, and Paul also preserved that link and unity with the Church in Jerusalem by reporting back after each of his missionary journeys. Luke tells us Paul appointed leaders in every church. In Paul's letters, we also see leaders in his churches, though there is fluidity in their designations at first. Throughout this study I use "Church" for the Church universal and "church" for a local church, for example a church established by Paul. An examination of Paul's writings displays what could be described as his "priestly" consciousness. In Catholic theology we talk of the apostles being ordained priests by Christ during the Last Supper. If we can talk of the apostles as priests, can we not also talk of Paul as a priest? The Pastoral Letters show a development as now it is "the overseer" and presbyters and deacons. This is anticipating the post-New Testament development of the threefold rank with which we are familiar, a bishop leading a college of presbyters in a local church assisted by deacons. The Pastoral Letters give more attention to Church leaders than any other book of the New Testament as they list the necessary qualities in an overseer, presbyters, and deacons. The laying on of hands is the means whereby mission is transferred; the apostles laid hands on the seven new deacons and Paul laid hands on Timothy. Either explicitly or implicitly, the laying on of hands is usually stated to also confer the Holy Spirit.

Chapter 5 concludes this study by showing that God's promise in Exodus 19:6 that Israel would be a priestly people is fulfilled when Christians are baptized. Five New Testament texts declare all Christians priestly and show how they exercise this priesthood: 1 Peter 2:5; 1 Peter 2:9; Revelation 1:4–6; Revelation 5:9–10; and Revelation 20:6. The priestly people precede the ministerial priests; the apostles were disciples before they were called a second time to be apostles. The two priesthoods are intimately connected since both are a response to Christ and bound together. The ministerial priesthood is serving the priestly people, and the priestly people receive the sacraments from the ministerial priesthood.

Each chapter concludes with an examination of relevant liturgical texts from the Roman Missal or the Roman Pontifical showing how the Scripture examined in that chapter, or the theology of that chapter, is reflected in the liturgical texts. By the end of this study, my hope is that I will have demonstrated that a hierarchical structure in the Church around the turn of the first century, and the application of priestly language to the Church's ministers a century or more later, was making explicit what was already there from the beginning. Christ had given the apostles everything necessary for ministry and we see this unfolding gradually in the ministry of the apostles, and of their successors and assistants in subsequent decades and centuries.

CHAPTER 1

OLD TESTAMENT PRIESTHOOD

W E BEGIN BY EXAMINING the Old Testament priesthood because it gives a necessary context to the New Covenant priesthood, helping us see the novelty in the New Covenant priesthood. There is both continuity and discontinuity between the Old and New Testament. The discontinuity is seen above all in the priests of the tribe of Levi, the Levitical priests, having to continually offer sacrifices for sins whereas the one sacrifice of Christ on the Cross suffices for all time. When expressing the continuity between the Old and New Testament we often use the terminology of "fulfillment." The Levitical priesthood was fulfilled in Christ, in his self-sacrifice on the Cross, his priestly sacrifice. Sometimes we also use the term "transcended" and say the Levitical priesthood is transcended in Christ's priesthood. There is merit to Paolo Prosperi's suggestion that "transfiguration" is an appropriate term to describe this continuity and discontinuity between the Old and New Testament:

> The biblical idea of fulfillment thus implies an interplay between continuity and rupture, such that the words we use to refer to the Old Testament figures and to the mystery of

Christ who fulfills them can be the same, while at the same time their meaning is transformed. Perhaps the least inappropriate theological term we can use to indicate this complex phenomenon of transignification is transfiguration, if by this we mean a change of aspect that does not damage the exterior form of the reality illuminated, but rather exalts it, conferring on it a splendor that radiates from within and that had remained hidden within its depths before rising to the surface.[1]

Thus, we could say that the Levitical priesthood is transfigured in the priesthood of Christ.

The Old Testament depicts three ranks in the tribe of Levi: high priest, priest, and Levite, but these are to be seen transfigured or fulfilled in Christ and not in the three ranks of bishops, priests, and deacons. Joseph Ratzinger writes, "The absolute claim of Jesus Christ means that the types of the Old Testament are to be interpreted in reference to him, not to the minister who is the temporary incumbent of an office."[2] The three ranks in the New Covenant of bishop, priest, and deacon are a participation in the one priesthood of Jesus Christ that transfigures the Levitical priesthood. The transfiguration of Levitical priests into the New Covenant priesthood will be all the clearer when we examine the Letter to the Hebrews in the next chapter. There is certainly a typological relationship between the three ranks of Old Covenant priesthood and the three ranks of New Covenant priesthood in that the high priest is a typological foreshadowing of a bishop, a Levitical priest is a typological anticipation of a priest, and a Levite is a typological prefiguring of a deacon, but the ranks in the priesthood of Levi are actually transfigured only in Christ. We will return to this at the end of this chapter. That "for many liberal Protestant theologians and commentators in the nineteenth and early twentieth century, and residually up to the present, the Israelite priesthood embodied all that they found dis-

---

[1]   Paolo Prosperi, "Novum in Vetere Latet. Vetus in Novo Patet: Towards a Renewal of Typological Exegesis," *Communio: International Catholic Review* 37 (2010): 396.

[2]   Joseph Ratzinger, *Principles of Catholic Theology: Building Stones for a Fundamental Theology*, trans. Mary Frances McCarthy (San Francisco: Ignatius Press, 1987), 282.

tasteful in contemporary Roman Catholicism or Judaism or both"[3] betrays a misunderstanding of Catholic priesthood. Catholic priesthood is not simply a continuation of Levitical priesthood, nor is it Jewish priesthood under a revised form. It is a new creation, whose discontinuity is captured by the term transfiguration, as we will see in subsequent chapters. Indeed, the misapprehension among non-Catholics that there are no priests in the New Testament except Christ, because New Covenant ministers are not yet called priests in the New Testament, reflects the element of discontinuity in the transfiguration of the Old Covenant priesthood into the New Covenant priesthood.

Worship of God before the Institution of the Levitical Priesthood

The firstborn son had a unique role in Israel. There is much evidence to show that the firstborn son, once he became the father of his own family, performed the role of priest in the family prior to the Levitical priesthood.[4] (Judg 17:10 links the role of father and priest.) In Numbers 3:11–13, we see the firstborn had a special position in Israel before the priesthood of the Levites replaced the priesthood of the firstborn. The firstborn received the blessing from his father and in turn bestowed this blessing on his firstborn before his death.[5] Isaac intended to give his blessing to Esau, his firstborn (Gen 27:4), but unknowingly gave it to Jacob instead (Gen 27:18–29). However, this birthright to receive the father's blessing could be lost (as in the case of Esau in Gen 27:5–38 and Reuben in Gen 49:3–4), but once the father had blessed his son, the blessing could not be revoked, as in the case of Isaac, who received his father's blessing instead of Esau by

---

[3]   Joseph Blenkinsopp, *Sage, Priest, Prophet: Religious and Intellectual Leadership in Ancient Israel* (Louisville, KY: Westminster John Knox Press, 1995), 67.

[4]   Scott W. Hahn, *Kinship by Covenant: A Canonical Approach to the Fulfillment of God's Saving Promises*, Anchor Yale Bible Reference Library (New Haven, CT/London: Yale University Press, 2009), 136–142.

[5]   On the power of this blessing, see Johannes Pedersen, *Israel: Its Life and Culture* (London: Oxford University Press, 1926), 1:199–200.

deception (Gen 27:30–38).[6] For more on the priesthood of Shem as firstborn, see Appendix 1.

The firstborn offered sacrifice. Abel offered sacrifice in Genesis 4:4, Noah in Genesis 8:20, Abraham in Genesis 22:13, and Jacob in Genesis 31:54, and again in 46:1, after he had been renamed as Israel. L. Ginzberg, who compiled the Aggadot from the Mishnah, the two Talmuds and Midrash into *Legends of the Jews*, wrote that, before entering the ark, Noah functioned as a priest when offering sacrifice. His son Shem performed the priestly duties after leaving the ark because Noah was injured by a hungry beast on the ark and, suffering from a defect, was unable to offer sacrifice as a priest.[7] Another example is Abraham being asked by God to sacrifice his son Isaac (Gen 22:2), which entailed Abraham acting as a priest. In the Aggadot, Abraham asked, "Am I fit to perform the sacrifice, am I a priest? Ought not rather the high priest Shem to do it?" to which God responded, "When thou wilt arrive at that place, I will consecrate thee and make thee a priest."[8]

Not only the firstborn, but also occasionally the king in the early years of the monarchy, as father of the nation, performed the priestly act of offering sacrifice (e.g., 1 Sam 13:9; 2 Sam 6:17; 1 Kings 9:25). However, "in the legal normative literature, which has its roots in the premonarchic period . . . the king has no function in the cult."[9] Samuel rebuked Saul in 1 Samuel 13:13 for the sacrifice he had offered in 1 Samuel 13:9. The last reference to the firstborn serving as priests is Exodus 19:22, 24, according to Jewish commentators.[10] After the golden calf incident, the priesthood was restricted to the tribe

---

[6]   Since that blessing was received by deception, it is confirmed later by a second blessing in Genesis 28. Jacob/Israel in turn gave his blessing to his grandson Ephraim, the son of Joseph (Gen 48:17–20). This displeased Joseph, since Manasseh was Joseph's firstborn, not Ephraim. Jacob/Israel gave this blessing to his grandson because the actions of his son Reuben had forfeited it (Gen 49:3–4).

[7]   Louis Ginzberg, Henrietta Szold, and Paul Radin, *Legends of the Jews*, 2nd ed. (Philadelphia, PA: Jewish Publication Society, 2003), 149–150.

[8]   Ibid., 225.

[9]   Moshe Weinfeld, *Deuteronomy 1–11: A New Translation with Introduction and Commentary*, Anchor Yale Bible 5 (New Haven, CT/London: Yale University Press, 2008), 422.

[10]   Nahum M. Sarna, *Exodus*, The JPS Torah Commentary (Philadelphia, PA: Jewish Publication Society, 1991), 107.

of Levi by divine decree (Num 3:11, 40–51; 8:16). "After the golden calf episode, and probably because the Israelite firstborn sons were involved in the idolatrous worship, these priestly tasks became the exclusive responsibility of the Levites."[11]

Establishment of the Levitical Priesthood

Old Testament scholarship believes the origin and development of priesthood in the tribe of Levi is much more complex than the biblical account. Critical scholarship considers that the depiction of the Levitical priesthood in the Old Testament reflects how it was centuries later rather than how it historically evolved. The issue is a minefield, and no critical reconstruction of the historical development of the Israelite priesthood has won the approval of all, and every reconstruction is at best very tentative.[12] It is beyond the purpose of this study, which is primarily concerned with the priesthood of Christ and his New Covenant ministers, to get involved in historical reconstructions that would remain hypothetical at best. With this limitation, we will examine the biblical account of the institution of the priesthood in the tribe of Levi, as it gives us the theology of the Levitical priesthood.

Ordination of the High Priest and the Priests

The instructions for the ordination of the high priest and priests are given by God to Moses in Exodus 28–29 and carried out during the ordinations in Leviticus 8. The directives are included in a long list of liturgical commands Moses receives from God following the covenant at Sinai (Exod 25–31). Aaron and his sons are to serve as priests (Exod 28:1). The ordination of the first high priest, Aaron, occurs simultaneously with the ordination of his sons as priests. The ordi-

---

[11]   Scott W. Hahn, *The Kingdom of God as Liturgical Empire: A Theological Commentary on 1-2 Chronicles* (Grand Rapids, MI: Baker Academic, 2012), 36.

[12]   Critical scholarship generally believes that, at first, the priesthood was not limited only to the tribe of Levi, but was confined to the Levites after some centuries and later again further limited to those Levites descended only from Aaron.

nation instructions do not specifically declare that Aaron is the first high priest; that designation makes its first appearance later (Lev 21:10; Num 35:25), but Aaron is certainly singled out for special attention by comparison with his sons. For a fuller account of the ordination, see Appendix 2.

The most important part of the ordination instructions given to Moses is at the conclusion, the sprinkling of the priests and their garments with the anointing oil mixed with blood gathered up after scattering it on the altar (Exod 29:21; Lev 8:30). Both Exodus 29:21 and Leviticus 8:30 say it is this action that consecrates Aaron and his garments, and his sons and their garments. However, the difference between the high priest and the other priests is that Aaron, the high priest, received a special anointing on his head (Exod 29:7; Lev 8:12), but not his sons. Leviticus 8:12 refers to this anointing as consecrating Aaron.

The high priest wore four additional vestments not worn by the other priests (Exod 28; see also Appendix 2). So there are two distinguishing elements in the ordination of the high priest: vestments and anointing. This reflects the different duties expected of the high priest and the other priests. All priests had the duty of offering sacrifice every day but only the high priest could enter the Holy of Holies and only once a year on the Day of Atonement/Yom Kippur.

We read about prophets being specially called by God (e.g., Amos 7:14–15) but not the priests, since the priesthood, so to speak, ran in the family. The males descended from Aaron were automatically priests. For that reason, Old Testament priesthood has been described as an office rather than a vocation.[13] The number of priests increased with the passing of time as the number of descendants of Aaron increased, so that by the time of King David, priests were divided into twenty four divisions, with each division serving twice a year (1 Chron 24:1–19). By the time of Christ, there were so many priests that each priest would have the honor of burning incense in the Holy Place only once in his lifetime (like Zechariah in Luke 1:9).[14]

---

[13]   Roland de Vaux, *Ancient Israel: Its Life and Institutions* (New York: McGraw-Hill, 1961), 346.

[14]   Darrell L. Bock, *Luke*, vol. 1, *1:1–9:50*, Baker Exegetical Commentary on the New Testament (Grand Rapids, MI: Baker Academic, 1994), 79.

Succession of High Priests

The high priesthood was passed to one of the sons of the high priest, usually to his firstborn though that has been debated. Thus Eleazar, the son of Aaron, became high priest after the death of Aaron in Numbers 20:25–29 (see Deuteronomy 10:6),[15] and his son Phinehas, grandson of Aaron, is the next high priest (Josh 24:33 and Judg 20:28). Succession in a direct line was important for the high priest as is clear from the genealogies of high priests. The Hebrew Scriptures provide us with five genealogies of high priests: 1 Chronicles 5:29–41 (6:3–15 in some English translations), 6:35–38 (6:50–53 in some English translations), and 9:11, Ezra 7:1–5, and Nehemiah 11:10–11, the most extensive being the first one in Chronicles.[16] First Chronicles lists the high priests using a formula beginning in 5:30 (6:4): X was the father of Y, Eleazar was the father of Phinehas, Phinehas the father of Abishua and so forth. Since the genealogy of high priests in 1 Chronicles 5:29–41 is the most extensive, obviously the other four lists are incomplete. Still, they make the point that for the high priesthood a direct line of descent was expected. The omissions from the list in Ezra 7:1–5 have been considered accidental.[17] There have been suggestions that the line of succession was broken when King David appointed Zadok as high priest (1 Kings 2:35), due to confusion over his genealogy in 1 Samuel. However, 1 Chronicles 5:29–34 (6:3–8) traces Zadok's descent from Aaron's high priestly line of succession through Eleazor, Aaron's son. 1 Chronicles 6:35–38 (6:50–53) also puts Zadok in a direct line of descent from Aaron. Furthermore, recent research indicates that, early in the second century BC, being a Zadokite meant belonging to the family of high priests.[18] The direct line of succession of Aaronic high priests was broken when Jason, the brother of the legitimate high priest Onias III, bribed the new Syrian ruler over Palestine, Antiochus IV Epiphanes, to appoint him as high priest instead in 175 BC (2 Macc 4:7). A few years after being

---

[15]   Eleazar was Aaron's third son, but the first two were killed in Leviticus 10:1–2. They had used profane coals for the censer instead of coals taken from an altar.

[16]   For a comparison of the five genealogies, see Roddy L. Braun, *1 Chronicles*, Word Biblical Commentary 14 (Dallas, TX: Word, 2002), 84–85.

[17]   H. G. M. Willamson, *Ezra-Nehemiah*, Word Biblical Commentary 16 (Dallas, TX: Word, 2002), 91–92.

[18]   Geza Vermes, *Scrolls, Scriptures, and Early Christianity*, Library of Second Temple Studies 56 (London/New York: T&T Clark, 2005), 32.

deposed, the legitimate high priest Onias III was murdered. The cutting off of an anointed one in Daniel 9:26 and the sweeping away of a prince of the covenant in Daniel 11:22 are usually understood to refer to his murder around 171 BC (2 Macc 4:30–38). Until this time the high priest had served in office until death, but that also came to an end at this time. In 172 BC, Menelaus, not even from a high priestly family or the tribe of Levi but from the tribe of Benjamin,[19] succeeded in getting himself appointed high priest by Antiochus IV Epiphanes (2 Macc 4:23–29). According to traditional accounts, eighteen high priests served in succession during the First Temple period (960—586 BC) and sixty high priests served during the Second Temple period (516 BC until the temple's destruction in AD 70).[20] Not all of these high priests are mentioned in Scripture and attempts to reconstruct the list of high priests are difficult.[21]

Levites Set Apart for Service of the Lord

The high priest and priests were ordained during a liturgy, the most important part of which was the anointing with oil. The remainder of the tribe of Levi were also set apart for service to the Lord, but they were not ordained during a liturgy. There are different accounts of this coming about. The first account is in Exodus. While Moses was up Mount Sinai receiving the instructions in Exodus 25–31, the people sinned by creating and worshipping the golden calf. When Moses asked who was on the Lord's side it was the tribe of Levi who responded (Exod 32:26). Moses asked them to slaughter the idolaters, and the Levites slew 3,000 men (Exod 32:28). As a result, Moses spoke of the Levites as ordaining themselves to service of the Lord that day (Exod 32:29). The Semitic idiom for ordination "fill the hand" (see Appendix 2) in the Hebrew of Exodus 32:29 confirms their being set apart for God.[22] Because of their faithfulness to God

---

[19]   His brother Simon is from the tribe of Benjamin, according to 2 Macc 3:4.

[20]   Geoffrey Wigoder, Fred Skolnik, and Shmuel Himelstein, *The New Encyclopedia of Judaism* (New York: New York University Press, 2002), 363.

[21]   A list of high priests is given in Emil G. Hirsoh, "High Priest," in *The Jewish Encyclopedia: A Descriptive Record of the History, Religion, Literature, and Customs of the Jewish People from the Earliest Times to the Present Day*, ed. Isidore Singer (New York/London: Funk & Wagnalls, 1906), 6:391–392.

[22]   The verb tense in Hebrew is ambiguous, so it is variously translated in the present, past, or imperative; see Noel D. Osborn and Howard Hatton,

they have become dedicated to God's service. Yet the manner of their being ordained surely implies an imperfection, to say the least, in their "ordination." The imperfection of the Levitical priesthood will be contrasted in the Letter to Hebrews with the perfection of Christ's priesthood.

A second account of the Levites being set apart for the Lord's service is Moses speaking in Deuteronomy 10:8–9, which may be taken as referring to the same event although it does not use the terminology of ordination. It enumerates three duties of the Levites: to carry the Ark of the Covenant, to serve the Lord, and to bless in his name. A third account of the Levites being set apart for God's service is Moses' blessing them in Deuteronomy 33:8–11, which speaks of all the Levites in priestly terms.

The firstborn had a special position before God until the rebellion with the golden calf at Sinai (Exod 13:2; Num 3:13). Following that rebellion, God decreed that the Levites would substitute before him instead of the firstborn (see Num 3:11, 40–51; 8:16). In place of relying on priestly service by the firstborn, the Levites are now linked with every family. But before the Levites could serve the Lord they had to be purified (Num 8:5–22). Their duties included assisting the priests (Num 3:5–10; 8:3, 13, 19; 18:2–6), but Numbers 18:3 makes clear that only the priests and not the Levites could come near the sacred vessels and altar. While the Levites as a whole had the duty of carrying the ark (Deut 10:8; 31:25; 1 Sam 6:15; 2 Sam 15:24; 1 Chron 15:2, 12, 15; 16:4; 2 Chron 5:4; 35:3), especially the Kohathites of the Levites, one of the three divisions of the tribe of Levi (Num 3:14–17), the priests had to cover the sacred objects first so that the Kohathites might not touch them (Num 4:5–15).[23] In Numbers 4:20 the Kohathites were not even to see the sacred objects for a moment. The Kohathites served from the age of thirty up to fifty (Num 4:3).

A Handbook on Exodus, UBS handbook series/Helps for translators (New York: United Bible Societies, 1999), 771. If imperative, then it would be "ordain yourselves today . . . to bring a blessing upon you"; see Friedrich Wilhelm Gesenius, Gesenius' Hebrew Grammar, ed. E. Kautzsch and Sir Arthur Ernest Cowley, 2nd English ed. (Oxford, UK: Oxford University Press, 1910), 351.

23   Numbers 4 outlines different duties for the different sections of the tribe of Levi.

Holiness Demanded of the Priests

Holiness for Levitical priests was different from our idea of holiness. For us, holiness is being imbued with supernatural charity compelling us to engage the world to make it holy. We see this above all in Christ who was a friend of gluttons and drunkards, tax collectors and sinners (Matt 11:19; Luke 7:34). Sinners felt comfortable approaching Christ (Luke 15:1). But for the Levitical priests, holiness had much to do with the externals, and to be holy meant keeping separate from the profane. This is evident in the temple where only priests could enter the Holy Place and only the high priest could enter the Holy of Holies.

The ordination of the Levitical priests required their holiness. Ordination means being put in an order[24] and holiness was expected of the order of the priesthood. Much more was expected of the high priest, because Leviticus 4:3 says if he sinned he brought guilt on the people. The holiness of the priesthood is emphasized in Leviticus 10, holiness that must not be violated. Priests cannot violate the holiness of the sanctuary, and if they do death will follow. Two of Aaron's sons, Nadab and Abihu, were consumed by heavenly fire because they offered unholy fire to God (Lev 10:1-2).

The sanctity of those ordered in the priestly office was to be respected by observance of specific laws in Leviticus 21-22. Laws for all priests are in 21:1-9, and the more stringent laws for the high priest are in 21:10-15. Bodily defects rendered a priest unable to offer sacrifice but he could eat the priestly portions of the sacrifices (Lev 21:16-24). However, if the priest became impure he could not eat the sacred food (Lev 22:4-9). The laws concerning ritual cleanness and ritual uncleanness in Leviticus 11-15 are applied to priests in 22:4-9. A priest was rendered impure through emission of seminal fluid (Lev 22:4; all men in Lev 15:16-18), so a priest had to maintain sexual abstinence on the day he officiated at his sacred duties, and the time of continence began at sunset the previous evening. Priests were also to abstain from alcohol before their duties (Lev 10:8-9). Even when ritually pure, priests were also to purify themselves when approaching the altar by washing beforehand (Exod 30:17-21).

---

[24]   For a brief explanation of the etymology of "order" and "ordination," see Aidan Nichols, *Holy Order: The Apostolic Ministry from the New Testament to the Second Vatican Council* (Dublin: Veritas Publications, 1990), 52.

The holiness of the priesthood entailed the priests being given different responsibilities from the Levites, seen especially in the transport of the Ark of the Covenant when priests had to cover the sacred objects so the Levites did not touch them. Sometimes those who carried the Ark of the Covenant are specified as "the Levites the priests" often translated as "the Levitical priests" (Josh 3:3, 8:33), a phrase that has been much debated. In the remainder of Joshua 3, it is the priests who are specified many times as the bearers of the ark. When the ark was being transferred to Jerusalem by King David, the oxen pulling the ark stumbled and Uzzah reached out and touched the ark to steady it and he died beside the ark (2 Sam 6:6–7; 1 Chron 13:9–10), apparently because he was not a Levite and broke the prohibition of Numbers 4:15.

There are other examples of different duties assigned to priests and Levites. The Levites would have provided music at liturgies, but only the priests would have blown the trumpets for special occasions (Josh 6:4, 8, 9, 13, 16; 1 Chron 15:24; 16:6; 2 Chron 5.12; 7:6; 13:12, 14; 29:26). When King Hezekiah asked the Levites to sanctify the temple and carry out the filth, only the priests went into the inner part of the temple and brought out the filth and then the Levites took it to the Kidron brook (2 Chron 29:15–16). After the Exile it was the priests rather than the Levites who built the new altar in the reconstructed temple (Ezra 3:2).

God was the Levites' Portion and Cup

The Book of Joshua reports the distribution of land among the tribes after entering Canaan. The tribe of Levi received no share of the land because the Lord was to be Levi's inheritance (Josh 13:14; 18:7; Num 18:20; Deut 10:8–9; 18:1–8; Ezek 44:28).[25] Not having land allowed the Levites to be free to concentrate on their liturgical duties. Psalm 16 makes most sense if understood as prayed by a Levite—for example, "God is my portion and cup" (Ps 16:5). Most of the priests lived in Jerusalem, but of the forty-eight cities given to the tribe of Levi (Josh 21; Num 35:1–8) thirteen were given to the priestly families (Josh 21:13–19). All priests left their cities to assist in the temple in Jerusalem during the major feasts.

Since the Levites did not have land or its accompanying income, they were to receive their income from serving in the temple. Deu-

---

[25]   Gen 49:5–7 offers an alternate explanation.

teronomy 18:1–2 states that all the tribe of Levi is to be supported from the offerings to God and 18:3–5 explains the entitlement of the priests. Priests were entitled to a part of every animal sacrificed except the burnt offering. Leviticus 6–7 give the rules concerning which parts of sacrifices may be consumed by the priests. They were also entitled to the first fruits of grain, new wine, oil, and the first wool after sheep shearing (Deut 18:4) and further priestly gifts are listed in Numbers 18:8–19.

Numbers 18:21 states that the tithes were to go to the tribe of Levi in return for their liturgical services. The tribe of Levi was also to tithe from the tithe they received and give it to the priests (Num 18:25–28), so the priests received one percent of the produce. Other offerings to be given to the priests are listed in Leviticus 27.

Duties of Levitical Priests

The priestly duties could be categorized in the three chief duties in Deuteronomy 33:8–10—discerning God's will, teaching the Torah, and offering sacrifices. However, we could summarize the priests' duties by simply saying they were obligated to keep all the people conscious of being a priestly people before God.

The Levitical Priests' Duty to Keep the People Conscious of Being a Priestly People

When God offered the Hebrews the covenant through Moses, among the promises God made was that if they would obey him they would be to him a kingdom of priests (Exod 19:5–6). This meant Israel had a duty to be priestly to other nations, to bring them to knowledge of God. The holiness expected of Israel on their part, the separateness they are to maintain that is the counterpart of the unique role given them by God in his plan for the world, is expressed in many other Old Testament passages: the people are holy to God (Deut 7:6; 14:2, 21; Jer 2:3); they are God's possession (Deut 26:18). Jean Colson observes that the role of the Levitical priests was to ensure the people remained conscious of being a priestly people and that they conducted themselves as such to give glory to God.[26] However, neither did the people live up to this charge, nor did the priests help them. If we take Isaiah 60–62 to refer to the Jews' return from Babylon to Jerusalem after the exile, then in Isaiah 61:6 the prophet is looking to the returning exiles to resume their priestly role among the nations once again, as he tells them they shall be called priests of the Lord. Clearly, between Exodus 19:6 and Isaiah 61:6 the priestly role of the people had not been taken seriously—they endured shame (Isa 61:7)—and their priestly role must be rekindled once again by God's prophet. The prophet prompts them once again to serve the nations spiritually as God had originally planned for them in Exodus 19:6. An allusion to Exodus 19:6 can be found in 2 Maccabees 2:17 in a letter from Jews in Jerusalem to Jews in Egypt sharing the good news of the rededication of the temple after its desecration in 167–164 BC. Because of that rededication, the letter expects the priestly promise of Exodus 19:6 to be fulfilled in the people.

The Greek Old Testament distinguishes between the priesthood of the people and the priesthood of the Levitical priests by employing different Greek vocabulary, with one exception. It is only in Isaiah 61:6 that the Greek Old Testament uses the same Greek word, *hiereus* (ἱερεύς), for the people as priests as it does for the Levitical priests. In the other two instances in Exodus 19:6 and 2 Maccabees 2:17, which refer to "priesthood" rather than "priest," the Septuagint distinguishes between the Levitical priesthood and the priestly role of all the people by utilizing different Greek words. The word *hierateuma* (ἱεράτευμα) describes the priestly role of the people in Exodus 19:6 and 2 Maccabees 2:17, whereas *hierateia* (ἱερατεία) describes the priestly office of the Levitical priests, for example, in Exodus 29:9; 40:15.[27] This distinction is disturbingly evident in Numbers 16. A rebellion led by a Levite named Korah against the leadership of Moses in the wilderness was seen by Moses as Korah seeking the priesthood for himself (Num 16:8–10). Moses challenged Korah and his

---

[26] Jean Colson, *Ministre de Jésus-Christ ou le Sacerdoce de l'Évangile, étude sur la condition sacerdotale des ministres chrétiens dans l'Église primitive*, Théologie historique 4 (Paris: Beauchesne et ses fils, 1965), 185.

[27] This distinction between the Levitical priests and priesthood of the people is only evident in the Greek Old Testament, not in the Hebrew. Exod 19:6 and Isa 61:6 both use the single word "priests" in the Hebrew, and 2 Macc is only in Greek.

supporters to offer incense before the Tabernacle the next day and let God decide. God ordered Moses to separate Korah and his followers from among the congregation and they suffered God's punishment. Another illustration of the difference between priest and non-priest is in what could also be seen as rebellious when King Jeroboam set up shrines in the northern kingdom in opposition to the temple in Jerusalem and chose non-Levites as priests (1 Kings 12:32), which was seen as sinful (1 Kings 13:34).

The Priests' Duty to Discern God's Will

The priest was sometimes expected to discern God's will. Occasionally, especially before the time of the prophets, this was done by utilizing the Urim and Thummim. While not much is known about the Urim and Thummim, they must have been two small objects, because the high priest was able to carry them on his breast in his garments (Exod 28:30; Lev 8:8). They are believed to have been two dice-like objects that were thrown by the priests, with the arrangement as they fell giving an answer to a question (Num 27:21). From 1 Samuel 14:41, it is surmised that a simple "yes" or "no" answer was given to a question by means of the Urim and Thummim, and likewise also from 1 Samuel 23:9–12 and 30:7–8 (the breastpiece carrying the Urim and Thummim was connected to the ephod). Only a priest could use these instruments of discernment (Deut 33:8; Ezra 2:63; Neh 7:65). Ecclesiasticus considers them as dependable as the Torah (Sir 33:3). However, on one occasion they did not give an answer (1 Sam 28:6), which is probably to be understood as a consequence of Saul having murdered the priests at Nob (1 Sam 22:17–19). It is difficult to say when exactly during Old Testament times the Urim and Thummim ceased to be used for consulting God's will. It may be that their demise came about as "God was weaning His people away from a physical means of revelation to a greater dependence on His word as written or as spoken by the prophets."[28]

We might be tempted to regard this practice nowadays as superstitious and similar to a lottery ball. However, in the thinking of the time, the Urim and Thummim revealed God's will. Perhaps we

---

[28]   C. Van Dam, "Urim and Thummim," in *The International Standard Bible Encyclopedia*, rev. and ed. Geoffrey W. Bromiley (Grand Rapids, MI: Eerdmans, 1988), 4:957.

could say it was appropriate for their faith at that time but they later moved beyond it, especially during the time of the prophets as the prophets declared God's will to them. The casting of lots in Acts 1:26 to choose the replacement for Judas has precedent in the use of the Urim and Thummim. Acts suggests it was God who made the choice and displayed his choice through the lots. It is worth noting that this was the time before Pentecost, and we do not see this practice again after Pentecost.

The Priests' Duty to Teach the Torah

Priests were the teachers of Israel transmitting the faith, handing down the teaching revealed to Moses, and every seven years they were to read the Torah to all Israel at the Festival of Booths (Deut 31:9–11). 2 Chronicles 15:3 refers to a "teaching priest." Priests were expected to teach on moral and liturgical matters. They were to teach the people all the commandments of God (Lev 10:11), and on liturgical matters the priests were to teach the people on the difference between clean and unclean (Ezek 22:26; 44:23). Deuteronomy 33:10 mentions the duty of teaching before that of sacrificing. This teaching "refers to the full range of priestly instruction in ritual, judicial, and civil matters, such as worship, distinction between sacred and profane, clean and unclean, judicial decisions, and division of territory."[29] After the exile, priests concerned themselves more with liturgical matters and scribes concerned themselves with the Torah.

The Priests' Duty to Offer Sacrifice

The Levitical priests had a duty to offer sacrifice to God. The animal was slaughtered by its owner petitioning God and the priest threw the blood around the altar (Lev 1:1–5; 3:1–2, 7–8, 12–13; 4:13–18, 22–25, 27–30, 32–34). If a bird was being offered, the priest himself would slaughter the bird on the altar (Lev 1:14–15; 5:7–10), and if the priest was offering a sin offering for himself, he would also kill the animal as well as sprinkle its blood around the altar (Lev 4:1–7). This is because the life is in the blood (Lev 17:11). The Israelites would have come to this understanding from seeing people and animals expire

---

[29] Jeffrey H. Tigay, *Deuteronomy*, The JPS Torah commentary (Philadelphia, PA: Jewish Publication Society, 1996), 325.

after losing blood.[30] Blood poured around the altar expiates for sin, not the altar by itself, or the blood poured elsewhere (Lev 17:11). It is not even the blood itself that expiates, but as Leviticus 17:11 makes clear, the blood makes atonement by means of its life. Blood offered upon the altar expiates for the life of Israel and ransoms Israel. Leviticus 17:11 assumes that "animal blood substitutes for human life on the altar . . . [and] that substitution was instituted by God himself."[31] Apart from sprinkling blood, the priest's duties at the sacrifice also entailed quartering the sacrifice, washing it, and burning it.

In the texts of Leviticus dealing with sacrifice (1:4; 3:2, 8, 13; 4:4, 15, 24, 29, 33), it is the one providing the sacrifice, rather than the priest, who laid one hand on the head of the animal prior to its slaughter.[32] Opinions differ as to the meaning of this. Some believe the imposition of a hand indicates transference of sin to the animal, while others believe it means the benefits of the sacrifice redound to the one making the offering.[33] On Yom Kippur, the high priest laid both hands on the head of the scapegoat, confessed the sins of the people over the goat, and sent it out into the desert to die on behalf of the people's sins (Lev 16:21). This is the only text requiring the laying on of both hands.

Priests' Other Sacred Duties

All liturgical matters came within the remit of the priests. The priests had to ensure that the feasts stipulated in Leviticus 23 were properly celebrated. They had to make sure that the fire on the altar of burnt offering never went out, day or night (Lev 6:12). On that altar, they

---

[30]   John E. Hartley, *Leviticus*, Word Biblical Commentary 4 (Dallas, TX: Word, 2002), 274.

[31]   N. Kiuchi, *Purification Offering in the Priestly Literature: Its Meaning and Function* (Sheffield, UK: Sheffield Academic Press, 1987), 109. See also Baruch A. Levine, *Leviticus*, The JPS Torah Commentary (Philadelphia, PA: Jewish Publication Society, 1989), 115.

[32]   The imposition of a hand on the sacrifice is also indicated by Lev 8:14, 18, 22. In these texts, the sons of Aaron lay the hand, so the text refers to "hands" rather than hand. These offerings are brought by the sons of Aaron before they are ordained priests and by Moses, who subsequently sprinkles the blood.

[33]   For a summary of interpretations of the laying on of hands on a sacrificial victim, see Hartley, *Leviticus*, 19–21.

offered a one-year-old lamb as a burnt offering to God every morning and evening (Exod 29:38–42; see also 2 Chron 13:11). This became known as the "Tamid" after the exile.[34] A lamp was to be kept burning outside the veil before the Holy of Holies as a symbol of God's presence. It symbolized the presence of God so it had to be made from the best oil (Exod 27:20) and it was to be kept burning all night (Exod 27:21). Every household extinguished its lamp when retiring at night, but since God does not sleep it would have been inappropriate to allow the lamp of God's presence to go out.[35]

Priests had a duty to guard what was holy, so in Leviticus 10:10 the priests are told to distinguish between the holy and the common, between clean and unclean, and Leviticus 11 gives the guidelines for clean and unclean. Leviticus 13–15 concern priests making decisions about skin diseases and other types of uncleanness and pronouncing a person clean or unclean.

Priests were to bless people in the name of God (Deut 10:8; 21:5; Lev 9:22; 1 Chron 23:13).[36] The priests were to "put God's name upon the people" and then God would bless them (Num 6:27). The priest pronounced the words but it was God who gave the blessing, so the blessing of the priest was the blessing of God. This is apparent in the divine name standing at the head of each of the parts of the blessing in Numbers 6:24–26. For the same reason, invoking the name of God was part of a sacrificial ritual (Exod 20:24). The high esteem in which the priestly benediction was held is demonstrated by the discovery of two amulets in a phylactery in the excavations of Ketef Himmon near Jerusalem from the seventh or sixth century BC containing two versions of the priestly blessing of Aaron in Numbers 6:24–26.[37] One version is almost identical to the priestly blessing of Aaron and the second shorter version combines the second and third part of the blessing. These would have been worn as amulets or as a burial pendant. The Mishnah reports that when priests gave this blessing in the temple they held their hands high up over their heads, but when the blessing was given outside of the temple they held their

---

34   Sarna, *Exodus*, 192.

35   Douglas K. Stuart, *Exodus*, The New American Commentary 2 (Nashville, TN: Broadman & Holman Publishers, 2007), 600.

36   Kings also sometimes blessed people: 2 Sam 6:18 and 1 Kings 8:14, 55.

37   Gabriel Barkay, *Ketef Hinnom* (Jerusalem: Israel Museum, 1986), 29–31.

hands up only as far as their shoulders (m. Sotah 7:6; m. Tamid 7:2).[38] The same Mishnah passages also report that in the temple the blessing was given as one blessing but outside of the temple as three separate blessings. The blessings in the Psalms (115:14–15; 121:7–8; 128:5; 134:3) were likely to have been uttered by the priests.

Discontent with the Levitical Priesthood and Hopes for Renewal

Here we briefly examine the discontent of the prophets with the priests and the hopes for a renewed priesthood in both biblical and non-biblical texts, which give us the immediate background or context to see Christ fulfilling and transfiguring the Old Covenant priesthood that we will see in the next chapter. Levitical priesthood was not the full answer to the people's need for sanctification; the answer was still awaited, and that answer would be Christ and his priesthood.

Prophetic Critique of the Levitical Priesthood

The prophets critiqued all sectors of society who were not obedient to the covenant. No one was beyond their censure and the priests were also subject to their reproaches. It is possible that rivalry between prophets and priests contributed to this situation as prophets had a special calling from God and priests held a hereditary office, but both were God's representatives.[39] We saw above that one of the priests' duties was to teach their people, but reading the prophets shows they became derelict in this duty. Hosea 4:4–10 condemns the priests because their people are without knowledge (of God), the priests have forgotten the law of God and have abandoned God. Isaiah 28:7 condemns the priests and false prophets because they are

---

[38]   All Mishnah references are from Jacob Neusner, *The Mishnah: A New Translation* (New Haven, CT: Yale University Press, 1988).

[39]   Lester L. Grabbe, "A Priest is without Honor in his Own Prophet: Priests and Other Religious Specialists in the Latter Prophets," in Lester L. Grabbe and Alice Ogden Bellis, *The Priests in the Prophets: The Portrayal of Priests, Prophets and Other Religious Specialists in the Latter Prophets* (London: T & T Clark: 2004), 90.

drunk and giving false judgments. All the leaders of Israel, including the priests, are condemned in Micah 3:9–11 because they carry out their duties for bribes, their devotion to God was not authentic, and their teaching was governed by money. In Zephaniah 3:1–4 there is criticism of Jerusalem and its officials, including its priests. Zephaniah 3:4 accuses the priests of doing the opposite of what they were enjoined by Leviticus 22:15, as they were profaning the sacred. The prophet Jeremiah, a priest (Jer 1:1), condemned the priests many times along with others in society (e.g., 2:8; 4:9; 5:31; 6:13; 8:10; 13:13; 32:32; 34:19). He is famous for his "temple sermon" in which he denounced the presumption that worshiping in the temple could cover over sins of injustice (Jer 7). Even idols had been set up in the temple (Jer 7:30) which could not have happened without the consent of the priests. In response to his condemnations, the priests, false prophets, and all the people wanted Jeremiah dead (Jer 26:8, 11). Jeremiah proclaimed that priests and false prophets had no knowledge (Jer 14:18) and were ungodly (Jer 23:11). The priests, along with others, were condemned for their greed in Jeremiah 6:13 and 8:10. One particularly wicked priest had Jeremiah beaten and tied up (Jer 20:1–2). The prophet Ezekiel, also a priest (Ezek 1:3), declared that the law had disappeared from the priests and they were offering no guidance (Ezek 7:26). While denouncing Jerusalem, he condemned the priests because they did not respect the holy as separate from the profane and they disrespected the Sabbath (Ezek 22:26). Malachi 1:6–14 is God's complaint through the prophet about the insincerity of worship, which could be seen as an indirect reproof of the priests. That becomes direct and blunt in Malachi 2:1–9 where he condemns priests for being unfaithful and their instruction being the downfall of many (Mal 2:8). Altogether it is not a pretty picture. The fact that the priesthood was hereditary, rather than a vocation, and that priests were assured of their sustenance from sacrifices and tithes, probably contributed in no small degree to the decay in the Levitical priesthood. Reform was needed. Prophecy had come to an end long before the events of the 170s BC when the direct line of succession of high priests came to end with Jason supplanting his brother, and Menelaus, not even from the tribe of Levi, taking the office after him, and the widespread degeneracy in the priesthood described in 2 Maccabees 4:13–15. Had the prophets been ministering during that and subsequent decades, we would, no doubt, have special prophetic words on the priesthood to read!

Hopes for a Renewed Priesthood

There were many texts in Judaism looking forward to a renewal in the priesthood. Not only were there hopes for a renewed priesthood, but there was also the expectation that the Messiah would be a royal personage and also a priestly figure.[40]

Biblical Texts Looking Forward to a Renewal of the Priesthood

The prophet Malachi, after condemning the Levitical priests for their lack of fidelity (1:6–2:9), foresaw a new priesthood in the future even if, presumably, he did not fully appreciate what he foresaw: "I send my messenger to prepare the way before me, and suddenly there will come to the temple, the Lord whom you seek . . ." (Mal 3:1). The messenger coming before the Lord is understood by Mark (1:2) and by Jesus himself in Matthew 11:10 and Luke 7:27 as John the Baptist. This means Jesus himself is the Lord coming to his temple in Malachi 3:1. Malachi tells us that when the Lord comes to his temple he will purify and refine the Levites so that they will offer a pure sacrifice pleasing to the Lord (Mal 3:3–4). Based on this, Malachi, even if unknown to himself, foresees Christ and his priests of the New Covenant offering the Eucharist as the one and only pure sacrifice pleasing to God. Earlier, Malachi offered another fascinating prophecy that everywhere from east to west a sacrifice and pure offering would be offered to God (Mal 1:11). Based on this understanding of Malachi 3:1–4, it makes perfect sense that the early Christians, the Didache (14:1–3) tells us, saw Malachi's prophecy of a pure sacrifice and offering from east to west as a prophecy of the sacrifice of the Eucharist.[41]

---

[40]   Crispin H. T. Fletcher-Louis, "Jesus as the High Priestly Messiah: Part 1," JSHJ 4 (2006): 7–15.

[41]   On the sacrifice in Mal 1:11 achieving fulfillment in the Eucharist, see Dieter Böhler, "The Church's Eucharist, the Lord's Supper, Israel's Sacrifice: Reflections on Pope Benedict's Axiom 'Without its coherence with its Old Testament heritage, Christian liturgy simply cannot be understood,'" in *Benedict XVI and the Roman Missal: Proceedings of the Fourth Fota In-*

So Malachi prophesies that the Lord will enter his temple, there will be a renewed priesthood, and there will be a pure sacrifice—the Eucharist—offered worldwide and pleasing to God.

In Isaiah 56:6–7, God announces through the prophet that foreigners will offer burnt offerings and sacrifices on his holy mountain and God will accept them on his altar. This is looking beyond priesthood confined to the tribe of Levi and instead to Gentiles offering sacrifices in Jerusalem. It is looking forward to something major happening in the future that will involve a massive change in the temple liturgy and the Levitical priesthood. We will return to this text at greater length early in the next chapter on Christ's priesthood.

Non-Biblical Literature Looking Forward to a Renewed Priesthood and Only the Thanksgiving Sacrifice

A number of non-biblical texts expected a renewed priesthood.[42] Some of these documents are from Qumran, the headquarters of the Essenes who lived a monastic life by the Dead Sea and whose scrolls were discovered in 1947.[43] We have accounts of their community in Philo, Josephus, Pliny, and Hippolytus. This Jewish group had separated themselves from mainstream Judaism and regarded themselves as the true Israel. They were opposed to the Jerusalem temple priesthood since the Zadokite (Aaronic) line of high priests was broken in Jerusalem[44] and maintained their own Zadokite line. It is unknown who was the high priest in Jerusalem during the decade beginning 160 BC, but one possibility is that the Qumran founder had been the legitimate Zadokite high priest in Jerusalem 160/159–150/149 BC who was forced from office in Jerusalem, and became the Qumran high priest called the Teacher of Righteousness in his newly founded Qum-

---

ternational Liturgical Conference, 2011, ed. Janet E. Rutherford & James O'Brien, Fota Liturgy Series (Dublin/New York: Four Courts Press/Scepter Publishers, 2013), 107–123.

[42] Albert Vanhoye, *Old Testament Priests and the New Priest: According to the New Testament* (Persham, MA: St. Bede's Publications, 1986), 44–47.

[43] The enumerations of the Qumran texts here follow Florentino García Martínez and Eibert J. C. Tigchelaar, *The Dead Sea Scrolls Study Edition (Translations)*, vol. 1 (Leiden and New York: Brill, 1997–1998).

[44] Jerome Murphy-O'Connor, "The Essenes and their History," *RB* 81 (1974): 228.

ran community.[45] The Qumran community named the high priest
in Jerusalem the Wicked Priest (1Qphab).[46] The Qumran texts (see
Appendix 3 for details) and the Testaments of the Twelve Patriarchs[47]
identify a future high priest with the messiah.[48]

Not only do extra-biblical Jewish documents look forward to a
change in the priesthood, a major change is also anticipated in the
Jewish sacrifices.[49] The thanksgiving offering, called the *tôdâ* (תּוֹדָה),
is described in Leviticus 7:11–15 under the peace offerings. It involved offering both unleavened and leavened bread (7:12). These offerings were made in thanksgiving after salvation from death, illness,
or threats to one's life. One's family and friends would have been
present at the sacrifice in a spirit of unity to consume the sacrificed
animal and bread not retained by the priest, and to give thanks to
God for deliverance. Leviticus Rabbah, homiletic midrashic explanation of the book of Leviticus passed down by Jewish exegetes for a
thousand years before its final fixing by rabbis about AD 400–425,
foresaw a time when all sacrifices would cease except the *tôdâ*. A text
critical study of Leviticus Rabbah 9:7 translates the relevant text: "In

---

[45] James C. Vanderkam, "2 Maccabees 6, 7A and Calendrical Change in Je-
      rusalem," JSJ 12 (1981): 72. See also Murphy-O'Connor, "Essenes and their
      History," 229.

[46] For various proposals on the identity of the "Wicked Priest" of the Jerusa-
      lem priesthood, see Vermes, *Scrolls*, 22–28.

[47] The Testament of the Twelve Patriarchs is a pseudepigraphical document
      giving the last speeches of Jacob's twelve sons. It has been debated for a
      few centuries whether it is a pre-Christian Jewish document with addi-
      tions made to it later by Christians or is a Christian document based on
      Jewish documents. It contains similar ideas to those of Qumran about the
      priestly and kingly messiah; see Paolo Sacchi, *Jewish Apocalyptic and its
      History*, trans. William J. Short, JSPSS 20 (Sheffield, UK: Sheffield Aca-
      demic Press, 1990), 161–162. The Aramaic Levi Document, fragments of
      which were found in Qumran, is earlier than the Testament of the Twelve
      Patriarchs. On its royal and priestly characteristics in a Levitical messiah,
      see Jonas C. Greenfield, Michael E. Stone, and Ester Eshel, *The Aramaic
      Levi Document: Edition, Translation, Commentary* (Leiden: Brill, 2004),
      20–21, 35–39, 187–188.

[48] Oscar Cullmann, *The Christology of the New Testament* (Philadelphia, PA:
      Westminster Press, 1963), 86.

[49] This paragraph and the following first appeared in very similar form
      in Thomas Lane, "The Jewish Temple is Transfigured in Christ and the
      Temple Liturgies are Transfigured in the Sacraments," *Antiphon* 19 (2015):
      22–23, and are used here with permission.

time to come all offerings will come to an end, but the thanksgiving offering will not come to an end. All forms of prayer will come to an end, but the thanksgiving prayer will not come to an end."[50]

For a Jew, the *tôdâ* would have been the appropriate Jewish way to give thanks to God for Jesus' Resurrection. Ratzinger accepts that the Eucharist is the Christian transposition of the *tôdâ*; in the *tôdâ* the one who had been saved sacrificed an animal and gave thanks, and in the Eucharist the Christian community gives thanks that Christ who sacrificed himself is risen, and the food represented by bread is the body of Jesus.[51] Furthermore, the word "Eucharist" is the Greek translation of the Hebrew word *tôdâ*. During the *tôdâ*, the one giving thanks to God raised the cup praising God for his salvation, and in the Eucharist drinking from the cup is sharing in the New Covenant.[52] The Eucharist is the *tôdâ* in which Christians celebrate the death and Resurrection of Jesus. The *tôdâ* that continued after all other sacrifices ceased is the Eucharist.

Promises of Perpetual Levitical Priesthood Transfigured in the Priesthood of Christ

In Exodus 29:9, God tells Moses that the priesthood of Aaron and his sons will endure by a decree whose quality is described as *ʿôlām* (עוֹלָם), which translators often render as "perpetual," that is, the priesthood will endure by a "perpetual" statute. However, the Hebrew word *ʿôlām*, apart from some late Old Testament texts in Ecclesiastes, does not carry the idea of perpetuity but rather of a very long time.[53] So in Exodus 29:9, God declared that Aaron and his sons will have the priesthood by a statute that will last a long time. The Babylonian Talmud, written centuries after the Jerusalem priesthood ceased sacrificing when the temple was destroyed in AD 70,

---

50 Jacob Neusner, *Judaism and Scripture: The Evidence of Leviticus Rabbah* (Chicago: University of Chicago Press, 1986), 240–241.

51 Joseph Ratzinger, *The Feast of Faith: Approaches to a Theology of the Liturgy*, trans. Graham Harrison (San Francisco: Ignatius Press, 1986), 51–60. Ratzinger is building on the research of Hartmut Gese, *Essays on Biblical Theology* (Minneapolis, MN: Augsburg Publishing House, 1981), 117–140.

52 Gese, *Essays on Biblical Theology*, 135.

53 Ernst Jenni and Claus Westermann, *Theological Lexicon of the Old Testament* (Peabody, MA: Hendrickson Publishers, 1997), 853.

sees this meaning that they are priests as long as they are wearing their priestly garments, which must mean the Talmud saw this statute lasting only until AD 70 (b. Sanh. 83B [9:6]).[54] In Exodus 40:15, God promises that the anointing of Aaron and his sons will admit them to a priesthood that translators often render as "perpetual," but again the Hebrew word ʿôlām is utilized in this text, so I would suggest that in Exodus 40:15 God is promising Aaron and his sons will be admitted to a priesthood that will last a long time. In Numbers 25:10–13, God promised Phineas and his descendants a covenant of priesthood (see Sir 45:23–24), again described by the word ʿôlām, so it is a priesthood that will last a long time, not eternally.[55] In Sirach 45:7 and 45:15, the Greek text refers to a covenant of priesthood that God gave to Aaron and his descendants using the word aiōnos (αἰῶνος), which also in the Septuagint does not in itself carry the idea of perpetuity.[56] The Levitical priesthood lasted a long time, not forever, because it was transfigured into the priesthood of Christ, the high priest of the New Covenant, who shared his priesthood with his New Covenant ministers.

Through the prophet Jeremiah, God broadened the promise of priesthood beyond Aaron's sons to the Levites, promising that the priests of Levi would never be lacking (Jer 33:18). This promise follows another where God says through Jeremiah that there will always be a descendant of David on the throne of Israel (Jer 33:17). But the monarchy came to an end in 587 BC, so God's promise is fulfilled in some other way. Jesus is the descendent on David's throne fulfilling the promise of a son always on David's throne. In Luke 1:32–33, the archangel Gabriel announces the birth of Jesus to Mary in words that fulfil God's promise to King David through the prophet Nathan

---

[54] Jacob Neusner, *The Babylonian Talmud: A Translation and Commentary* (Peabody, MA: Hendrickson Publishers, 2011), 16:436. All further citations of the Babylonian Talmud are to be found in Neusner's edition.

[55] In 1 Sam 2:35, God promises he will raise up a faithful priest who will go in and out before his anointed king forever. This is normally seen as Zadok and the priests of his line after him replacing the wicked sons of Eli. The high priestly line of Zadok continued not just to the end of the monarchy but until the second century BC, when the legitimate Zadokite priest was ousted in the 170s BC.

[56] T. Holtz, "αἰών," *Exegetical Dictionary of the New Testament*, ed. Horst Robert Balz and Gerhard Schneider, vol. 1 (Grand Rapids, MI: Eerdmans, 1990), 44.

promising a descendant on his throne forever (2 Sam 7:9, 13–16).[57] The archangel does not say how Jesus will sit on that throne forever, but in Acts 2:32–36 Peter says that, after his Ascension, Jesus sat at the right hand of the Father. That is how Jesus sits on the throne of David forever, and so the promise in 2 Samuel 7, which seemed broken at the collapse of the monarchy in 587 BC, is fulfilled in a much more marvelous way in Jesus exalted in heaven. Jeremiah 33:17 and 2 Samuel 7 promise a descendant of David on the throne forever, which is fulfilled in Jesus. Immediately following this promise, in Jeremiah 33:18, God promises that Levitical priests would never be lacking. If fulfillment in Christ is the correct way to understand Jeremiah 33:17, the Christological implications carry over into Jeremiah 33:18 and also refer to the time of Christ, to the New Covenant priesthood. So even though the Levitical priesthood ceased liturgically in AD 70 with the destruction of the temple, God's promises in Jeremiah 33:18 were fulfilled in another way, in the transfiguration of the Levitical priesthood into the priesthood of Christ and his New Covenant ministers. It is Christ, the high priest of the New Covenant, who fully satisfied the people's need for sanctification, which we will take up in the next chapter.

Some Echoes in Catholic Liturgy

I stated at the beginning of this chapter that there is both continuity and discontinuity between the Levitical priesthood of the Old Covenant and the priesthood of Christ participated in by his New Covenant ministers, and that the term "transfiguration" has been proposed as an appropriate way of capturing both the continuity and discontinuity between the Levitical priesthood and the priesthood of Christ. While the Levitical priesthood is transfigured only in the priesthood of Christ, there is a typological relationship between the three ranks of Old Covenant priesthood and the three ranks of New Covenant priesthood in that the high priest is a typological foreshadowing of a bishop, a Levitical priest is a typological anticipation of a priest, and a Levite is a typological prefiguring of a deacon, but those

---

57   This is easily seen in a graph in Joseph A. Fitzmyer, *The Gospel According to Luke I-IX: Introduction, Translation, and Notes*, Anchor Yale Bible 28 (New Haven, CT/London: Yale University Press, 2008), 338.

three ranks of Levitical priesthood are transfigured in Christ. When describing a bishop, priest, and deacon, the Catholic liturgical texts employ biblical phrases from both Old and New Testaments. We will look at the New Testament phrases at the conclusion of the chapters commenting on the New Testament, and here we look at the Old Testament allusions in the liturgy.

The Ordination Prayer (Prayer of Consecration), following immediately after the laying on of hands during ordination liturgies, is different for Catholic bishops, priests, and deacons and alludes to events in both the Old and New Testaments. The Ordination Prayer for bishops does not specifically refer to Levitical high priests, but to God establishing rulers and priests and not leaving the sanctuary without ministers.[58] Giuseppe Ferraro tells us that Moses and Aaron are the prototypes of these rulers and priests.[59]

The Ordination Prayer for priests following the laying on of hands contains two Old Testament references. It recalls the seventy elders assisting Moses and Aaron (Num 11:16–17): "you chose men next in rank and dignity to accompany them and assist them in their task."[60] The second reference recalls Aaron's sons receiving the priesthood, on whom God "poured an abundant share of their father's plenty, that the number of the priests prescribed by the Law might be sufficient for the sacrifices of the tabernacle."[61]

The Ordination Prayer following the laying on of hands for deacons refers to the Levites who assisted the priests: "as once you chose the sons of Levi to minister in the former tabernacle, so now you establish three ranks of ministers in their sacred offices to serve in your name."[62] In the longer form of the Easter Proclamation (Exsultet) sung by the deacon during the Easter Vigil, a prayer to God for the deacon invokes the mercy of God "who has been pleased to number me, though unworthy, among the Levites."[63]

---

[58]   Congregatio de Cultu Divino et Disciplina Sacramentorum, Vox Clara Committee, *The Roman Pontifical* (Vatican City: Vox Clara Committee, 2012), 34, 54.

[59]   Giuseppe Ferraro, *Le preghiere di ordinazione al diaconato, al presbiterato, all'episcopato* (Naples, IT: Edizioni Dehoniane, 1977), 186.

[60]   *Roman Pontifical*, 78, 94, 160.

[61]   Ibid., 78, 94, 160.

[62]   Ibid., 116, 132, 156.

[63]   Catholic Church, *Roman Missal, Renewed by Decree of the Most Holy Second Ecumenical Council of the Vatican, Promulgated by Authority of Pope*

While the Ordination Prayer for bishops does not specifically reflect the typological relationship between the bishop and high priest, the following liturgical texts make that connection. The Collect of the Mass for the Ordination of a Bishop, when the presider at the Eucharist is the principal ordaining bishop, refers to the newly consecrated bishop, "whom you have raised up among your people to be High Priest."[64] The Mass for a bishop, in the Prayer over the Offerings, once again refers to the bishop, "whom you have raised up among your people to be High Priest."[65] Pope St. Clement I is called "Martyr and High Priest" in the collect for his memorial on November 23rd.[66] In the Mass for a pope, the entrance antiphon is based on Sirach 50:1 and other texts and refers to high priest,[67] and the Mass for a deceased pope calls the pope "High Priest over your flock."[68]

Apart from references and allusions in the liturgical texts, we can see other resonances of Old Testament cult in Catholic liturgy. The Levites were not allowed to touch the sacred utensils or Ark of the Covenant (Num 4:15), and only the priest may carry the consecrated hosts after Holy Communion back to the place where the Eucharist is reserved.[69] Altar servers who carry the bishop's crozier and miter wear a vimpa over their shoulders extending to their hands so they do not touch the episcopal pontificalia. A lamp burned day and night outside the Holy of Holies as a reminder of God's presence (Exod 27:20–21), and a sanctuary lamp burns day and night beside every tabernacle, reminding all that Jesus is present. The Levitical priests were sprinkled with anointing oil mixed with blood during their ordination liturgy (Exod 29:21), but only Aaron, the first high priest, was anointed with oil on his head (Exod 29:7). Catholic priests are anointed on their palms by the bishop with holy chrism during the ordination liturgy,[70] and the head of a bishop is anointed during

---

Paul VI and Revised at the Direction of Pope John Paul II, 3rd typical ed. (Washington, DC: United States Conference of Catholic Bishops, 2011), 349, 354.

64   Ibid., 1139.

65   Ibid., 1246.

66   Ibid., 999.

67   Ibid., 1071.

68   Ibid., 1402.

69   *General Instruction of the Roman Missal* §163 (*Roman Missal*, 50).

70   *Roman Pontifical*, 80, 96.

his ordination liturgy.[71] All Levitical priests wore four liturgical garments, but the high priest wore four additional liturgical garments (see Appendix 2). Catholic bishops receive liturgical insignia during their ordinations that are worn only by bishops, the ring on the ring finger of the right hand, the miter, and the crozier.[72]

---

[71]   Ibid., 35, 56.

[72]   Ibid., 35–36, 56–57.

CHAPTER 2

THE PRIESTHOOD
OF CHRIST

O UR STUDY OF THE LEVITICAL PRIESTHOOD in the previous chapter examined the salient features of the Levitical priesthood and concluded by showing the need for a new priesthood. We saw the Old Testament depicting God bestowing the priesthood on and confining it to men descended from Aaron in the tribe of Levi from the time of the Sinai covenant in a three-tier hierarchy: the high priest, the other priests, and the remainder of the tribe of Levi who served as the priests' assistants. Their ordination liturgies included anointing with oil on their palms and, for the high priest, anointing on his head also. The high priesthood was passed on in a direct line of succession from father to son, but this broke down about the 170s BC, which was only one of many problems that beset the Levitical priesthood in the last centuries before Christ. There was growing discontent with the priesthood as the centuries passed. This was plainly evident in the prophets' critiques of the priesthood, and biblical texts and non-biblical texts alike looked forward to a renewal in the priesthood. This chapter offers the answer to and resolution of that growing longing for something better. The hopes for a renewed priesthood were fulfilled in Christ, the high priest of the New Covenant. Christ was the one to whom all those longing for a better priesthood looked toward.

In this chapter we will see that Jesus was a priest, though of a different kind from the Levitical high priest. The first part of this chapter examines Gospel passages implying that Jesus is a priest. Jesus' actions and words in the temple are particularly relevant from this perspective and have implications for the Levitical priesthood— for example, when Jesus suggests he is the fulfillment of the Jewish liturgies, we can expect the Levitical priesthood's days of service in the temple are numbered because God has something much better in store in Jesus. Jesus' prayer in John 17 has been identified for centuries as his high priestly prayer. There are strong priestly undertones—for example, in the garment Jesus wore to the Cross and in Luke closing his Gospel with Jesus blessing like a priest. The second part of this chapter examines the Letter to the Hebrews, the only New Testament document that designates Jesus as high priest, not just once, but again and again. It describes Jesus' death in terms of the Yom Kippur/Day of Atonement liturgy. It was only during that liturgy, once every year, that the Jewish high priest entered the Holy of Holies sprinkling a bull's blood to atone for sins, but when Christ, the high priest of the New Covenant died, he took his blood into the heavenly sanctuary to gain salvation for us. Christ's death was his self-sacrifice that brought his priesthood to its perfect realization. Christ's death opened the way for us to enter God's sanctuary, and Hebrews invites us to enter through the flesh and blood of Jesus. Formerly, only the high priest could enter the Holy of Holies once annually, but we enter the heavenly sanctuary, the true Holy of Holies, through the Eucharist.

No one would ever have associated priesthood with Jesus because he was not from the priestly tribe of Levi, but rather from the tribe of Judah (Heb 7:14). The New Testament contains abundant references to Jesus being a descendant of King David (tribe of Judah), and, consequently, not from the tribe of Levi (e.g. Matt 1:1; Luke 1:32, 69; Rom 1:3; 2 Tim 2:8; Rev 5:5; 22:16). It is because Joseph was of the tribe of Judah, King David's tribe, that he had to go to Bethlehem for registration (Luke 2:3–4). More than that, the Gospels give Christ various titles such as Son of Man, Christ, Lord, and Son of God, but never high priest, and Jesus never described himself as a priest. Nevertheless, there are many intimations throughout the New Testament that Jesus was a priest of a different kind, and to these we now turn.

Indications of Christ's Priesthood in the Gospels

The Temple and Its Liturgies Are Transfigured in Jesus

The Levitical priests served in the temple and each time we see Jesus making statements about the temple or its liturgies, they deserve our attention for the implications they might hold for the Levitical priesthood. Christ's actions and statements in the temple suggest he will fulfill the temple and its liturgies, or to continue using the terminology of chapter 1, that the temple and its liturgies will be transfigured in him, and that automatically means the Levitical priesthood also must be transfigured in him, though that is not stated explicitly.[1] In Matthew 12:6, Christ says he is greater than the temple. As we will see, Christ made the same point in many different ways by his words and actions in the temple, and the logical consequence is that, if the temple and its liturgies are transfigured/fulfilled in Christ, the Levitical priesthood also will be transfigured in Christ.

In all four Gospels Jesus cleanses the temple by driving out the money-changers, but in John 2:19 Christ says, "Destroy this temple and in three days I will raise it up." John refers to raising the temple again, not rebuilding it. To be certain that there is no confusion, the evangelist adds, "He spoke of the temple of his body" (2:21). At Jesus' Resurrection, the raised body of Jesus will be the transfigured temple. It seems that in Matthew and Mark the listeners mistakenly thought Jesus was referring to rebuilding the Herodian temple and could not at that time have known Jesus was talking of his future Resurrection. This misunderstanding was used as a false charge against Jesus during his trial before the Sanhedrin in Matthew 26:61 and Mark 14:58.

---

[1]   For more on this, see Mary L. Coloe, *God Dwells with Us: Temple Symbolism in the Fourth Gospel* (Collegeville, MN: Michael Glazier, 2001); Paul M. Hoskins, *Jesus as the Fulfillment of the Temple in the Gospel of John* (Eugene, OR: Wipf and Stock Publishers, 2007); and Alan Kerr, *The Temple of Jesus' Body: The Temple Theme in the Gospel of John*, Journal for the Study of the New Testament Supplement Series 220 (New York: Sheffield Academic Press, 2002).

Jesus cleansing the temple, together with his teaching about raising it again, is a sign of the coming destruction of the temple and anticipates the transfiguration of the Herodian temple into the resurrected body of Jesus. To use the thought of Matthew 12:6, Jesus is greater than the temple.

In the Synoptic accounts of the temple cleansing in Matthew 21:13, Mark 11:17, and Luke 19:46, Christ refers to God's house being a house of prayer. That reference to "house of prayer" occurs in Isaiah 56:6–7, where the prophet, Third Isaiah (as we commonly call him), foresaw major changes in the temple liturgy in the future, changes so major that Levitical priests would not be the only ones offering sacrifices. In Isaiah 56:6–7, God announces through the prophet that foreigners will offer burnt offerings and sacrifices on his holy mountain (where the Jerusalem temple is located) and that God will accept them on his altar. This is looking beyond priesthood confined to the tribe of Levi. It is looking forward to something major happening in the future that will involve a massive change in the temple liturgy and the Levitical priesthood. The shock in Isaiah 56:6–7 is its prediction that foreigners will come to minister in the temple, because the word used for minister/serve in 56:6, *šārat* (שָׁרַת), typically refers to liturgical service.[2] The prophet sees Gentiles offering sacrifices in Jerusalem. This is omitted from Isaiah 56 in the Dead Sea Scrolls, perhaps because this idea was so repugnant.[3] It is highly suggestive that as Christ cleanses the temple he quotes part of a Scripture passage referring to foreigners undertaking priestly sacrificial duties in the temple. Brant Pitre observes that Christ "is not only awaiting a new Temple, but a new priesthood in which both Israel and the Gentiles will act as priests in the eschatological age."[4]

The first half of the Gospel of John, commonly called the Book of Signs, contains a number of discourses given by Christ at major Jewish feasts. Significantly, during these discourses Jesus indicates that

---

[2]   Francis Brown, Samuel Driver, and Charles Briggs, *Enhanced Brown-Driver-Briggs Hebrew and English Lexicon* (Oak Harbor, WA: Logos Research Systems, 2000), 1058.

[3]   John N. Oswalt, *The Book of Isaiah, Chapters 40–66*, The New International Commentary on the Old Testament (Grand Rapids, MI: Eerdmans, 1998), 460.

[4]   Brant Pitre, "Jesus, the New Temple, and the New Priesthood," *Letter & Spirit* 4, *Temple and Contemplation: God's Presence in the Cosmos, Church, and Human Heart* (2008): 73.

he is the fulfillment of these feasts. Christ entered the temple during the Feast of Tabernacles (John 7:14). The Mishnah (m. Suk. 4:7) gives details of a daily morning water liturgy during Tabernacles in which the (high) priest would go to Siloam, fill a flask with water, and upon returning to the temple fill a silver bowl with the water, which was used as a water libation around the altar. On the last day of the feast, Christ proclaimed, "If anyone thirst let him come to me and drink" (John 7:37), indicating that he is the fulfillment of Tabernacles' daily morning water liturgy. Naturally, this has implications for the Levitical priesthood.

The Mishnah also describes a daily evening light liturgy during Tabernacles (m. Suk. 5:2–4). Priests lit four giant candelabras in the Court of Women whose light was said to enlighten every courtyard in Jerusalem. When Jesus stated, "I am the light of the world; he who follows me will not walk in darkness, but will have the light of life" (John 8:12), he also suggested he is the fulfillment of this evening light liturgy of Tabernacles just as he is the transfiguration of its daily morning water liturgy. As if to confirm this, Jesus' miraculous healing of the blind man during Tabernacles (John 9:1–7) also shows that he is the transfiguration of Tabernacles' evening light liturgy. During that miracle Jesus proclaimed, "As long as I am in the world I am the light of the world" (John 9:5). Christ is the fulfillment of these liturgies, which must have consequences for the Levitical priesthood.

The Feast of Dedication (John 10:22–39) celebrated the re-dedication or re-consecration of the temple in 164 BC (1 Macc 4:52–59) when the temple was purified after a three-year-long desecration by invading Seleucids. During this feast, Christ declared that he had been consecrated by the Father (John 10:36). The feast celebrated the re-consecration of the temple, but Christ is now the Consecrated One. Consequently, he must be seen as fulfilling/transfiguring the temple and its liturgies. This explains why, earlier, Christ declared to the Samaritan woman that the hour was coming when worship would be offered to the Father neither on Mount Gerizim of the Samaritans nor in Jerusalem of the Jews, but would be offered to the Father in spirit and truth (John 4:21–23).

Since Jesus is the transfiguration/fulfillment of the temple and its liturgies, we would also expect to see indications of Jesus replacing the priestly sacrifices of the Old Covenant in the temple. The Jewish scholar Jacob Neusner does not disagree that Jesus overturning the money-changers' tables signifies the destruction of the temple, but he does offer an additional interpretation.[5] The money-changers in the temple and throughout Israel facilitated the collection of the half-shekel temple tax paid by all Israelites during the month of Adar for the Tamid or daily whole-offerings during the year ahead.[6] It was a sacrifice to please God and to make atonement. It is given various names, such as the "burnt offering" (Exod 29:18) and the "burnt sacrifice" (Ps 20:3). It is also called the "whole burnt offering" (Deut 33:10; Ps 51:19) because it was the only sacrifice wholly or completely burnt on the altar. In Exodus 29:42 and Numbers 28:6 it is called the "continual burnt offering." Because it was to be offered "continually"—in Hebrew, tāmîd (תָּמִיד)—this sacrifice is called "Tamid" in rabbinic documents. The Tosefta, which is a little later than the Mishnah, regards the half-shekel temple tax as atonement for sin, and Neusner believes that must have also been the case at the time of Christ, based on Exodus 30:16. Payment of the half-shekel temple tax allowed people, wherever they were, to participate in the daily whole-offering in the temple in atonement for sin. Neusner writes:

> For the overturning of the money-changers' tables represents an act of the rejection of the most important rite of the Israelite cult, the daily whole-offering, and, therefore, a statement that there is a means of atonement other than the daily whole-offering, which now is null. Then what was to take the place of the daily whole-offering? It was to be the rite of the Eucharist: table for table, whole-offering for whole-offering. It therefore seems to me that the correct context in which to read the overturning of the money-changers' tables is not the destruction of the Temple in general, but the institution of the sacrifice of the Eucharist, in particular.[7]

Based on Neusner's understanding, the overturning of the money-changers' tables indicates that priestly sacrifices of the Old Covenant would be replaced/transfigured by Jesus' onetime sacrifice of him-

5   Jacob Neusner, "Money-Changers in the Temple: the Mishnah's Explanation," NTS 35 (1989): 287–290.

6   See Jacob Neusner, "Sacrifice and Temple in Rabbinic Judaism," in *The Encyclopedia of Judaism*, ed. Alan J. Avery-Peck and William Scott Green (Leiden/Boston/Köln: Brill, 2000), 3:1294.

7   Neusner, "Money-Changers in the Temple," 290.

self in the New Covenant. The faithful of the New Covenant would participate in the salvific effects of Jesus' priestly self-sacrifice every time they participate in the Eucharist. Jesus overturns the money-changers' tables in Matthew 21:12, Mark 11:15, and John 2:15. It is easier to apply Neusner's argument to Matthew and Mark because in Matthew 26:26–28 and Mark 14:22–24 Jesus institutes the Eucharist. It is more difficult to apply Neusner's argument to the Gospel of John because the footwashing in John 13 substitutes for the institution of the Eucharist in John, although in John 6:51c, "the bread that I shall give for the life of the world is my flesh" parallels "This is my Body" in the institution narratives in the Synoptics.

All the examples above of temple liturgies transfigured/fulfilled in Jesus implicitly anticipate the ending of the Levitical sacrifices and liturgies in the temple.[8] These pave the way for the understanding of Christ as priest that would come to full flower in the Letter to the Hebrews. Christ, the high priest of the New Covenant, brought all the liturgies of the Old Covenant to fulfillment in himself, transfiguring them in the New Covenant.

Jesus Understands Psalms Fulfilled in Himself

In each of the Synoptics, Christ playfully asks how the Messiah can be David's son, because David called the Messiah his lord when David wrote Psalm 110 (Matt 22:41–45; Mark 12:35–37; Luke 20:41–44). Christ quoted Psalm 110:1:

> The Lord says to my lord:
> "Sit at my right hand,
> till I make your enemies your footstool."

It is complex, but we may begin unraveling it by rephrasing it in this way:

> The Lord (God) says to my Lord (the Lord over David):
> "Sit at my right hand,
> till I make your enemies your footstool."

---

[8]   Parts of this section on the temple and its liturgies transfigured in Jesus appeared in similar form in Thomas Lane, "The Jewish Temple is Transfigured in Christ and the Temple Liturgies are Transfigured in the Sacraments," *Antiphon* 19 (2015): 14–28, and are used here with permission.

Christ then asks how someone who is Lord over David can also be David's son/descendant, meaning "how can someone who is superior to David also be his descendant?" The reverse would have been expected because David was remembered as the ideal king, even though his sins were known, since God had made the promise of a descendant on his throne forever through the prophet Nathan in 2 Samuel 7 (see end of the previous chapter). Peter gives the answer in his Pentecost Sermon: Christ is both David's son (i.e. his descendant) and also his lord, since Christ is the Messiah, and Jesus' exaltation to the right hand of the Father after his Ascension proves this (Acts 2:32–36; see Rom 1:3–4). Jesus himself is the answer to the riddle. The Psalm could only be correctly interpreted in relation to Jesus himself. Now we can rephrase Psalm 110:1 in this way:

> The Father says to Jesus (the Lord over David):
> "Sit at my right hand,
> till I make your enemies your footstool."

It is highly significant that a few verses later in the same Psalm we read of God swearing an oath: "you are a priest for ever after the order of Melchizedek" (Ps 110:4). Already in Jesus' understanding, the first verse of the Psalm can be correctly explained only in relation to himself; he is the Lord at the right hand of the Father, and it is appropriate to think that Christ considered the Father's oath of eternal priesthood in verse 4 also applicable to himself.

In Mark 14:62 and Matthew 26:64, Jesus stood before the high priest, and when asked if he is the Messiah, the Son of God, he answered affirmatively and said they would "see the Son of man sitting at the right hand of Power, and coming with the clouds of heaven." Jesus' answer combines a partial citation of Psalm 110:1 ("sitting at the right hand") with Daniel 7:13 on the coming of the son of man. We find similar phraseology in Luke 22:67–69. Since, as we have seen, Psalm 110 is fulfilled in Christ as priest, this statement by Oscar Cullmann is very relevant: "Is it not significant that Jesus applies to himself a saying about the eternal High Priest precisely when he stands before the Jewish high priest and is questioned by him concerning his claim to be the messiah?"[9] Two priests are face to face in

---

9   Oscar Cullmann, *The Christology of the New Testament* (Philadelphia, PA: Westminster Press 1963), 88–89.

this scene in Mark 14:62, the old and the new, the high priest of the Levitical priesthood and Christ the high priest of the New Covenant who will fulfill the Levitical priesthood.

Jesus Prays as High Priest in John 17

John 17 allows us to listen in on Jesus praying to the Father during the Last Supper. The prayer is known as the High Priestly Prayer, a title first given it by David Chyträus, a Lutheran theologian of the sixteenth century, and it has been so called since then by both Protestant and Catholic theologians.[10] Even before then, its priestly character had long been highlighted.[11] Many structures for the prayer in John 17 have been proposed. In *The Priesthood of Christ and His Ministers*, André Feuillet proposes that John 17 has the same structure as the high priest's prayers on Yom Kippur, the Day of Atonement.[12] On Yom Kippur, in Leviticus 16:6–11 and 16:15–16, the high priest offered the sacrifices in atonement for:

1. himself (Lev 16:6),
2. his "house," i.e. fellow priests (Lev 16:6),
3. and all people (Lev 16:15–16).

In John 17 Jesus prays:

1. for himself (17:1–5), asking the Father to enable him to continue glorifying the Father,
2. for his disciples (17:6–19),
3. and for those who will believe through his disciples that they may be united (17:20–26).

There is value to Feuillet's conclusion that the "threefold prayer of Christ in John 17 shows Christ is the high priest of the New Covenant."[13]

---

[10]   Ibid., 105.

[11]   Joseph Ratzinger, *Jesus of Nazareth. Holy Week: From the Entrance into Jerusalem to the Resurrection* (San Francisco: Ignatius Press, 2011), 76.

[12]   André Feuillet, *The Priesthood of Christ and His Ministers* (Garden City, NY: Doubleday, 1975), 207–208.

[13]   Ibid., 208.

Apart from similarity in structure, there are other resemblances between Christ's prayer in John 17 and the Day of Atonement liturgy. The Day of Atonement was the only day in the year during which the high priest could utter the divine name Yahweh, and then only inside the Holy of Holies. Accordingly, Feuillet finds Jesus' declaration that he has manifested the Father's name to the disciples amplifying the connection between John 17 and the Day of Atonement liturgy (John 17:6, 26).[14] Two other mentions of the Father's name also amplify the parallel: Jesus kept the disciples in the Father's name (17:12), and prayed that the Father keep them safe in his name (17:11).

Even those who question Feuillet's interpretation have said of his results that "those who have found priestly allusions in the text are not simply fantasizing"[15] and that there is a significant gesture in John 17 toward the world of the high priest.[16] Joseph Ratzinger believes Feuillet has given us the key to a correct understanding of John 17.[17] I think it is fair to say that in John 17 Jesus prays before commencing his Passion in such a way so as to recall the Levitical high priest because the Levitical priesthood will be transfigured in him in his priestly self-sacrifice on the Cross.

Sacrificial Language during the Last Supper

Many times before his Passion, Christ made it clear to his disciples that his life would end violently.[18] Just as the Old Covenant was sealed by animal's blood (Exod 24:8), the New Covenant would be sealed by Christ's blood shed during his Passion and death. Jesus' words at the institution of the Eucharist during the Last Supper contain

---

[14] Ibid., 62–69.

[15] Harold W. Attridge, "How Priestly Is the 'High Priestly Prayer' of John 17?" *CBQ* 75 (2013): 11.

[16] Ibid., 12.

[17] Ratzinger, *Jesus of Nazareth: Holy Week*, 77.

[18] The Synoptics record three "Passion Predictions" by Christ (first prediction: Matt 16:21; Mark 8:31; Luke 9:22; second prediction: Matthew 17:22–23; Mark 9:31; Luke 9:44; third prediction: Matthew 20:18–19; Mark 10:33–34; Luke 18:32–33). There is an additional prediction in Luke 17:25. There are also three "Passion Predictions" in John, though in a different format, showing the benefit of Christ's sacrificial death for the Church: John 3:14–15 (eternal life for those who believe); 10:11 (for the sheep); 12:24 (much fruit).

sacrificial tones anticipating his sacrifice on the Cross to establish the New Covenant. The words "body" and "blood" used by Christ during the institution of the Eucharist had a sacrificial tone easily recognizable by any Jew.[19] In Luke 22:19–20 and in the account of the Last Supper in 1 Corinthians 11:23–25, Christ says over the bread that it is his body "for you." Again in Luke and in the account in 1 Corinthians, Jesus says the cup is the "new covenant" in his blood. These are the only two texts in the New Testament citing Jesus' own words describing his death as the institution of the "New Covenant." In Matthew 26:28 and Mark 14:24, the word "covenant" is in the narrative instituting the Eucharist, but only Luke and 1 Corinthians 11 have "new covenant." The sharing of the cup during the Last Supper, and subsequently in remembrance of Christ's death (1 Cor 11:25), is a participation in the salvific effects of Christ's death instituting the New Covenant. In Luke and 1 Corinthians, the words "body," "blood," "for you," and "new covenant" anticipate Christ's sacrificial death.

The narratives instituting the Eucharist in Matthew and Mark also contain the words "body" and "blood" but link the atoning quality of Christ's death to the Last Supper with additional language. Christ says over the cup that it is the blood of the covenant poured out "for many" (Matt 26:28; Mark 14:24).[20] Christ's use of the word "many" suggests he saw himself as the fulfillment of Deutero-Isaiah's prophecy of a suffering servant (Isa 52:13–53:12) whose death would atone for the sins of "many" (Isa 53:11, 12). Additionally, in Matthew 26:28, Christ reveals that the consequence of the pouring out of his blood of the covenant is the forgiveness of sins.

All four accounts of the Last Supper—the parallel accounts of Matthew and Mark and those of Luke and its parallel in 1 Corinthians 11—associate Christ's death with the Last Supper and reveal the sacrificial nature of his death. The very words used by Christ during the Last Supper ("body," "blood," "for you," "new covenant," "many") reveal Christ's consciousness that his death would be a self-sacrifice in atonement and that he saw himself fulfilling the suffering servant of Isaiah who made atonement for the sins of many by his death.

---

[19]   Joachim Jeremias, *The Eucharistic Words of Jesus*, trans. John Bowden (London: SCM, 1966), 222.

[20]   Ratzinger offers an explanation: Jesus died for *all*, but *many* receive the Sacrament of the Eucharist (*Jesus of Nazareth: Holy Week*, 135–136).

Christ would be both the victim offered to institute the New Covenant and the priest offering himself as the victim.

Jesus' Seamless Robe

Jesus went to Calvary wearing a seamless undergarment or tunic, woven from top to bottom, beneath his outer garments (John 19:23). John sees great significance in this seamless robe, because he states in 19:23 that it was "seamless" and, at the end of 19:23, that it was "in one piece" (δι' ὅλου), though the latter is not obvious in all English translations. It certainly was a unique garment, because the tunic worn daily by men and women in Palestine was not seamless but made of two pieces of fabric sown together.[21]

John does not tell us the meaning of the symbolism but leaves it up to the reader to work it out. It is often taken to symbolize the unity of the Church, and certainly tearing a garment by a prophet was seen as a sign of disunity (see 1 Kings 11:29–33). I think we can also see it symbolizing Jesus' priesthood, the transfiguration of the Levitical priesthood. Admittedly, this is not without difficulties because of the word *chitōn* (χιτών), which John uses in 19:23 to describe Jesus' garment. The high priest wore two full length garments, the tunic/undergarment worn by all priests and, additionally, his priestly robe (or the ephod). *Chitōn* is the word in the Greek Old Testament for the tunic/undergarment worn by all priests, while a different word, *hypodytēs* (ὑποδύτης), is usually the word for the priestly robe. However, I believe there are possible ways around this difficulty.

Firstly, the wider context in John's Gospel—the passages we have already examined where we saw the temple liturgies transfigured in Jesus and Jesus' high priestly prayer in John 17 reflecting the structure of the high priest's prayer on Yom Kippur—indicates that, although the letter to the Hebrews is the only New Testament document describing Jesus as high priest, the Gospel of John also applies priestly theology to Jesus. Therefore, it would not be out of place in John to expect to see priestly associations in Jesus' Passion.[22]

---

[21]   James S. Jeffers, *The Greco-Roman World of the New Testament Era: Exploring the Background of Early Christianity* (Downers Grove, IL: InterVarsity Press, 1999), 43.

[22]   For a much more detailed examination of Jesus' tunic in the context of different passages in John, see John Paul Heil, "Jesus as the Unique High Priest in John," *CBQ* 57 (1995): 729–745.

Secondly, it would have been impossible for Jesus to wear a high priest's robe on the way to the Cross because he himself would never have been able to enter the priests' courtyard in the temple and no priest would ever remove the high priest's robe from its place inside the temple. The most the evangelist could do is make an association between the way Jesus went dressed to the Cross and the priestly garment of the high priest. How does John do this? The word *hypodytēs* in the Greek Old Testament for the high priest's robe literally means an undergarment, because it was worn under the high priest's ephod. Jesus' tunic was the garment he wore under his other clothes, which the soldiers took from him first (John 19:23). Those who doubt the priestly symbolism in Jesus' tunic in John 19:23 associate Jesus' tunic with the high priest's tunic (*chitōn*) rather than the high priest's robe (*hypodytēs*).[23] I would like to suggest that we consider associating Jesus' *chitōn* in John 19:23 with the *hypodytēs* or high priestly robe because Jesus wore his tunic under his other garments and the high priest wore his *hypodytēs* under the ephod.

Thirdly, John 19:23 tells us Jesus' tunic was seamless, and although the Old Testament does not tell us the high priest's robe was seamless, Josephus does: "Now this vesture was not composed of two pieces, nor was it sewed together upon the shoulders and the sides, but it was one long vestment so woven as to have an aperture for the neck."[24] The mere fact that the daily tunic worn by everyone and the tunic worn by the high priest under his priestly robe are also called *chitōn* does not compel us to associate Jesus' garment with them. To me it makes more sense to associate Jesus' seamless garment instead with the high priest's robe, which was also seamless. Ratzinger[25] also regards the reference to Jesus' tunic being seamless as signifying a

---

[23] Ignace de la Potterie associates Jesus' tunic with the priestly tunic, not his priestly robe, thus discounting its priestly connotation. However, this is not surprising, as he also does not see priestly theology applied to Jesus by John; see *The Hour of Jesus: The Passion and Resurrection of Jesus According to John* (New York: Alba House, 1989), 87 and 99.

[24] Flavius Josephus, *Antiquitates Judaicae* 3.161, in *The Works of Josephus: Complete and Unabridged*, trans. William Wiston (Peabody, MA: Hendrickson, 1987).

[25] Since Pope Benedict XVI wrote the three volumes of *Jesus of Nazareth* in a private capacity as a theologian rather than as ecclesial documents in his capacity as Pontiff, I entitle him Ratzinger here and in the following chapters to reflect this distinction. When speaking as Pontiff, I entitle him Pope Benedict XVI.

high priestly undertone, especially in view of John 17: "we may detect in the evangelist's passing reference an allusion to Jesus' high-priestly dignity, which John had expounded theologically in the high-priestly prayer of chapter 17. Not only is this dying man Israel's true king: he is also the high priest who accomplishes his high-priestly ministry precisely in this hour of his most extreme dishonor."[26]

Fourthly, John 19:24 tells us that the soldiers did not tear Jesus' robe. Exodus 28:32 forbade the tearing of the high priest's robe. Since everyone in Palestine wore a *chitōn* daily, saying Jesus went to his Passion wearing a *chitōn* would not have special significance, but saying that Jesus went to his Passion wearing a *chitōn* having two qualities similar to the robe of the high priest—seamless and not torn—allows us to see it containing symbolism associating it with the high priest's garment.

Fifthly, John points out another quality of Jesus' tunic in 19:23: it was woven from top to bottom, *anōthen* (ἄνωθεν). This word *anōthen* has great significance when used elsewhere in John. In John 3:31, Jesus is the one who comes from above (*anōthen*), and in 19:11 Pilate would have no power over Jesus were it not given him from above (*anōthen*). Both Matthew 27:51 and Mark 15:38 tell us the curtain in the temple was torn in two from top to bottom (*anōthen*) when Jesus died. These usages of the word *anōthen* indicate divine origin: Pilate's power has been given him by God and the curtain in the temple is torn by God. Surely it is not by chance that John 19:23 tells us Jesus' *chitōn* was woven from top to bottom (*anōthen*). It must mean something. This garment is not just any garment, but is drawing attention to some divine connection. Could it not be another clue to strengthen John's intimation to see priestly significance in Jesus' garment?

Jesus' Priestly Death

Every priest offers sacrifice to God, and Jesus' death was his priestly sacrifice. Ratzinger sees Jesus' priestly self-giving already commencing when submitting to the Father on the Mount of Olives.[27] The priestly aspect of Christ's death is implied a number of times in the New Testament letters when they state that Christ gave himself up for our sins

---

[26]   Ratzinger, *Jesus of Nazareth: Holy Week*, 216–217.

[27]   Ibid., 164.

(Rom 5:8; 8:32; 1 Cor 5:7; 15:3; Gal 1:3–4; 2:20; Eph 5:2; 1 Thes 5:9–10; 1 Tim 2:5–6; Titus 2:14; 1 Pet 1:18–19; 3:18).

Jesus' Priestly Blessing

Only Luke tells us that as Christ ascended to the Father he raised his hands and blessed (Luke 24:50–51). The two actions combined, raising hands and blessing, recall two priestly blessings in the Old Testament. The priest Aaron lifted up his hands and gave a blessing when concluding the sacrifice eight days after his ordination (Lev 9:22). There are also similarities between Christ's blessing and the priestly blessing of Simon in Sirach 50:20–21.[28] Both Simon and Christ bestow their blessing after an atoning sacrifice, Simon after the atoning sacrifice on the Day of Atonement[29] and Christ after his atoning sacrifice on the Cross.

Summarizing the chapter thus far, we could say that while Jesus never used the word "priest" to describe himself, his words and actions show that he is a priest of a different kind from the Levitical priesthood. He is the transfiguration of the temple and its liturgies where the Levitical priests ministered. He saw Psalm 110:1 about David's Lord sitting at God's right hand fulfilled in himself, and surely also saw its fourth verse about priesthood forever in the line of Melchizedek fulfilled in himself. His prayer during the Last Supper in John 17 has so many links with the high priest on the Day of Atonement that it has been called his high priestly prayer. During the Last Supper, Christ's words over the bread and cup had sacrificial meaning anticipating his death on Calvary. Christ went to his death dressed in a garment with the same two qualities as the high priest's robe—it was seamless and was not torn. Before his Ascension, Christ raised his hands and blessed as did the Levitical priests after offering sacrifice. Yet in all these examples, the priesthood of Christ is implied but never explicitly stated. The Letter to the Hebrews explicitly describes Christ as a priest many times, the only New Testament book to do so. To that we must now turn.

---

28 Andrews G. Mekkattukunnel, *The Priestly Blessing of the Risen Christ: An Exegetico-Theological Analysis of Luke 24, 50–53*, European University Studies 23/714 (Bern, CH: Peter Lang, 2001), 184–188.

29 Fearghus Ó Fearghail believes the sacrifice is the Daily Whole Offering; see "Sir 50, 5–21: Yom Kippur or The Daily Whole-Offering?" *Bib* 59 (1978): 301–316.

The Priesthood of Christ in the Letter to the Hebrews

The Letter to the Hebrews satisfies a most important need not addressed by any other New Testament document. It shows that Christ was a high priest of a different order and that his death was his priestly self-sacrifice. We will trace the theme of Christ's priesthood in the sections of the letter in 2:17–10:18, where it is most clearly expressed. Although we now regard Jesus' death as a priestly self-sacrifice, initially Jesus' death would not have been seen as a priestly act. A Jewish priest sacrificed a life other than his own, but Jesus' death, on the other hand, was a punishment and was unaccompanied by a solemn priestly liturgy. Hebrews has a unique way of describing Christ's death on Calvary. It sees Christ's death as the transfiguration/fulfillment of the Old Testament Day of Atonement/Yom Kippur liturgy. That was the only day of the year when the Levitical high priest entered the Holy of Holies to sprinkle blood to atone for sins (Lev 16:11–14). According to Hebrews, when Christ offered himself to the Father on the Cross, he entered the heavenly Holy of Holies once for all time to atone for our sins, and not only that, but now the way into the heavenly Holy of Holies is open for all Christians, giving us access to the Father through Christ. In demonstrating that Jesus was a priest, that his death was a priestly self-sacrifice, Hebrews also shows Jesus as the realization of the Jewish hopes for a renewed priesthood that surfaced in the centuries leading up to Christ. Hebrews shows that Jesus is the answer to those expectations and, in so doing, satisfies a need not accomplished by any other New Testament document.

The contents of Hebrews show that the letter expected the listeners to be familiar with Jewish liturgy and the Levitical priesthood, indicating that it was addressed to Jewish converts to Christianity. However, some of these converts were straying away from their new Christian faith. Some were not meeting with the Christian community (10:25); they were drifting away (2:1). They had an unbelieving heart (3:12), their faith was weak (12:12–13), and they were apostatizing (6:6). Most likely they are returning again to the practice of Judaism, especially its sacrifices. Hebrews responds to this, showing that in Christ and Christianity we have everything we need spiritually. We now have a New Covenant, with a new priesthood, the priesthood of Christ, and no longer need animal sacrifices because the sacrificial death of Christ suffices for all time.

This suggests that the letter was written before the destruction of the temple in Jerusalem in AD 70, even though the letter never mentions the temple. Instead, the letter refers to the Levitical priesthood and the sacrifices that were offered in the Tabernacle/Tent in the desert and that continued in the temple in Jerusalem. It does at first seem strange that the letter so often refers to the Tabernacle/Tent which was long gone, rather than to the temple presumably still standing in Jerusalem. Even so, the Tabernacle and temple had the same divisions: the Holy Place where only the priests could enter and the Holy of Holies where only the high priest could enter once yearly on Yom Kippur. Perhaps the letter mentions the Tabernacle rather than the temple because the detailed instructions for the construction of the Tabernacle were received as part of God's covenant with Moses, and Hebrews will point out that in Christ we have a new better covenant (Heb 8:7–13).

When the Letter to the Hebrews is read in the Church, it is introduced as "A Reading from the Letter to the Hebrews" because there is no agreement about who is its author. To reflect this unconfirmed authorship when referring to this letter, I will simply refer to Hebrews or its author. For most of the history of the Church, the author was commonly thought to be St. Paul, due in part to this book being included in the early manuscripts with St. Paul's letters. Who are the Hebrews to whom the letter is addressed? Suggestions are varied, but the proposal by Ceslas Spicq that the Hebrews are a group of Jewish priests who converted to Christianity has been followed by many.[30] One such group of Jewish priests who accepted Christ is mentioned in Acts 6:7.

Hebrews 1–2

The first two chapters of Hebrews set out to prove that Jesus is greater than the angels. We take Jesus' superiority to the angels for granted, but for Hebrews it is important because Judaism believed Moses received the covenant from God through the intermediary of angels

---

[30] Ceslas Spicq, *L'Épître aux Hébreux*, Études bibliques (Paris: Gabalda, 1952–1953), 29–31.

(Heb 2:2). The New Covenant is given to us through the mediation of Jesus, the Son of God, so it is far greater, since Jesus is a greater intermediary than an angel. Consequently, the New Covenant and its liturgy are not to be dismissed to return to the Jewish temple liturgies of the Old Covenant given through angels. This first section of Hebrews, proving the superiority of Jesus to the angels, concludes with the first explicit mention of Jesus as high priest in 2:17.[31] Albert Vanhoye believes that the name given to Jesus in 1:4, which is superior to those of the angels, while never explicitly stated there, is the name "high priest" that is ascribed to him in 2:17.[32]

Christ a Merciful and Trustworthy High Priest Like His Brothers in Every Respect (2:17–18)

Christ had to be like his brothers in all respects so that he would be a merciful and trustworthy high priest (2:17). Because Jesus has been tempted, he can help us when we are tempted (2:18). Hebrews 4:15 adds that, although Jesus was tempted in every way, he did not sin. The same verb, *peirazō* (πειράζω), denoting the tempting of Christ in both Hebrews 2:18 and 4:15 is used in the Synoptics for Satan tempting Jesus in the desert (Matt 4:1, 3; Mark 1:13; Luke 4:2). Christ really was tempted like us. Christ did not assume a mere resemblance to humanity but took on our human nature itself. He truly is like us in every respect except sin. Christ's solidarity with us, sharing our humanity, first appeared in Hebrews 2:10–16, but it is only in 2:17 that Hebrews says it was a necessity for Christ's priesthood. It enabled him to be a compassionate priest. Because Christ has the same flesh and blood as we have (2:14), he calls us his brothers (2:11–12). After the collapse of the direct line of descent of the high priesthood following the Maccabean Revolt, ambition became the way to achieve the Levitical high priesthood. Christ's path to the high priesthood was the total opposite. Vanhoye points out, better than any, the radicalism of what the author of Hebrews has achieved in describing Christ's solidarity with us:

---

[31]   The priesthood of Christ is implied in 1:3 in the statement about Christ having made purification for sins.

[32]   Albert Vanhoye, *Old Testament Priests and the New Priest: According to the New Testament* (Persham, MA: St. Bede's, 1986), 85–86.

It never enters his head to exclude physical wounds or contact with death; on the contrary, he sees them as included in the road that leads to priesthood: it was necessary for Jesus to suffer, it was necessary for him to suffer death. What a reversal of attitudes! It would be difficult to imagine a more radical one.[33]

Christ's solidarity with us made him the perfect priestly mediator between God and mankind.

Hebrews 2:17 tells us the purpose of Christ's assimilation of the human condition was that he might have two qualities, mercy (toward us) and trustworthiness (to his Father). The first quality, mercy, is never associated in the Old Testament with the Levitical priests. Christ's second quality, *pistos* (πιστός), often translated as "faithful," denoting that Christ was faithful to the mission given him by his Father, could also be translated as "trustworthy" or "worthy of trust." The latter has the advantage of emphasizing Christ's ongoing relationship with his Father rather than a onetime act of fidelity in the past, which suits Christ's role in 8:1–2, where he sits at the right hand of the Father conducting a liturgy in the heavenly sanctuary. The word *pistos* has a similar meaning, "trustworthy," in 1 Corinthians 7:25 and 1 Timothy 1:15. Two qualities of Christ's priesthood are highlighted in Hebrews 2:17: he is merciful and trustworthy.

Next, 2:17 proclaims Christ's priestly mission was to expiate the sins of the people, to reconcile us with God. "Expiate" translates the Greek verb *hilaskomai* (ἱλάσκομαι). It is the verbal form of the Greek word used to denote the "mercy seat," the lid over the Ark of the Covenant in the Holy of Holies in Exodus 25:17 21. It was from the mercy seat on top of the ark that God communicated with Moses (Exod 25:22). The high priest sprinkled blood on the mercy seat once a year on the Day of Atonement/Yom Kippur to atone for sins (Lev 16:12–14). It is surely no accident that Hebrews describes Christ's mission of expiating our sins using the verb *hilaskomai*, recalling the mercy seat. Christ's priestly self-sacrifice on Calvary is the New Covenant transfiguration of the Levitical priest sprinkling blood on the mercy seat each year on Yom Kippur, but once is sufficient for all time. Hebrews 9 will explain the efficacy of Christ's onetime act of expiation. Romans 3:25 describes Christ as the mercy seat, although

---

[33] Ibid., 73.

that is not usually evident in English translations. Based on that, we could say that the mercy seat on top of the Ark of the Covenant was anticipating Christ, the true mercy seat of the New Covenant.

Hebrews 2:18 explains that Christ's sufferings and temptations had a consequence, his compassion/mercy, the first of his two characteristics of 2:17. Because Christ suffered and was tempted, he is able to help those who are tempted now. Hebrews recaps this again later in 4:15–16, declaring that Christ is not a high priest unable to sympathize with us, and so we can confidently draw near to receive mercy. Such closeness of a priest to his people is novel compared to the Levitical priests, who were separated from their people by tribe and by a special part of the temple into which only they could enter to sacrifice and worship God. God had intended the Levitical priests to be close to the people, but there is no statement in Judaism paralleling the compassion attributed to the Levitical priests in Hebrews 5:2. The thought of Hebrews 5:2 is influenced by Hebrews' reflection on the compassion of Jesus and describes what God planned for the Levitical priesthood, rather than what transpired.[34]

The first two chapters, proving that Jesus is superior to the angels, conclude with the first reference to Christ as high priest in 2:17. The next two units (3:1–4:14 and 4:15–5:10) expound in reverse order the two attributes of Jesus in 2:17, his mercy and trustworthiness:

Jesus is a merciful and trustworthy high priest (2:17)	
Jesus' trustworthiness (3:1–4:14)	Jesus' mercy (4:15–5:10)

Jesus Our Trustworthy High Priest (3:1–4:14)

The trustworthiness of Jesus' priesthood is expanded in 3:1–4:14, which opens and closes referring to Jesus as high priest (3:1; 4:14). Hebrews 3:1–4:14 encourages readers to have faith in Christ because

---

34   William L. Lane, *Hebrews 1–8*, Word Biblical Commentary 47A (Dallas, TX: Word, 1998), 116. For more on the gradation between priests and people, see Philip Peter Jenson, *Graded Holiness: A Key to the Priestly Conception of the World*, JSOTSup 106 (Sheffield, UK: Sheffield Academic Press, 1992), chapter 5.

he is trustworthy, and this is especially stressed in 3:1–6. This reassurance to trust in Christ follows from reflecting on Christ's humanity in 2:17–18, which is why 3:1 commences with "therefore." The text begins by asking us to reflect on Jesus the apostle and high priest "of our confession" (3:1), which I take to mean that Jesus is the object of our confession, the one whom we profess.[35] In Greek, the word *apostolos*, "apostle" (ἀπόστολος), means one who has been sent, and Jesus is the one who has been sent from the Father. Jesus was trustworthy to the Father who appointed him for his earthly mission, just as Moses was trustworthy when God appointed him over the house of Israel (Hebrews 3:2, 5; see Num 12:7). But Jesus was deemed much more trustworthy, because Moses was a trustworthy servant in the house while Jesus was a trustworthy son in the house (Heb 3:3–6). In 3:6, it is clarified that now the Church is Christ's house. So anyone tempted to revert to Judaism should know that the house is no longer the house of Israel, as in the day of Moses, because now the house is the Church and Jesus is over our house. He is the apostle sent by the Father, our high priest, and he is worthy of our trust.

The conclusion in 4:14 again encourages to hold fast to the confession of faith, since we have a great high priest, Jesus, who has passed through the heavens. The letter describes Jesus as high priest many times, but this is the only verse describing Jesus as a "great high priest," and while this is uncommon, it is not unheard of as a description of the Levitical high priest (e.g., 1 Macc 13:42).

Jesus Our Merciful High Priest (4:15–5:10)

Jesus Is Our Sympathetic Priest—Let Us Approach God's Throne (4:15–16)

The second quality of Jesus' priesthood, his mercy, is developed in 4:15–5:10. The explanation commences in 4:15–16 by reiterating what was already stated in 2:17, that Jesus' sympathy for our weaknesses arises out of his being tempted in all respects like us, and adds that Jesus did not sin. This is the first use of the word *sympatheō*, "show sympathy" (συμπαθέω), in the New Testament (Hebrews 4:15) and is eminently suitable for Jesus' solidarity with us. It is a composite Greek word composed of σύν + πάσχω ("with" + "suffer"), mean-

---

[35]   Vanhoye believes it means we bring our profession of faith through Christ to the Father (*Old Testament Priests and the New Priest*, 97–98).

ing to *suffer with* someone, to share the same suffering or emotion. When we suffer weakness, we can remember that Christ is sympathetic to us because he has already experienced our weaknesses. He is with us and also suffered like us, though he did not sin. The verb "tempt" was in the aorist tense (past action) in 2:18 to indicate Christ's past trials, but here in 4:15, it is in the perfect tense, indicating the continuing effects of those trials on Christ, that he has not forgotten his trials even though he is now sitting at the right hand of the Father in heaven (Heb 8:1; Acts 2:33). That is why Jesus is merciful and sympathetic.

Since Christ is merciful and sympathetic, Hebrews encourages us to approach the throne of grace (4:16). Jesus our priest, in his once-for-all-time act of expiation, has opened access for us to the throne of God. Previously, only the high priest could approach God's throne once a year, the mercy seat alluded to in 2:17, inside the Holy of Holies. Now, Hebrews 4:16 encourages approaching the throne spiritually through Christ. God's throne now welcomes all. Through Christ's priestly sacrifice, the veil guarding the way into the Holy of Holies has been torn down (Matt 27:51; Mark 15:38; Luke 23:45) and we have access to the Father in heaven. The exhortation is obviously not to encourage listeners to enter the Holy of Holies in the temple, but rather to commune spiritually with the Father in heaven through Christ, since Christ is now the way to the Father. Hebrews 10 will explain that we can approach the throne through the Eucharist.

The sense of the exhortation in 4:16 is that there is now complete freedom to approach the Father through Christ. The Greek word *parrēsia* (παρρησία) in 4:16, often translated as "confidence," is a composite word formed by joining two words, *pas* (πᾶς) + *rhēsis* (ῥῆσις), "all" + "speech," thus meaning freedom to speak and so, in this context, referring to complete freedom to draw near to God's throne. It is noteworthy that the author of Hebrews uses this word in encouraging the letter's recipients to draw near to God, because in Judaism no one was allowed to pronounce the divine name "Yahweh" with the exception of the high priest, who could do so only once a year inside in the Holy of Holies on the Day of Atonement/Yom Kippur. Now, by contrast, there is freedom of speech to approach the Father through Jesus to obtain mercy and grace.

How the Levitical High Priest and Christ Became High Priests (5:1–10)

The author of Hebrews aimed to convince his readers in 4:15–16 that Christ is a sympathetic high priest. Following that, he proceeds to explain how one becomes a high priest. The Levitical high priest was appointed by God rather than choosing the high priesthood for himself (5:1–4), and likewise, Christ was appointed high priest by the Father (5:5–10).

How One Became the Levitical High Priest (5:1–4)

The Levitical priests have been superseded by Christ, yet the great respect of Hebrews for them is clearly evident. Every high priest does not take the honor of high priesthood on himself but is appointed by God (5:1, 4). This is remarkable in that the position of high priest was such that one was in effect born into that position, since it was passed from father to the eldest son. Even though the Levitical office of high priest was passed on in that hereditary manner until the Maccabean period, Hebrews wants us to understand that this was God's plan and those who received the office of high priest in this way did so because they were in fact called by God (5:4). Every high priest is appointed by God as mediator between God and his people, and the high priest acts on behalf of men in the service of God, offering sacrifices for sins (5:1).

How Christ Became a Priest—Decreed by the Father (5:5–6)

How did Christ become high priest? Hebrews explains in 5:5–10. The first word in Greek in 5:5 already indicates the reasoning that will be used, *houtōs* (οὕτως), "in the same manner." In the same manner as the Levitical high priests, Christ did not exalt himself before the Father to become a high priest, but rather the Father appointed him high priest (5:5–6).

Hebrews uses a two-step approach to prove that the Father appointed Christ a high priest, each step making use of an Old Testament quotation. Firstly, Hebrews 5:5 quotes Psalm 2:7—"You are my son, today I have begotten you." Psalm 2 was a hymn for a royal coronation reflecting the Jewish understanding that their king was adopted by God as his son on the day of his coronation. In verse 6 of the Psalm, God proclaims that he has installed his king, and the king responds in verse 7, quoting God's decree to him, "You are my Son, today I have begotten you." This reflects the Davidic theology in 2 Samuel 7:12–14 where God decreed to David that there would be a king on the throne of David forever. After the termination of the monarchy in 587 BC, royal psalms such as Psalm 2 could no longer be prayed in reference to a king on the throne. Then such psalms had to be read, prayed, and understood in a new way and were seen anticipating the coming of the Messiah. This explains why the New Testament sees Psalm 2:7 fulfilled in Christ (Acts 13:33; Heb 1:5; 5:5). For the New Testament writers, Psalm 2:7 is the Father's decree to Christ, "You are my son, today I have begotten you."

Secondly, Hebrews 5:6 cites Psalm 110:4 as if also spoken by the Father to Christ. Psalm 110, like Psalm 2, is a royal psalm from before the collapse of the monarchy in 587 BC. A divine oracle from God to the king is preserved in verse 4, "You are a priest forever after the order of Melchizedek." (The author will explain Christ's priesthood after the order of Melchizedek in Heb 7.) The author of Hebrews first cited Psalm 2:7, well known by the early Church in its messianic sense, as if the Father is speaking to the Son of his begetting, and then in parallel fashion quotes Ps 110:4 as an analogous decree by the Father bestowing the priesthood on the Incarnate Christ. Sonship is bestowed on Christ by the Father (Ps 2:7), and in parallel fashion, the priesthood is also bestowed on Christ by the Father (Ps 110:4). The author of Hebrews found, in the Old Testament, precise texts to suit his purpose perfectly to prove that the Father bestowed the priesthood on Christ. The author began with what was already common— the Sonship of Christ—which allowed him to prove the priesthood of Christ by a Christological interpretation of Psalm 110:4 analogous to the Christological interpretation of Psalm 2:7. Applying Psalm 110:4 to Christ in this way was not a big leap in Hebrews 5:6 because Christ had already applied verse 1 of Psalm 110 to himself about sitting at his Father's right hand (Matt 22:44; Mark 12:36; Luke 20:42–43). Peter did likewise during his Pentecost Sermon (Acts 2:34–35), and Hebrews 1:13 had also already done so.

In 5:1–6, Hebrews has shown that both the Levitical high priest and Christ did not take the priesthood on themselves but were appointed by the Father. Later, Hebrews will add a detail to distinguish the Father's appointment of Christ as high priest: the Father made

Christ a priest by oath, which did not occur in the case of the Leviti-cal priests (7:20–22). Are we to understand that Christ was a priest from the moment of his Incarnation? Jean Galot writes, "the priest-hood of Christ had its beginning at the Incarnation but attained its full reality only at the moment in which he entered into heaven."[36]

Christ's Priestly Offering of Himself (5:7–10)

High priests were appointed to offer gifts and sacrifices to God (5:1), and Christ as priest also made offerings to his Father, his prayers and entreaties (5:7). Even the same verb for making an offering— *prospherō* (προσφέρω)—was chosen by the author of Hebrews for the high priest's offering in 5:1 and for Christ's offering in 5:7. Jesus' prayers and petitions were offered with loud cries and tears to God who could save him from death (5:7). Jesus' prayers and tears began in Gethsemane and continued as he died on the Cross. His priestly self-offering already commenced in Gethsemane.

Jesus' prayers were heard because of his *eulabeia* (εὐλάβεια) be-fore God (5:7). The Greek word *eulabeia* cannot easily be translated into English in one word. It means "reverent awe in the presence of God."[37] The idea conveyed is that Christ prayed with complete open-ness to the Father, willing to accept whatever outcome to his prayer the Father decided. Jesus' prayer of petition is a model for our prayer of petition. Jesus' prayers, cries, and tears were answered by the Fa-ther in Jesus' Resurrection.

As Jesus makes his priestly offering to his Father, he does so in solidarity with our human nature, "in the days of his flesh" (5:7). Sharing our humanity, Jesus learned obedience through his suffer-ing (5:8). St. Thomas Aquinas explains it in this way: "Christ . . . was

---

[36] Jean Galot, *Theology of the Priesthood* (San Francisco: Ignatius Press, 1985), 59.

[37] William Arndt, Frederick W. Danker, and Walter Bauer, *A Greek-English Lexicon of the New Testament and Other Early Christian Literature*, 3rd ed. (BDAG), rev. and ed. F. W. Danker (Chicago: University of Chicago Press, 2000), 407. It is one of the seven gifts of the Spirit of Isa 11:2–3 (LXX) that the bishop prays confirmandi receive during the Sacrament of Confirma-tion. In the bishop's prayer, it is "wonder and awe" in the presence of God; see Congregatio de Cultu Divino et Disciplina Sacramentorum, Vox Clara Committee, *The Roman Pontifical* (Vatican City: Vox Clara Committee, 2012), 361.

ignorant of nothing and as a consequence did not learn . . . but there is also the knowledge of experience, and according to this . . . [he] learned obedience by the things which He suffered . . . He learned obedience, that is, how burdensome it is to obey since He obeyed in the most burdensome and difficult matters, for He obeyed even unto the death of the cross."[38] That humility of Christ, who humbled himself by becoming human, becoming obedient to death, even death on a cross, is praised in Philippians 2:8. Hebrews makes it abundantly clear that Christ's priestly offering involved Christ's own personal sacrifice and suffering. It was a necessity that Vanhoye explains in this way:

> But our nature "of flesh and blood" which he had agreed to share (2:14) had been deformed by disobedience and needed to be set right. It was necessary for it to be melted down again in the crucible of suffering and transformed by the action of God. No man, however, was in a position to welcome this terribly trying divine action in the way required. Only Christ, who had no need of it for himself, was capable of it . . . In him, therefore, a new man has been created who corresponds perfectly to the divine intention.[39]

We see then that the path to priesthood for Christ was twofold: being appointed a priest by the Father (5:5) and also being obedient while undergoing human suffering (5:7–8). There is also a dual path to priesthood for those ordained Catholic priests sharing in Christ's priesthood today: they are called by God and obedient to formation in seminary.

Hebrews 5:9 tells us Christ's obedient offering of himself in his Passion had two consequences: Christ's priesthood attained its perfect fulfillment and he became the source of our salvation (5:9). Taking up the first point, the Greek of 5:9 says Christ was made perfect (in his priesthood). This does not mean there was imperfection in Christ previously, but that Christ's priesthood is fully manifested or realized in his sacrifice on the Cross. The verb *teleioō* (τελειόω) in 5:9, translated as "make perfect," signifies priestly ordination in the

---

[38]   Thomas Aquinas, *Commentary on the Epistle to the Hebrews* (South Bend, IN: St. Augustine's Press, 2006), 116–117.

[39]   Vanhoye, *Old Testament Priests and the New Priest*, 129.

Greek Pentateuch[40] (e.g., Exod 29:9, 29, 35). Christ's "perfection" is bringing his priesthood to its proper end through his self-sacrificial offering. This perfection/transformation of Christ on Calvary can be seen in his disciples not recognizing him after his Resurrection (Luke 24:15–16; John 20:14–15) and Jesus appearing and disappearing suddenly (Luke 24:31, 36; John 20:19, 26). Although the verb "perfect" is used of the ordination of the Levitical priests in the Pentateuch, Hebrews uses the verb "perfect" only of Christ's priestly self-offering on Calvary. That is why, in 5:1, Hebrews says the Levitical priests were "appointed," using the verb kathistēmi (καθίστημι), which refers to installation in any office. But in 5:9, Hebrews uses the verb "perfect," teleioō (τελειόω), of Christ's priestly self-offering on Calvary.[41] In this way the author of Hebrews is teaching that the Levitical priests were never transformed by their ordination but Christ was existentially transformed and perfected in his priesthood by his Passion. The Father had already decreed Christ was his Son and a priest forever, therefore we might say that 5:9 describes Christ enacting his priesthood perfectly in his self-sacrificial offering on Calvary, just as a Catholic priest enacts his priesthood when he concelebrates Mass with his bishop just minutes after his ordination.

The second consequence of Christ's obedient self-offering is that Christ is the source of our salvation—Christ saves us (5:9)—but we have to wait until 10:1–18 for Hebrews to expand on that. Hebrews concludes this unit of the letter by repeating the thought of 5:5–6—Christ was designated a priest by the Father after the order of Melchizedek (5:10).

Christ a Priest after the Order of Melchizedek (Hebrews 7)

Hebrews 5:1–6 showed that the Levitical high priest and Christ did not take the honor of high priesthood on themselves but were appointed by the Father. Now in Hebrews 7, the author sets about showing that Christ's priesthood is superior to that of the Levites. Hebrews' argument may be summarized as follows:

---

[40] Ibid., 133; see also 165–166. This is the Greek verb used to translate the Hebrew idiom "fill the hand" we looked at in chapter 1 and will examine in Appendix 2.

[41] Ibid., 138, 141.

a) Melchizedek's priesthood is superior to the Levites (7:1–10);

b) Christ is a priest after the order of Melchizedek (7:11–19);

c) and therefore Christ's priesthood is superior to the Levites (7:20–28).

a) Melchizedek's priesthood is superior to the Levites (7:1–10)

Hebrews 7:1 is a brief summary of the meeting between Melchizedek and Abraham recounted in Genesis 14:18–20. Melchizedek was king of Salem, which is often identified with Jerusalem. He was a priest of God Most High. He blessed Abraham when Abraham returned after defeating marauding kings, and Abraham in turn tithed to Melchizedek. Hebrews then plays with the etymology of Melchizedek's name (7:2). The name Melchizedek is a composite word formed by joining two words, *melek* ("king"; מֶלֶךְ) + *ṣedeq* ("righteousness"; צֶדֶק), so Hebrews says his name means "King of Righteousness." Since the word "Salem" is related to "Shalom," regularly translated as "peace," this leads Hebrews to play with words and say Melchizedek is "king of Salem"—"king of peace" (7:2).

Hebrews 7:3 then interprets the account of Melchizedek in Genesis in a way that shows his distinction from the Levitical priesthood and makes him anticipate Christ. Hebrews says Melchizedek has no father or mother or genealogy. That is understood by some exegetes to be an argument from silence.[42] It could be explained as follows. Melchizedek is presented in Genesis 14:18 without any prior introduction, and we do not read about him in the Pentateuch again afterwards, which prompts Hebrews to state that Melchizedek had no beginning or end. To our minds, this is an unusual way of interpreting Scripture, but this way of understanding Scripture was not uncommon in Judaism. For example, the Talmud says that until the time of Jacob there was no illness (b. Sanh. 107B [11:1])[43] because the first illness mentioned in Scripture is the illness of Jacob in Genesis

---

[42]   Ibid., 154. See also Craig R. Koester, *Hebrews: A New Translation with Introduction and Commentary*, Anchor Yale Bible 36 (New Haven, CT/London: Yale University Press, 2008), 348.

[43]   Jacob Neusner, *The Babylonian Talmud: A Translation and Commentary* (Peabody, MA: Hendrickson, 2011), 16:578. All further citations of the Babylonian Talmud are to be found in Neusner's edition.

48:1. The same Talmud passage also says that no one showed signs of old age until Abraham because signs of old age are first mentioned in Genesis 24:1 (previous passages in Genesis mentioned Noah's age—e.g., 5:32—but not that he was showing signs of age). It was essential for the Levitical priests to be able to show their genealogy in order to be allowed to serve as priests. Priests returning to Jerusalem after the exile in Babylon who could not prove their priestly descent due to lack of genealogical documentation were barred from serving (Ezra 2:61–62; Neh 7:63–64). But Hebrews saying that Melchizedek had no father, mother, or genealogy meant Melchizedek was not in a line of priestly succession. Not only is Melchizedek introduced suddenly in Genesis without mention of his parents, but also his death is not related in Genesis. This also leads Hebrews to say that Melchizedek is not only without beginning of days but also without end of life and therefore resembles Christ.

Hebrews 7:1–3 showed that lack of ancestry distinguishes Melchizedek's priesthood from the Levites, and in 7:4–10 the author makes use of a clever argument to show the superiority of Melchizedek's priesthood over the Levites. Melchizedek blessed Abraham, and Abraham tithed to Melchizedek. The greater one gives the blessing, so Melchizedek blessing Abraham reveals that Melchizedek was superior to Abraham. When Abraham tithed to Melchizedek, that also displayed Melchizedek's superiority. The Levites were descended from Abraham, so in the person of Abraham, the Levites paid tithes to a greater one, Melchizedek. Melchizedek's priesthood is therefore superior to the Levitical priesthood. The mere fact that the Levitical priesthood came later than the priesthood of Melchizedek does not mean it was greater. Melchizedek's priesthood is greater, though preceding the Levitical priesthood.

b) Christ is a priest after the order of Melchizedek (7:11–19)

Following the demonstration of the superiority of Melchizedek's priesthood over the Levitical priesthood, the inferiority of the Levitical priesthood by comparison with Christ's priesthood is established in 7:11–19. The Levitical priesthood was lacking in perfection. It remained in an unrealized condition "if perfection were by way of the Levitical priesthood" (7:11). The Greek word *teleiōsis* (τελείωσις), translated as "perfection," refers to the ordination of a priest in the

Greek Pentateuch (e.g., Exod 29:22, 26, 27), as does its verbal form already encountered in Hebrews 5:9. Although the word "perfection" was used in the Old Testament for the ordination of the Levitical priests, Hebrews is stating there was something lacking in their ordination "if perfection were by way of the Levitical priesthood" (in Hebrews 5, Hebrews avoided using "perfection" when discussing the Levitical priests and employed it only for Christ's priesthood). That is why priesthood in another order, the order of Melchizedek, was necessary. Inadequacy in the Levitical priesthood has been replaced by perfection in the priesthood of Christ. Vanhoye explains 7:11 in this way:

> In short, it is the necessity for the Passion and Resurrection of Christ that appears again here. In order that another priest could be "raised up," it was necessary for Christ to submit himself to the transformation of his human self, achieved in his Passion and manifested in his Resurrection.[44]

Since there is a change in the priesthood from Levitical priesthood to Christ, there must also be a change in the divine law (7:12), because the Levitical priesthood was governed by God's law given to Moses in the Old Covenant (Exod 29). With a new priesthood, there must now be a new law. The change in the priesthood accompanies the New Covenant. The change in the law is obvious when one considers the laws concerning priestly succession. In the Old Covenant, the priesthood was reserved to those descended from Aaron in the tribe of Levi, but Jesus is from the tribe of Judah, which has no priestly connection (Heb 7:13–14). In Jesus, therefore, there has been a radical transformation in the priesthood.

Jesus became a priest not because he satisfied a law requiring physical descent from Aaron, but by what Hebrews 7:16 calls "an indestructible life." Jesus' Resurrection gave him indestructible life and his priesthood of intercession in heaven. In heaven, interceding for us at the right side of the Father (Heb 8:1–2), Christ's priesthood reaches its fulfillment. It is worth recalling again what Galot wrote: "the priesthood of Christ had its beginning at the Incarnation but attained its full reality only at the moment in which he entered into

---

44   Vanhoye, *Old Testament Priests and the New Priest*, 167.

heaven."[45] The next verse (7:17) once again cites Psalm 110:4 and applies it to Christ: he is a priest forever after the order of Melchizedek. Two consequences follow from all of the above, one negative and one positive. The Levitical laws on hereditary priesthood are annulled (7:18) and there is a new way to draw near to God (7:19). This new way is through Christ our high priest.

c) Christ's priesthood is superior to the Levites (7:20–28)

The Levitical high priests were called by God even though they held a hereditary office (5:4). Yet God did not swear an oath confirming them in their priesthood (7:21), but the Father did swear an oath in Psalm 110:4 confirming Christ's priesthood (7:20–21). For Hebrews, this means the New Covenant is better (7:22). Hebrews uses a juridical term, "surety," to describe Jesus as the guarantee of the New Covenant in 7:22. If a parent acts as guarantor or surety for a child's loan, the parent promises to pay the loan if the child fails to do so. For the author of Hebrews, Christ is the surety or guarantee of the New Covenant. Christ took all the obligation of the New Covenant on himself on Calvary. He is the surety of a better covenant because his sacrifice was once for all time, in contrast to the continual sacrifices of the Old Covenant.

The Levitical priests passed their priesthood from one to another as each one died; their time in office was limited. There had to be many priests because they died (7:23). But Christ's priesthood is permanent (7:24). Christ's priestly ministry interceding on our behalf continues forever, so he can save all those who approach the Father through him (7:25). That verse could be regarded as a summary of Christ's priestly office.[46]

The chapter concludes with a shout of praise for Christ the high priest, recapitulating the superiority of Christ's priesthood over the Levitical priests (7:26–28). The Levitical priests had to offer sacrifices for their own sins, but sinless Christ offered one sacrifice for all time (7:26–27). The Levitical high priests, with human weakness, were regulated by the law, but Christ was appointed Son by the Father's oath and has been made perfect forever (7:28). Levitical high

---

45   Galot, *Theology of the Priesthood*, 59.

46   Spicq, *L'Épître aux Hébreux*, 129.

priests were governed by the law, but Christ was ordained an eternal priest by his Father's oath. Christ's priesthood is superior to that of the Levitical priests.

Superiority of Christ's Sacrifice, the New Covenant, and Christ's Priestly Ministry in Heaven (Hebrews 8–9)

Hebrews 7 showed the superiority of Christ's priesthood in the order of Melchizedek over the Levitical priesthood. Now in chapters 8–9, Hebrews shows:

a) the superiority of Christ's sacrifice over the Levitical priest's sacrifice (8:1–6);
b) the superiority of the New Covenant that Christ mediates over the Old Covenant (8:7–13);
c) and the superiority of the heavenly temple where Christ now ministers as priest over the earthly temple of the Levitical priests (9:1–28).

Superiority of Christ's Sacrifice (8:1–6)

Chapter 8 commences by informing the reader we have arrived at the point Hebrews wants to make: Christ is a high priest sitting at the right hand of his Father in heaven (8:1). Hebrews describes Christ as a *leitourgos* (λειτουργός), a liturgist/minister conducting a sacred liturgy in heaven (8:2).[47] Hebrews describes God's heavenly sanctuary as the true tent (8:2). The Levitical priests were performing their liturgies in a tent on earth called the Tabernacle, but that earthly tent was merely a copy of the real sanctuary in heaven, God's heavenly dwelling (8:5; see Wis 9:8). Although that tent was replaced by the temple in Jerusalem, Hebrews continually refers to the tent rather than the temple. Before Moses constructed the Tabernacle/Tent God

---

47   Hebrews 8:2 describes God's dwelling in heaven simply as "the sanctuary." The Greek *ta hagia* (τὰ ἅγια) does not specify whether the sanctuary is the Holy of Holies or should be taken more generally. Commentators are split: some believe that "sanctuary" refers to the heavenly Holy of Holies and "tent" refers to the whole of God's heavenly dwelling, while others believe the text is not making this claim. This distinction is not significant here in Hebrews 8:2, but we will have occasion to comment on this when discussing Hebrews 9:12, so I draw your attention to it now.

gave him a revelation of the plan to follow for its construction. So the Tabernacle/Tent is not the ultimate end; it is only patterned after God's heavenly sanctuary.

Christ is a priest in God's true sanctuary in heaven. The duty of a priest is to offer sacrifice, and so Christ, being a high priest, must also have a sacrifice to offer (8:3). Since Jesus was not from the tribe of Levi, he could never become a priest in the earthly Tabernacle/Tent or offer sacrifices in the temple, as specified in Jewish law (8:4). But Christ's priestly service in heaven is as superior to the priestly service of the Levitical priests as the New Covenant is superior to the Old Covenant (8:6). This is because he offered himself, not animals, as the Levitical priests did, and Christ's sacrifice was once for all time, unlike that of the Levitical priests, which had to be continually repeated (9:24–28).

Superiority of the New Covenant (8:7–13)

The superiority of the New Covenant and Christ's priestly ministry in heaven (8:6) implies there is a deficiency in the Old Covenant (8:7), which allows Hebrews to introduce the quotation from Jeremiah 31:31–34 promising a New Covenant. Other Old Testament texts promised an "eternal covenant" (Jer 32:40), a "covenant of peace" (Ezek 34:25; 37:26), and an "everlasting covenant" (Ezek 16:60; 37:26), but Jeremiah 31:31–34 is the only Old Testament text to promise a "new covenant." The author of Hebrews has found the perfect Scripture passage to prove that even Scripture itself foretold the substitution of the Mosaic covenant by a better one. In Hebrews 5:6, the author used Scripture to prove that Christ became a priest by the will of the Father (Ps 110:4), and here in chapter 8, the author uses Jeremiah 31:31–34 to show that Scripture also predicted a new covenant better than its predecessor. Hebrews 8:6 reports a chorus of what is better: Christ is the mediator of a better covenant; his priestly ministry is better; and the New Covenant is founded on better promises. (These are the attributes of a better covenant because, as Hebrews 7:12 notes, a change in covenant automatically brings a change in priesthood and therefore a change in liturgy.) Hebrews does not elaborate on the difference between the promises of the Old and New Covenants, but the promises pertaining to the New Covenant follow in 8:10–12, in the last verses of the quotation from Jeremiah. The New Covenant will be internalized and will be characterized by God's mercy. Hebrews regards the First Covenant as growing old and superseded by the New Covenant (8:13).

Superiority of the Heavenly Temple Where Christ Now Ministers as Priest (9:1–28)

Following on naturally from the declaration in 8:13 that the First Covenant is growing old, Hebrews 9:1–10 explains that the liturgy performed by the Levitical priests could not bring salvation. The description of that liturgy is introduced in 9:1 with the statement that the First/Old Covenant had worship regulations and a sanctuary. Hebrews gives attention to the two distinct areas in the sanctuary, each preceded by a curtain, because Hebrews will later interpret these two areas spiritually. The first area, accessed by all priests, was the Holy Place (9:2), and the second area, entered by the high priest only once a year, was the Holy of Holies (9:3). The first area, the Holy Place, contained the seven-branched lampstand, called the menorah, and the holy table covered in gold on which was placed the bread of Presence in two rows of six loaves representing the twelve tribes. The bread was replaced each Sabbath by the high priest and consumed by the priests (see Lev 24:5–9). The second area, the Holy of Holies, contained the Ark of the Covenant and what Hebrews describes as either a censer for burning incense or the incense altar (9:4).[48] Hebrews 9:4 tells us that the Ark of the Covenant contained not only the stone tablets of the commandments but also an urn of manna (Exod 16:32–34) and Aaron's rod that budded (Num 17). Aaron's rod was the only one of twelve rods representing the twelve tribes that budded after a time of rebellion among the people. This confirmed God's choice of the Aaronic priesthood and Aaron's authority. The mercy seat was on top of the ark (9:5; see comments above on 2:17).

The explanation of the different components of the Holy Place and Holy of Holies in 9:1–5 is followed by a description of their dis-

---

[48]   It is unclear in the Greek which is meant, though it is usually taken to be the altar of incense even though most, but not all, believe it was situated in the first area, the Holy Place, and not the Holy of Holies, based on Exod 30:7; see Harold W. Attridge and Helmut Koester, *The Epistle to the Hebrews: A Commentary on the Epistle to the Hebrews*, Hermeneia—a Critical and Historical Commentary on the Bible (Philadelphia, PA: Fortress Press, 1989), 234–235.

tinct liturgies in Hebrews 9:6–7. The priests minister in the Holy Place (9:6), but only the high priest can enter the Holy of Holies and only once a year taking the blood of a sacrificed bull and goat as a sin offering (9:7; see Lev 16). Then 9:8–10 interpret these two distinct areas—the Holy Place and the Holy of Holies—and attribute the explanation to the Holy Spirit in 9:8. The first or outer area, the Holy Place, is a figure for the time before Christ when the sacrifices of the Old Covenant were being conducted, and the way into the Holy of Holies, the second or inner area—symbolic of the age of Christ and access through Christ to the heavenly sanctuary—had not yet been revealed (9:8–9a; see 9:11–12; 10:19–20). Hebrews negatively critiques the sacrifices of the Old Covenant: they were unable to perfect the conscience of the worshippers (9:9b-10). In other words, the worship of the Old Covenant was unable to bring about a personal transformation in the worshippers but the worship of the New Covenant produces such a personal transformation.[49] So the very structure of the tent, with entry forbidden into the second or inner area, the Holy of Holies, was symbolic of the ineffectiveness of the Old Covenant liturgy and its inability to sanctify those who worshipped. It dealt with only externals, food and drink and ritual washings (9:10). It was before the time of Christ, the time of "reformation," to use the language of Hebrews 9:10.

By contrast, in 9:11–28, and especially in 9:11–12, Hebrews emphasizes the effectiveness of Christ's onetime self-offering and describes Christ's death like no other New Testament document. The Levitical high priest sprinkled blood inside the Holy of Holies each year on Yom Kippur to make atonement for sin. Now Hebrews sees Christ's death as the transfiguration/fulfillment of the Yom Kippur liturgy. When Christ died, he took his own blood not into the Holy of Holies in the temple but into the heavenly sanctuary to gain salvation for us. Back in 6:19–20, Hebrews alluded to Christ as high priest entering behind the curtain into the Holy of Holies. That was already a strong indication that Jesus' Passion and death were a transfiguration/fulfillment of the Yom Kippur liturgy, but Hebrews leaves the full explanation until 9:11–28. Christ's acceptance of his death as a sacrifice of reconciliation is the perfect fulfillment of his priesthood (5:9–10). It is best described by Vanhoye:

---

[49]   Vanhoye, *Old Testament Priests and the New Priest*, 187.

At the beginning of his offering, Christ was on earth like the other priests, but at its completion he has left the world. His offering has resulted in an effective transformation, which has transported him to another level of existence. It is not a question of a ceremony, but of an existential fulfillment.[50]

Ratzinger describes Christ's passage from the Cross to the heavenly temple in this way:

Jesus stepped, not in the limited arena of the liturgical performance, the Temple, but publicly, before the eyes of the world, through the curtain of death into the real temple, that is, before the face of God himself, in order to offer, not things, the blood of animals, or anything like that, but himself.[51]

Hebrews 9:12 says Christ entered the heavenly sanctuary. However, we might have expected Hebrews would instead say Christ entered the heavenly Holy of Holies, since in 9:1–5 the author distinguishes between the Holy Place and Holy of Holies. But 9:12 says Christ entered the "sanctuary," *ta hagia* (τὰ ἅγια), which is translated in many Bibles as "the Holy Place." In 8:2, the same Greek term, *ta hagia*, refers to the heavenly sanctuary, so it seems more appropriate to translate it as "sanctuary" also here in 9:12. If we were to translate it as "Holy Place," that would seem strange after Hebrews clearly distinguished between Holy Place and Holy of Holies in 9:1–5. That would beg the question of why Christ would not take his blood into the heavenly Holy of Holies like the Levitical high priest but stopped in the Holy Place, unless one were to understand "Holy Place" as referring to the entire heavenly sanctuary. Instead, Hebrews does not distinguish between Holy Place and Holy of Holies in God's heavenly temple, simply referring to God's sanctuary, even though 8:5 states that the earthly temple is a copy of God's heavenly temple. It seems that Hebrews was specific in 9:1–5 about the division between the Holy Place and Holy of Holies in the earthly tent to make the point in 9:8–9a that the Holy Place is symbolic of the Old Covenant and the Holy of Holies is symbolic of the New Covenant.

---

[50]   Ibid., 180.

[51]   Joseph Ratzinger, *Introduction to Christianity*, trans. J. R. Foster, revised ed. (San Francisco: Ignatius Press, 2004), 286.

Christ's offering was effective once for all time because he took his own blood into the sanctuary, not animals' blood (9:12). That effectiveness is highlighted in 9:14, which describes Christ as blameless, meaning he was sinless (as in 4:15). The value and effectiveness of the blood offered derives from the one who offered it, which is why Christ's offering is effective for all time. A second reason for the effectiveness of Christ's self-offering is that he made it through the Spirit (9:14). Christ's sacrificial offering resulted in the purification of Christians' consciences to serve God (9:14). It caused the transformation of Christians before the Father, whereas the sprinkling of animals' blood and ashes only brought purification from ritual uncleanness (9:13; see Num 19).

The superiority of Christ's self-sacrifice over the animal sacrifices (9:11–14) has consequences: Christ is the mediator of a New Covenant (9:15).[52] Hebrews had already reflected on the New Covenant in chapter 8 and meditates on it again in 9:15–22. There is a play on the double meaning of the Greek word *diathēkē* (διαθήκη) in 9:16 that affects the understanding of the remainder of the chapter. The word *diathēkē* meant "testament" or "last will" in secular Greek, but the Greek Old Testament used the word *diathēkē* to mean "covenant." This double meaning was surely evident to the listeners of Hebrews. A last will (*diathēkē*) does not come into effect until the death of the one who made the will (9:16–17). Similarly, the Old Covenant (*diathēkē*) did not come into effect without death demonstrated by the blood, so Moses sprinkled the blood of goats and calves on the book of the covenant, the people, the tent, and sacred vessels (9:18–22). The death of the animals in some way substituted for God, but in the New Covenant the death of God's Son would take place. Death brings a last will or testament (*diathēkē*) into effect, and death brought the Old and New Covenants (*diathēkē*) into effect, animals' death the Old Covenant and Christ's death the New Covenant. Diagrammatically, it can be represented in this way:

---

[52] For more on the mediating role of Christ, see Joseph Ratzinger, *Principles of Catholic Theology: Building Stones for a Fundamental Theology*, trans. Mary Frances McCarthy (San Francisco: Ignatius Press, 1987), 269–273.

1. *diathēkē* (in the secular sense meaning "last will") comes into
    effect upon the death of the one who made the will (9:16–17).
2. *diathēkē* (meaning "covenant").
    a. The Old Covenant came into effect by death dem-
        onstrated by Moses sprinkling the blood of animals
        (9:18–22).
    b. The New Covenant came into effect by the death of
        Christ (9:23–28).

What is the point of 9:15–28? It demonstrates the necessity of the
death of Jesus for what we inherit spiritually, "eternal redemption" in
9:12 and a purified conscience in 9:14.

Salvific Effects of Christ's Priestly Sacrifice (Hebrews 10)

The meditation on Christ's priesthood draws to a conclusion in 10:1–
18, where Hebrews emphasizes the salvific benefits of Christ's priestly offering for the faithful. It is introduced in 10:1–4 stating that the
sacrifices of the Levitical priests were unable to perfect/transform
the worshippers of the Old Covenant. If those animal sacrifices had
been effective in removing consciousness of sin from the worshippers, they would not have had to continually repeat those animal
sacrifices every year on Yom Kippur.

Following this introduction, there are three Old Testament quo-
tations surrounded by Hebrews' comments, one each in 10:5–10, in
10:11–14, and in 10:15–18, which Hebrews sees fulfilled in Christ:

1. Firstly, in 10:5–7, Hebrews quotes Psalm 40:6–7 in such a way
    that the author sees Christ reciting the Psalm when Christ
    became incarnate (10:5–7). When the Son became incarnate,
    the Father did not want animal sacrifices and they were abol-
    ished, to be replaced by the perfect priestly sacrifice of Christ
    (10:9b–10).
2. In 10:12b–13, the second quotation is from Psalm 110:1.
    When Christ made his single sacrifice for all time, in the
    words of Psalm 110:1, he sat down at the right hand of God
    waiting for his enemies to be subject to him. Then follows a
    crucial statement in 10:14: by that one sacrifice, Christ has
    perfected/transformed the faithful for all time. Christ's ac-

ceptance of his death as a sacrifice of reconciliation is not only the perfect realization of his priesthood before the Father (see comments above on 5:9) but also *transformed us* before God because now, in Christ, we have true forgiveness of sins and are able to enter into God's presence (4:16; 10:19).

3. Thirdly, in 10:16–17, Hebrews quotes Jeremiah 31:33–34, a shorter form of the quotation in 8:10–12. It critiques the Old Covenant because there is now a New Covenant characterized by being written on people's hearts rather than stone and effecting forgiveness of sins. This marks the conclusion of Hebrews' teaching on Christ's priesthood.

Following the conclusion of the teaching on Christ's priesthood, we are provided with an exhortation beginning in 10:19 and continuing to the end of the chapter. Of interest to us is 10:19–25, which commences with an invitation to enter God's sanctuary, an invitation already issued in 4:16. However, here the reader is told specifically how to enter into God's sanctuary. Christ is a great priest over God's house (10:21) because he has opened the way to God's sanctuary by his death on Calvary, and we can enter "by the blood of Jesus" (10:19) and through the curtain, "through his flesh" (10:20). Obviously, we see entering through the flesh of Jesus as an allusion to the Eucharist. Hebrews is teaching that the celebration of the Eucharist is now the way to enter God's sanctuary. Unlike Yom Kippur, where only the high priest could enter the Holy of Holies, now all Christians are invited into God's sanctuary through the flesh and blood of Jesus. Hebrews 6:20 says Jesus entered before us as our forerunner, meaning we are to follow him. But before approaching God's heavenly throne in the celebration of the Eucharist, Hebrews asks Christians to be prepared in three ways: to have full faith, no evil in our conscience, and bodies washed with pure water, which I take to mean having received Baptism (10:22). We enter the sanctuary through Christ, through his flesh and blood, the celebration of the Eucharist when Christians meet together (10:25). We can enter the sanctuary every day as we join in the daily celebration of Mass. Christ was sacrificed once for all time, but we benefit from the salvific effects of Christ's death on Calvary as we meet for the daily celebration of the Eucharist. Although Hebrews continues for another three chapters,

we have reached the end of Hebrews' instruction on the high priesthood of Christ.

Since Christ is a high priest in the order of Melchizedek and we
are to enter the sanctuary through the Eucharist, would we not expect to find some anticipation of the Eucharist in Melchizedek? In
drawing parallels between Melchizedek and Christ (Heb 7), Hebrews
does not mention the bread and wine brought out by Melchizedek
(Gen 14:18), and Genesis does not say the bread and wine were for
sacrifice, and scholars generally see it as an offering on the part of
Melchizedek to feed Abraham's army. Of course, anything offered
to Abraham was indirectly offered to God, but the bread and wine
offered by Melchizedek in Genesis 14:18 may have been a priestly
sacrifice.[53] One translation of the Hebrew, taking into account the
Hebrew text and context, is "Melchisedech brought out bread and
wine *since* he was a priest of the most high God."[54] From the Church
Fathers onwards, the offering of bread and wine by Melchizedek
has been seen prefiguring the Eucharist.[55] Eucharistic Prayer I also
sees Melchizedek's bread and wine prefiguring the Eucharist. The
prayer asks the Father to be pleased to accept the offering of bread
and wine just as once the Father accepted "the offering of your high
priest Melchizedek."[56] The Latin original of Eucharistic Prayer I
makes the foreshadowing of the Eucharist even clearer, as it states
that Melchizedek made the offering to God: "which your high priest
Melchizedek offered *to you*" (*tibi* in the Latin).

Jewish Tradition and Yom Kippur

According to Jewish tradition, on the day of Yom Kippur, "There
was a crimson thread tied to the door of the sanctuary. When the

---

[53]   Scott W. Hahn, *Kinship by Covenant: A Canonical Approach to the Fulfill-
       ment of God's Saving Promises*, Anchor Bible Reference Library (New Ha-
       ven, CT/London: Yale University Press, 2009), 131.

[54]   John F. X. Sheehan, "Melchisedech in Christian Consciousness," *ScEccl* 18
       (1966): 129.

[55]   Gerald O'Collins and Michael Keenan Jones, *Jesus Our Priest: A Christian
       Approach to the Priesthood of Christ* (Oxford, UK: Oxford University Press,
       2010), 117.

[56]   *Roman Missal, Renewed by Decree of the Most Holy Second Ecumenical
       Council of the Vatican, Promulgated by Authority of Pope Paul VI and Re-
       vised at the Direction of Pope John Paul II*, 3rd typical ed. (Washington, DC:
       United States Conference of Catholic Bishops, 2011), 641.

goat sent into the wilderness to die in atonement for sin had reached its destination, the thread would turn white" (m. Yoma 6:8).[57] According to the Babylonian Talmud (b. Yoma 39B [4:1]), this phenomenon ceased forty years before the destruction of the temple. The Babylonian Talmud also reports that the menorah lamps, which were supposed to be constantly lit reminding them of the pillar of fire at night in the desert (symbolizing God's presence), went out each night and that the doors of the temple opened mysteriously every night (b. Yoma 39B [4:1]). The Jerusalem Talmud likewise reports the same phenomena (y. Yoma 6:3, 43C).[58] The Jewish traditions do not connect these phenomena with the death of Christ—both Talmuds see them presaging the destruction of the temple—but it is remarkable that Jewish tradition reports these phenomena, seen auguring the end of the temple, occurring during the time span between the death of Christ and the destruction of the temple. Yom Kippur and all Jewish sacrifices were transfigured/fulfilled in Christ's death, and amazingly Jewish tradition reports events following Christ's death seen auguring the end of the temple.

Christ's Priesthood

Hebrews labors to prove that Christ is the high priest of the New Covenant. Christ's death on Calvary was a self-sacrifice that brought his priesthood to its perfect realization and brought about the perfection/transformation of the faithful for all time. The Levitical priesthood was unable to properly sanctify the people with their sacrifices, but Christ did this through his sacrifice. The Old Covenant priesthood and sacrifices were superseded by Christ's priesthood and sacrifice. Christ's priesthood in Hebrews is not metaphorical; the opposite is in fact the case. It is the Old Testament priesthood and its sacrifices that are shadows/metaphors of the real priesthood and real sacrifice of Christ. Again and again, Hebrews writes of Christ as a real priest: a merciful and trustworthy high priest (2:17); high priest of our confession (3:1); a great high priest (4:14); Christ is a high priest able to sympathize with us in our weaknesses (4:15); Christ

---

57 Jacob Neusner, *The Mishnah: A New Translation* (New Haven, CT: Yale University Press, 1988), 276.

58 All citations of the Jerusalem Talmud are from Jacob Neusner, *The Jerusalem Talmud: A Translation and Commentary* (Peabody, MA: Hendrickson Publishers, 2008).

did not seek the glory of high priest (5:5); he is a priest forever after
the order of Melchizedek (5:6); he has been named by the Father high
priest after the order of Melchizedek (5:10); high priest after the order of Melchizedek (6:20); another priest after the order of Melchizedek (7:11); another priest according to the likeness of Melchizedek
(7:15); has become [a priest] (7:16); a priest forever after the order of
Melchizedek (7:17); the Father swore an oath that he is a priest (7:21);
he holds his priesthood perpetually (7:24); it was becoming that we
have such a high priest (7:26); we have a high priest (8:1); it is necessary for this priest to have something to offer (8:3); not a priest in the
tribe of Levi prescribed by the law of Moses (8:4); high priest (9:11);
and we have a great priest (10:21). The Levitical priesthood, the sacrifices, the Tent/Tabernacle were imperfect and were shadows of the
real priesthood of Christ, his once-for-all-time priestly sacrifice, and
God's sanctuary in heaven (7:11; 8:2, 5; 10:1). Even the Old Testament
critiqued itself and pointed forward to something better than itself
(Heb 8:8–13; Jer 31:31–34). This is best expressed by Galot: "Before
Christ, the Jewish priesthood is just a shadow, a figure, with no self-
contained value. Only in Christ can we discover the genuine significance of the priesthood."[59]

Theology of Hebrews in Catholic Liturgy

Christ is referred to as High Priest in the Catholic liturgical documents, both in the Apostolic Constitution *Missale Romanum* and
in the *General Instruction of the Roman Missal*.[60] The texts of the
prayers in the Roman Missal refer to Christ as High Priest a number of times. In the Roman Missal there are twenty-four references
to high priest, all but five of them to Jesus as our High Priest. (The
others reflect the typological relationship between the bishop and
high priest; see the end of the previous chapter.) For example, in the
Chrism Mass after the priests renew their promises, the bishop asks
the people to pray for their priests that the Lord may "keep them
faithful as ministers of Christ, the High Priest,"[61] and the Preface to

---

[59]   Galot, *Theology of the Priesthood*, 65.

[60]   See Pope Paul VI, Apostolic Constitution *Missale Romanum* (1969; *Roman
       Missal*, 15), and the *General Instruction of the Roman Missal* (ibid., 4, 387).

[61]   *Roman Missal*, 291.

the Eucharistic Prayer of the Chrism Mass, entitled *The Priesthood of Christ and the Ministry of Priests*, in addressing the Father, says, "you made your Only Begotten Son High Priest of the new and eternal covenant."[62] The Collect on Thursday of the Second Week of Easter refers to "Christ our High Priest, interceding on our behalf."[63] Part of the Prayer over the Offerings at the Vigil Mass for the Ascension of the Lord states, "O God, whose Only Begotten Son, our High Priest, is seated ever-living at your right hand to intercede for us."[64] One Votive Mass is the Votive Mass of Our Lord Jesus Christ, the Eternal High Priest.[65]

The Missal also reflects the theology of the Letter to the Hebrews in describing Christ's death as the sacrifice transfiguring and fulfilling the Old Covenant sacrifices. The Prayer over the Offerings of the Sixteenth Sunday begins, "O God, who in the one perfect sacrifice brought to completion varied offerings of the law . . ."[66] The Prayer over the Offerings for Thanksgiving mentions the "perfect sacrifice of Jesus."[67] In Eucharistic Prayer IV, we pray, "we offer you his Body and Blood, the sacrifice acceptable to you."[68] The third Mass for the Common of Virgins refers to "the one unblemished sacrifice."[69] Finally, an excerpt of the Preface V of Easter, preceding the Eucharistic Prayer, mirrors the theology of Hebrews:

> By the oblation of his Body,
> he brought the sacrifices of old to fulfillment
> in the reality of the Cross
> and, by commending himself to you for our salvation,
> showed himself the Priest, the Altar, and the Lamb of sacrifice.[70]

---

[62]   Ibid., 295.

[63]   Ibid., 400.

[64]   Ibid., 431.

[65]   Ibid., 1330.

[66]   Ibid., 476.

[67]   Ibid., 1004.

[68]   Ibid., 660.

[69]   Ibid., 1095.

[70]   Ibid., 566.

CHAPTER 3

JESUS CALLED TWELVE APOSTLES OUT OF HIS MANY DISCIPLES AND CONSECRATED THEM

The Old Testament depicts the priesthood confined to the male descendants of Aaron in the tribe of Levi from the time of the Sinai covenant, but in the centuries leading up to Christ there was an expectation of a renewed priesthood. That hope was fulfilled in Christ, whom the previous chapter showed was the high priest of the New Covenant. We saw that, although Jesus was not from the tribe of Levi, in many different ways the New Testament intimated that Christ was a priest of a different kind. That came to full flowering in the Letter to the Hebrews, which designates Christ the high priest of the New Covenant again and again. The Letter to the Hebrews describes Jesus' death in terms of the Yom Kippur/Day of Atonement liturgy. That liturgy was the only one in the year when the Jewish high priest entered the Holy of Holies sprinkling animals' blood to atone for sins, but Hebrews tells us that when Christ—the high priest of the New Covenant—died, he took his blood into the heavenly sanctuary to gain salvation for us. Christ's acceptance of his death as a sacrifice of reconciliation was the perfect realization of his priesthood. His death opened the way for us to enter God's sanctuary, and Hebrews invites us to enter through the flesh and blood of Jesus, through the Eucharist.

This chapter builds on the previous chapter by showing Jesus sharing his priesthood with the apostles. We will see that Christ specially prepared the twelve apostles to continue his ministry. Jesus called the twelve apostles out of the disciples; it is portrayed as a second calling following their first calling to be disciples. The Twelve can be understood in terms of the Jewish idea of agency whereby the agent acted with the authority of the one who sent him and was his representative. Christ gave Peter primacy over the Twelve, symbolized by the language of bestowing on him the keys of the kingdom of heaven and binding and loosing. Jesus sent the Twelve on a mission with his same powers and they preached, worked miracles, and exorcised demons as Jesus did. Their ministry was an extension of Jesus' ministry. Jesus asked the Father to consecrate the apostles during the Last Supper (John 17:17), which, as we will see, was a sharing in Jesus' own priesthood. He gave them the authority to offer the Eucharist—"Do this in memory of me"—and the authority to forgive sins in the name of God and commissioned them to preach, teach, and baptize. Christ had a specific intention when choosing the Twelve, to empower them to lead the new worship in spirit and truth (John 4:23) of the New Covenant. After Pentecost, they continued the ministry of Jesus, the high priest of the New Covenant, as Jesus' consecrated ministers of the New Covenant, as his priests, as we would say today.

Jesus called many disciples, but the Gospels give attention to the call of those who would later become the apostles. The Synoptics give special attention to Jesus calling Peter, Andrew, James, and John in Matthew 4:18–22, Mark 1:16–20, and Luke 5:1–11, and in addition, we read of the call of Philip and Nathanael in John 1:35–51.[1] On the presumption that Levi is the same disciple as Matthew, his call is related in Matthew 9:9, Mark 2:13–14, and Luke 5:27–28. Even as soon as Jesus calls these disciples, there is a hint of what will happen to them later when Christ says he will *make* them *become* fishers of men (Mark 1:17). They will become—they will undergo a change. When God calls, he speaks to us in language we can understand, so Jesus used their own language, fishing language, when he called them. Simon and Andrew left their livelihoods to follow Jesus (Mark 1:18;

---

[1]   There is not agreement on whether Nathanael became one of the Twelve. If he was later called into the Twelve, he is identified with "Bartholomew."

Matt 4:20), and James and John made a bigger sacrifice, leaving the family business (Mark 1:20; Matt 4:22). What is striking in these accounts is that they left everything immediately to follow Jesus. The evangelists present them as examples of how to respond when Christ calls, leaving everything to follow Christ. Their obedience and submission to Jesus, the Word of God, gave them the freedom to let go of their former lives, not just their professional lives, but also to some extent their familial lives.

Jesus Called Twelve Apostles out of the Many Disciples

In the four Gospels Jesus chooses twelve of the disciples to become the twelve apostles. Each evangelist narrates this differently. In Mark and Luke, Jesus calls twelve out of the crowd of disciples, and then we are given the list of their names. Matthew likewise records Jesus choosing the Twelve, but more subtly. In John, the Twelve are presented suddenly without any prior introduction; they have already been chosen out of the disciples. Mark and Luke have most in common in their presentation of the Twelve and are the most unequivocal in describing twelve disciples called to be apostles from the gathering of all disciples.

Mark 3:13–19

Mark commences his account with Jesus going up the mountain and calling to him those whom he willed (3:13). Mark wants us to understand that the choice of these particular twelve disciples is not arbitrary but is the will of God. The verb "willed," *thelō* (θέλω), means their choice is not just a desire on the part of Jesus but his unambiguous decision. The other Greek verb for willing/wishing in the New Testament, *boulomai* (βούλομαι), almost always means human willing.[2] But the verb *thelō*, while having a variety of usages, signifies the will of God in Mark 3:13. Commenting on this verse, Joseph Ratzinger wrote, "You cannot make yourself a disciple—it is an event of election, a free decision of the Lord's will, which in its turn is

---

2   Hans-Joachim Ritz, "βούλομαι," in *Exegetical Dictionary of the New Testament*, ed. Horst Robert Balz and Gerhard Schneider (Grand Rapids, MI: Eerdmans, 1990), 1:225.

anchored in his communion of will with the Father."[3] Before Mark
takes us any further into the account of Jesus choosing the Twelve,
already Mark portrays this moment as coming from the heart of God.
Earlier, Jesus said he would make them become fishers of men, and
here too we know something big in God's plan is about to unfold. It is
ambiguous in Mark 3:13 whether only the Twelve were with Jesus on
the mountain or there was a crowd of disciples on the mountain from
whom Jesus chose the Twelve. In the parallel in Luke 6:13, there is
no ambiguity: the disciples were with Jesus and from them he chose
the Twelve.

Mark presents Jesus' appointment of the Twelve in 3:13–19 as a
second call. The first four were called to be disciples in 1:16–20, and
now those four and eight more are called a second time. Mark wants
us to see this as a second call, so he deliberately describes this second
call in parallel fashion to the first call. In both pericopes:

1. Jesus calls (1:17, 20; 3:13);
2. they respond (in Mark 1 they left everything and in 3:13 they
    came to Jesus);
3. and Jesus bestows an appointment on those called (in Mark
    1 they will become fishers of men and in Mark 3 they are
    "made" apostles).

Many English translations of Mark 3:14 say Jesus "appointed"
twelve, but that does not properly express what Mark conveys in his
Greek text. Mark says Jesus "created," epoiēsen (ἐποίησεν), twelve.
This is not just Jesus choosing or appointing twelve, but rather Jesus
is engaging in an act of creation. Just as the Father created the world
in Genesis, here Jesus created something new, twelve apostles to lead
the Church after Pentecost. Mark's use of the verb create/make (poieō/
ποιέω) reveals that he sees the choice of the Twelve as the institution
of a new office. In the Greek Old Testament, the verb "create"/"make"
was similarly used to depict people having office conferred upon them,
though that is not always evident, due to poieō being translated as "appointed," as in Mark.[4] In 1 Samuel 12:6, Moses and Aaron were spoken

3   Joseph Ratzinger, *Jesus of Nazareth: From the Baptism in the Jordan to the
      Transfiguration* (New York: Doubleday, 2007), 170.

4   Martino Conti, *La Vocazione e le vocazione nella Bibbia* (Brescia/Rome, IT:
      La Scuola Editrice and Edizioni Antonianum, 1985), 309.

of as appointed (to lead their people); in Exodus 18:25, Moses chose men and appointed them chiefs over the people; and in 1 Kings 12:31–32 (LXX), priests were appointed. The significance of Mark using the make/create verb for the Twelve is confirmed by the New Testament using the same verb, *poieō*, for the Father making Jesus both Lord and Messiah (Acts 2:36) and high priest (Heb 3:2). During their first calling in 1:17, Jesus had promised the apostles, "I will make you become fishers of men." The verb "become" in 1:17—*ginomai* (γίνομαι)—carried the idea of being born, or coming into existence, or being created, and so it pointed to their future transformation. That transformation commences in 3:14 and will continue right through the ministry of Jesus, with a particular highlight being their consecration during the Last Supper (John 17:17–19).

The unique event that occurred in the lives of the Twelve is reflected in them receiving the title "apostles." Some Greek manuscripts add "whom he named apostles" in the text of Mark 3:14. Many text critics regard this as a later addition to the Markan autograph (original text of Mark), but since it is in many ancient manuscripts, some English contemporary translations place "whom he named apostles" in parentheses rather than omit it. Even if "whom he named apostles" is an addition in 3:14, Mark does utilize the term "apostles" in 6:30. So at least once, and perhaps twice, Mark has designated the Twelve as "apostles."

Immediately following Jesus creating the Twelve, Mark gives us two reasons why Jesus did this. Firstly, they are created twelve *to be with Jesus*. Unlike the students of a rabbi, who study the Torah, Jesus' apostles are called to be with Jesus and enjoy spiritual communion with him, to study Jesus. The apostles' special time with Jesus allowed him to give them teaching not imparted to the other disciples. Jesus taught them the secrets of the kingdom of God, whereas the others were taught in parables (Matt 13:11; Mark 4:11; Luke 8:10). After Peter confessed that Jesus was the Messiah, Jesus warned the Twelve not to tell anyone (Matt 16:20; Mark 8:30; Luke 9:21), since the popular understanding of the Messiah was too much at variance with Jesus' mission and revealing his messianic identity would not be helpful.[5] Even though the Twelve were the privileged recipients of Je-

---

[5]   The term given to this is the "Messianic Secret," coined by William Wrede in *Das Messiasgeheimnis in den Evangelien: zugleich ein Beitrag zum Verständnis des Markusevangeliums* (Göttingen: Vandenhoeck & Ruprecht, 1901).

sus' teaching, we are often disappointed with their understanding (or we could say their misunderstanding) and actions. Nonetheless, that intimacy of Christ with the Twelve is evident throughout the Last Supper Discourse in John 13–17—for example, when Jesus declared them to be his friends in John 15:15.

The second reason Jesus created the Twelve is that they would later be sent out to preach (Mark 3:14) and cast out demons (3:15), the same activities of Jesus in the preceding chapters. But it is only after being with Jesus that they can be sent in Mark 6:7 to preach and to banish evil. They must be formed in Jesus' seminary before they can minister in the name of Jesus. We see a double duty falling to the Twelve: they must spend time with Jesus and be sent out to minister. In this they resemble the Son who was with the Father and sent by the Father to us. Being with Jesus does not exclude mission, and mission cannot be successful without time spent with the Lord. Mark follows the choosing of the Twelve with a list of their names in 3:16–19 (See Appendix 5: The Twelve Apostles).

Mark has shown that the apostles were first called to be disciples and later the apostles received a second calling from Jesus when they were called to be the twelve apostles. This is what we see played out in the Church now. All are called through Baptism to be disciples of Jesus, and some receive an additional calling to be ministerial priests of Jesus Christ. All disciples of Jesus receive the Sacrament of Baptism, but those who receive the calling to be Jesus' ministerial priests also receive the Sacrament of Holy Orders. The priesthood of the faithful arises out of our baptismal calling, but the ministerial priesthood, which is ordered to the service of the priesthood of the faithful, is conferred through the Sacrament of Holy Orders.

Luke 6:12–16

In Luke, Jesus spent all night in prayer before choosing the Twelve, a prayerful night vigil that bore fruit the following morning in the choice of the Twelve. Luke emphasizes Jesus' prayer preceding the choosing of the apostles. Luke mentions the prayer not just once, but twice in 6:12: Jesus went onto the mountain "to pray" and passed the night "in prayer to God." The implication is that the apostles were chosen by Jesus in prayerful union with his Father. Jesus' choice of the apostles is the culmination of his prayer and flows out of his relationship with his Father. We saw in Mark 3:13 that when Jesus called the Twelve it was an explicit act of will by Jesus. Reading Mark 3:13 with Luke 6:12, we can say that a definite willing of Jesus emanated from his prayerful union with his Father. All the apostles, even Judas, were chosen by the will of God. That is stated poignantly in John 6:70 when Jesus says he chose the Twelve and one of them is a devil.

Like Mark, Luke displays Jesus choosing the twelve apostles out of the crowd of disciples. In Luke, it is also their second calling, but Luke emphasizes more than Mark that the Twelve are called from the disciples. When it was day, Jesus called his disciples and chose twelve *out of them* (6:13). Luke clearly indicates that the Twelve were chosen from among all the other disciples present. The calling of the Twelve is a public act on the part of Jesus in the presence of all the disciples.

Luke says Jesus gave the name "apostles" to the Twelve (6:13) without specifying whether Jesus did so at this particular time. It is only in Mark 3:14 (in some manuscripts) and 6:30 and in Matthew 10:2 that the other Synoptics call them apostles. Luke describes the Twelve as apostles more frequently (Luke 9:10; 17:5; 22:14; 24:10). This is not surprising, since Luke's second volume—The Acts of the Apostles—describes the ministry of some of the apostles, especially that of Peter in the first half of the book. Luke uses the term "apostles" a total of twenty-eight times in Acts, and only two of those twenty-eight occurrences were for missionaries who did not belong to the Twelve, Paul and Barnabas, in Acts 14:4, 14. As Ratzinger says, in Luke, "apostle" is practically synonymous with the Twelve.[6] Like Mark, Luke follows the choosing of the Twelve with the list of their names in 6:14–16. (See Appendix 5: The Twelve Apostles).

Matthew 10:1–4

The Twelve are introduced in Matthew 10:1 for the first time. Matthew does not clearly portray this as his parallel to the choosing of the Twelve in Luke 6:12–13 and Mark 3:13–14, because there is no explicit statement about Jesus choosing the Twelve at this time out of all the disciples. Does Matthew intend us to understand that the Twelve have already been chosen by Jesus and are only being mentioned by

---

[6]　　Ratzinger, *Jesus of Nazareth: From the Baptism*, 169.

Matthew here for the first time?[7] On the contrary, many exegetes take 10:1 to be the moment of the choosing of the Twelve out of the disciples in Matthew.[8] That seems to me to be the best explanation for the following reasons:

1. The verb for the calling together of the Twelve in 10:1, *proskaleomai* (προσκαλέομαι), is also the verb in Mark 3:13 for Jesus calling the Twelve to him.

2. In Mark 3:15, just after Jesus created the Twelve, we are told their future mission includes the power to expel demons. Here in Matthew 10:1, we are also told Jesus gave that same power to the Twelve; it is expanded here to power and control over the demons, and the apostles also have the authority to heal.

3. Both Mark and Luke follow the account of the choosing of the Twelve with a list of the twelve names, and like Mark and Luke, Matthew also lists the Twelve in 10:2–4 after their calling.

4. The selection of the Twelve in Luke was the fruit of Jesus' night of prayerful union with his Father. Ratzinger takes the calling of the Twelve in 10:1 as an answer to Jesus' prayer immediately preceding, in 9:38, asking the Lord of the harvest to send laborers to his harvest: "The choice of the Twelve appears as the first answer to this prayer. It is as though Jesus himself were anticipating the response that the divine authority would subsequently make to the prayer of his disciples."[9] The context for the calling of the Twelve, therefore, in both Matthew and Luke is prayer.

In summary, Matthew, like Mark and Luke, depicts the Twelve receiving a second call from Jesus, though in a much more subtle

---

[7]   This is the view of Craig Blomberg, *Matthew*, The New American Commentary 22 (Nashville, TN: Broadman & Holman Publishers, 1992), 167.

[8]   David L. Turner, *Matthew*, Baker Exegetical Commentary on the New Testament (Grand Rapids, MI: Baker Academic, 2008), 264. See also Grant R. Osborne, *Matthew*, Zondervan Exegetical Commentary on the New Testament, 1 (Grand Rapids, MI: Zondervan, 2010), 370.

[9]   Joseph Ratzinger, *The God of Jesus Christ: Meditations on the Triune God*, trans. Brian McNeil (San Francisco: Ignatius Press, 2008), 80–81.

way than Mark and Luke. Each of the Synoptics shows them called out of the disciples, though using different terminology. They were the recipients of special formation by Jesus to continue his ministry after him.

John 6:66-71

John neither gives an account of Jesus calling the Twelve out of a crowd of disciples nor a list of names. He expects us to know this already. After Jesus taught on the Eucharist, many of his disciples stopped following him (6:66). Then the Twelve are introduced suddenly when Jesus asks if they also want to leave (6:67), as if the reader already knows all about them. During the conversation, Jesus refers to the moment in the past, not recorded in this Gospel, when he chose them: "Did I not choose you twelve and one of you is an adversary?" (6:70). The Greek verb "choose" in 6:70, *eklegomai* (ἐκλέγομαι), is the same verb used later in this Gospel when Christ said to the apostles during the Last Supper, "You did not choose me, but I chose you and appointed you that you should go and bear fruit" (John 15:16). Luke used *eklegomai* in 6:13 to describe Jesus choosing the Twelve out of the disciples, and again in Acts 1:2, 24 for choosing the apostles. So although John does not record the moment of the selection of the Twelve, as do the Synoptics, John introduces the Twelve who had been previously chosen. During a critical moment in Jesus' ministry when many disciples left Jesus, the evangelist highlights the fidelity of the Twelve by means of Peter's statement of faith ("to whom shall *we* go . . . *we* have believed"). There are two other references to the Twelve in John's Gospel: in 6:71 Judas is mentioned as a member of the Twelve, and in 20:24 Thomas is one of the Twelve. When Jesus created the Twelve in Mark 3:14, they were to be with Jesus and to be sent out to minister later. In John's Gospel, the Twelve received special teaching from Jesus during the extended Last Supper Discourse that runs from after the Last Supper in John 13 to the end of John 17.[10] During that discourse, in 15:4-7, Jesus asked the Twelve to remain in

---

[10]   The discourse bears a number of similarities with Farewell Discourses known in ancient Jewish writing including the Old Testament, e.g., Jacob's address to his sons in Genesis 48-49, Moses' speech in Deuteronomy 33, and Joshua's in Joshua 23-24; see George R. Beasley-Murray, *John*, Word Biblical Commentary 36 (Dallas, TX: Word, 2002), 222-223.

him just as he remains in them. The Greek verb *menō* (μένω), translated as "remain/abide," signifies "the closest possible relationship between Christ and the believer."[11]

We have seen the four Gospels emphasize in different ways the importance of the twelve apostles, especially through their second calling in the Synoptics, and their fidelity to Jesus during a critical moment in John's Gospel. Although sometimes "disciple" and "twelve" are used interchangeably, after their second calling—that is, after their creation as apostles—the Twelve are specifically mentioned many more times in the Gospels, underlining their importance (Matt 10:1–2, 5; 11:1; [implied in] 19:28; 20:17; 26:14, 20, 47; Mark 3:14; 4:10; 6:7; 9:35; 10:32; 11:11; 14:10, 17, 20, 43; Luke 6:13; 8:1; 9:1, 12; 18:31; 22:3; 22:47; John 6:67, 70, 71; 20:24). After the Gospels, the term is found only in Acts 6:2 and 1 Corinthians 15:5. The evangelists give such importance to the Twelve because they will carry on Jesus' ministry. The Twelve were called out of his disciples to engage in a special ministry, just as now ministerial priests are called out of all the baptized to receive a special ministry through the reception of Holy Orders.

The Twelve and the Restoration of Israel

Twelve is not an arbitrary number. By choosing twelve apostles, Jesus is deliberately recalling the twelve tribes of Israel scattered and disappeared since the invasion of the Northern Kingdom in the eighth century BC. Jesus' choice of twelve apostles is fulfilling Jewish hopes for the restoration of the twelve tribes, but in a totally unexpected manner. Matthew 19:28 and Luke 22:30 confirm this when Jesus promises the Twelve that they will sit on thrones judging the twelve tribes of Israel. For Jesus to show that he was establishing the new Israel, he could not choose seven apostles, which would have been the Jewish perfect number; he had to choose twelve. It is no coincidence that the Qumran Essenes were also governed by a council of twelve: "In the Community council (there shall be) twelve men and three priests" (1QS 8:1).[12] The Church is the fulfillment of the Jew-

---

[11]   K. Munzer and C. Brown, "Remain," in *New International Dictionary of New Testament Theology*, ed. Lothar Coenen, Erich Beyreuther, and Hans Bietenhard (Grand Rapids, MI: Zondervan Publishing House, 1986), 3:225.

[12]   Florentino García Martínez and Eibert J. C. Tigchelaar, *The Dead Sea Scrolls Study Edition* (Leiden: Brill, 1997–1998), 1:89.

ish hopes for restoration. It is precisely for this reason that Peter had to replace Judas before Pentecost: there had to be twelve apostles at Pentecost when the Church began its mission with its first preaching and baptisms. After Pentecost, there is no attention given to keeping the number twelve intact when the apostles began to be martyred.

The Lists of the Twelve

Mark 3:16–19 and Luke 6:14–16 list the Twelve following their selection/creation, and Matthew 10:2–4 following what may also be taken as their selection/creation in 10:1. Another list is given in Acts 1:13–14 without Judas. Comparing the lists of the Twelve reveals some differences in the names (see Appendix 5: The Twelve Apostles) but is best explained as an apostle having two names and being called one name by one evangelist and the other name by the other evangelist, or the apostle having his name changed, like Simon to Peter. The lists are in three groups of four: Simon is always first in the first four, Philip is always first in the second four, and James the son of Alphaeus is always first in the third four. The evangelists do not try to hide the embarrassment and shame Judas brought to the Church. Each list in the Synoptics mentions that Judas betrayed Jesus. There was no point in concealing what was already known, and it also served as a warning to future disciples. From the first moment Judas is introduced, he is tagged as the betrayer/traitor.

The Twelve Apostles as Agents of Jesus

Our English word "apostle" is derived from the Greek word *apostolos* (ἀπόστολος), which means someone who has been sent. Its corresponding verb, "to send," is *apostellō* (ἀποστέλλω). The other Greek verb "to send," *pempō* (πέμπω), is used for communicating important messages, but *apostellō* "is sharpened to focus on the purpose and goal of the event in question and hence on the sending forth and completion of the assignment; the verb assumes the meaning of *commission*."[13] Since *apostellō* includes that idea of commission, it is highly probable that the Jewish concept of agent, *šālîah* (שלח), lies behind the Greek word "apostle." In Judaism, the agent acted as the

---

13   J.-A. Bühner, "ἀποστέλλω," in Balz and Schneider, *Exegetical Dictionary of the New Testament*, 1:141.

representative of the one who sent him and acted on his authority. It seems plausible that *apostolos* in the New Testament had that meaning of agency, since the Greek Old Testament utilizes *apostellō* to translate the verb "send," *šālah* (שׁלח), in the Hebrew Old Testament. Examples of agency can be found in Jewish documents. For example, in the Mishnah, Jerusalem Talmud, and Babylonian Talmud, a man effects betrothal on his own or through his agent (likewise a woman), and a man betroths his daughter on his own or through his agent (m.Qidd. 2:1; b.Qidd. 41A [2:1]; y.Qidd. 2:1, 62A). Agents were also employed in divorce cases (b. Git. 29B [3:6]; 32A [4:1]), and leading prayer in one's stead (b. Ber. 34B [5:5]).[14] In the later New Testament period, the rabbis described someone who had been commissioned or authorized by God as a *šālîah*,[15] and both the Sanhedrin and rabbis commissioned agents to act on their behalf.[16] While some scholars are reticent to see agency as a background to the apostles, many are supportive—for example, Craig Keener, who points out that later Jewish texts regard the agent as the equivalent to his sender and that how one treats Jesus' messengers is how one treats Jesus (Matt 10:40–42).[17] The idea of agency shows itself when Jesus' teaching is reflected in the teaching of the Twelve (e.g., the apostles' proclamation of repentance mirroring Jesus' proclamation of repentance).[18] Ratzinger, viewing the apostles as agents of Jesus, describes their apostleship in this way:

> apostleship is a sharing in the mission of Jesus Christ; like Christ, the apostle proclaims the nearness of the kingdom of God, and, from Christ, he has the power to make the coming

---

[14] Hermann Leberecht Strack and Paul Billerbeck, *Kommentar zum Neuen Testament aus Talmud und Midrasch* (Munich: C. H. Beck, 1978), 3:2–4.

[15] Stephen P. McHenry, "Three Significant Moments in the Theological Development of the Sacramental Character of Orders: Its Origin, Standardization, and New Direction in Augustine, Aquinas, and Congar" (PhD diss., Fordham University, 1983), 38.

[16] Joseph A. Fitzmyer, *The Gospel According to Luke I–IX: Introduction, Translation, and Notes*, Anchor Yale Bible 28 (New Haven, CT/London: Yale University Press, 2008), 617.

[17] Craig S. Keener, *The Gospel of Matthew: A Socio-Rhetorical Commentary* (Grand Rapids, MI/Cambridge, UK: Eerdmans, 2009), 313–315.

[18] Joel Marcus, *Mark 1–8: A New Translation With Introduction and Commentary*, Anchor Yale Bible 27 (New Haven, CT/London: Yale University Press, 2008), 388.

visible by signs of power (Mk 3:14–19; Mt 10:7–9). The close relationship of Christ's mission and that of the apostle is summarized in two statements: "Anyone who listens to you listens to me; anyone who rejects you rejects me, and those who reject me reject the one who sent me" (Lk 10:16; cf. Mt 10:40).[19]

We could also add Mark 9:41, Luke 9:48, and John 13:20. It makes sense to understand the Jewish concept of agency behind the call of the apostles, and due to the mystical understanding of agency developed by some rabbis, the words of the apostles were really the words of Jesus.[20]

During the twentieth century, the origin of the twelve apostles was debated: did Jesus choose these twelve apostles during his ministry or did their office arise during the life of the early Church and the evangelists retroject them or impose them into the life of Christ when writing their Gospels? Many have defended the historicity of the Gospel accounts of Jesus appointing the twelve apostles, and among the most helpful is that by John Meier.[21] His defense of the Gospel accounts revolves around three arguments:

1. The various New Testament documents offer multiple attestation of the existence of the Twelve during the ministry of Jesus.
2. The scandal of Jesus being betrayed by one of the twelve he had chosen is not something the Church would have invented when struggling to succeed in the first years after Jesus.
3. If the Twelve had only come into prominence during the time of the Church, rather than during the ministry of Jesus, we would expect many examples of such prominence outside the Gospels in the New Testament and much less in the Gospels, but the opposite is the case. The Twelve are very prominent

---

[19]   Joseph Ratzinger, *Principles of Catholic Theology: Building Stones for a Fundamental Theology*, trans. Mary Frances McCarthy (San Francisco: Ignatius Press, 1987), 273.

[20]   Aidan Nichols, *Holy Order: the Apostolic Ministry from the New Testament to the Second Vatican Council* (Dublin: Veritas Publications, 1990), 7.

[21]   John P. Meier, *A Marginal Jew, Rethinking the Historical Jesus: Volume Three, Companions and Competitors* (New Haven, CT/London: Yale University Press, 2001), 128–147. See also Meier, "The Circle of the Twelve: Did It Exist During Jesus' Public Ministry?" *JBL* 116 (1997): 643–672.

in the Gospels and otherwise mentioned only from the beginning of Acts until Acts 6:2, and again only in 1 Corinthians 15:5.

We can safely conclude that the choosing of the apostles indeed goes back to Jesus, as the Gospels relate. The Church did not invent itself but was founded on the teaching and actions of Jesus and on the choice of the twelve apostles. Ratzinger says, "we can say that the New Testament consistently traces apostleship to a specified institution by the Lord and defines it as an act of calling (cf. Mark 3:13–19)."[22]

The calling of the twelve apostles out of the much larger assembly of all the disciples anticipates statements later in the New Testament where we read that God has given different responsibilities to different people: some were called to be apostles, some prophets, some evangelists, and so on (1 Cor 12:28–29; Eph 4:11). It also anticipates the priesthood of the faithful and the ministerial priesthood, the priesthood of the faithful that everyone shares by virtue of Baptism and the ministerial priesthood of those ordained in the Sacrament of Holy Orders.

The Primacy of Saint Peter

Christ gave Peter the responsibility and honor of primacy, being first in rank among the twelve apostles. As a result, Peter automatically became the leader of the apostles after Christ's Ascension as we see in the Acts of the Apostles. While Peter's primacy is seen in many places in the Gospels, three texts in particular show that Christ gave Peter the authority to govern: Matthew 16:18–19, Luke 22:32, and John 21:15–17.

Peter the Rock, on whom Jesus builds his Church, is given the keys (Matt 16:18–19)

Peter is the Rock on which the Church is built (Matt 16:18)
After Peter confesses Jesus to be the Messiah at Caesarea Philippi (Matt 16:16), Jesus declares, "You are Peter and on this rock I will build my Church" (Matt 16:18). It is a play on words, though the

---

22   Ratzinger, *Principles of Catholic Theology*, 273.

wordplay is not evident in English. In the Aramaic language in Palestine, the play on words would have been very apparent because "Peter" and "rock" are the same word in Aramaic, *kêpāʾ* (כֵּיפָא), so Jesus proclaimed, "You are *Kêpāʾ* and on this *kêpāʾ* I will build my church," "you are Rock and on this rock I will build my Church." The wordplay by Jesus is also evident in the Greek text of the evangelists because, in Greek, Peter is *Petros* (Πέτρος) and rock is *petra* (πέτρα). Two different words are necessary in Greek for the wordplay because *petra* is a feminine Greek noun and the masculine form necessary for a male name has to be *Petros*. Regardless of confession or Christian denomination, most biblical scholars agree that in this verse Peter is the rock intended by Christ, the rock on which Christ will build his Church. In the last century, interpretations were divided along confessional lines, but thankfully we have mostly gotten over that. A number of years ago, Protestant Scripture scholars underwent a sea change after studying the primacy of Peter in the New Testament and arrived at the conclusion that the New Testament does recognize the primacy of Peter.[23] Yet, there are still those who do not accept that Peter is the rock and instead see the rock as Jesus or Peter's confession of faith in Jesus as the Messiah in Matthew 16:16. But the natural way of reading the second *kêpāʾ* is with reference to the first *kêpāʾ*, Peter himself.

An objection raised is that *petra* refers to a stone rather than something suitable for a foundation, but in fact *petra* does refer to a massive rock.[24] The word in Greek for a small stone is *lithos* (λίθος; e.g., Matthew 3:9), and a stone that one stumbles over is a *skandalon* (σκάνδαλον). The same word, *petra*, is clearly used by Christ in Matthew 7:24 as a foundation stone: everyone who hears his words and does them will be like a wise man who built his house on rock (*petra*). It is exegetically sound, as the majority of biblical scholars of all confessions agree, to interpret Matthew 16:18 as Christ saying Peter is the rock on which he will build his Church.[25]

---

[23]   Rudolf Pesch, *Die biblischen Grundlagen des Primats* (Freiburg: Herder, 2001), 59.

[24]   William Arndt, Frederick W. Danker, and Walter Bauer, *A Greek-English Lexicon of the New Testament and Other Early Christian Literature*, 3rd ed. (BDAG), rev. and ed. F. W. Danker (Chicago: University of Chicago Press, 2000), 809. Rudolf Pesch, "πέτρα," in Balz and Schneider, *Exegetical Dictionary of the New Testament*, 3:81.

[25]   For example, the evangelical *New American Commentary* is in agreement (see Blomberg, *Matthew*, 252).

Another objection was that by proponents of the historical-critical method of Scripture interpretation who saw 16:17–19 as a later interpolation or addition into the Gospel because these verses are absent following Mark 8:29 and Luke 9:20 in the parallel passages. However, this objection is no longer defensible.[26] A doubt raised against the authenticity of this text was Christ proclaiming he would build his Church on Peter, the objection being that "my Church" was imposed on the Gospel rather than being a statement by Jesus himself. The claim was made that the word "Church"—*ekklesia* (ἐκκλησία)— occurs only here and in Matthew 18:17 in Jesus' statements and that such infrequency would not be expected if Jesus had really intended to found the Church. Again, the majority of scholars of all persuasions do not accept this thinking. Even though we do not imagine the Twelve envisioned the expansion of the Church we see occurring in the Acts of the Apostles when Jesus made the pronouncement to Peter, they were a gathering or assembly, and the word *ekklesia* in Matthew 16:18 is the word employed in the Greek Old Testament to translate the Hebrew word *qāhāl* (קָהָל) for the assembly of the Hebrews in the desert (e.g., Lev 8:4). An example of the widespread reaction against suggestions that this verse is a creation by the Church is: "It is hard to know what kind of thinking, other than confessional presupposition, justifies the tendency of some commentators to dismiss this verse as not authentic. A Messiah without a Messianic Community would have been unthinkable to any Jew."[27] In support of the authenticity of "Church" in Matthew 18:17, Ratzinger says, "the Protestant exegete A. [Albrecht] Oepke has drawn attention to the fact that one cannot be cautious enough with such verbal statistics. He points out, for example, that the word 'cross' does not occur in the whole of Saint Paul's Letter to the Romans, although the letter is imbued from beginning to end with the apostle's theology of the Cross."[28]

Paul's statement in 1 Corinthians 3:11 that Jesus is the foundation of the Church, the statement in Ephesians 2:20 that the apostles and prophets are the foundation and Christ is the cornerstone,

---

26   Pesch, *Die biblischen Grundlagen des Primats*, 16.

27   W. F. Albright and C. S. Mann, *Matthew: Introduction, Translation, and Notes*, Anchor Yale Bible 26 (New Haven, CT/London: Yale University Press, 2008), 195.

28   Joseph Ratzinger, *Called to Communion: Understanding the Church Today*, trans. Adrian Walker (San Francisco: Ignatius Press, 1996), 59.

and Revelation 21:14 stating that the New Jerusalem—the Church in heaven—is founded on the Twelve do not contradict Matthew 16:18. Rather, we could say that each of these texts emphasizes a different aspect of the foundation of the Church to make a point in its particular context, in much the same way that the four Gospels give us four slightly different but complementary portraits of Christ. In Matthew 16:18, the important role of Peter is what is emphasized, a point echoed elsewhere in the Gospels by their always placing Peter first in the lists of the Twelve, and always first in the list of three apostles who were present with Christ for special moments (raising of the dead girl in Mark 5:37 and Luke 8:51; Jesus' Transfiguration in Matt 17:1, Mark 9:2, and Luke 9:28; being near Jesus during his agony in Gethsemane in Matt 26:37 and Mark 14:33). Peter being first, his primacy, is specifically mentioned in Matthew 10:2: "first, Simon, who is called Peter." In that regard, Ratzinger writes, "In Matthew's Gospel, he is even introduced with the momentous word 'the first'—the root that in the later language of 'primacy' became the term for the special mission of the fisherman from Bethsaida makes itself heard here for the first time."[29]

Peter is given the keys (Matt 16:19)

The next verse (16:19) confirms Peter is the rock, since Christ gives him the keys of the kingdom of heaven and whatever he binds on earth will be bound in heaven and whatever he looses on earth will be loosed in heaven. Keys symbolized the office of the one who held them, clearly evident in Isaiah 22. Shebna was the master of the house of King Hezekiah (Isa 22:15–19), a duty also variously termed by scholars as "treasurer" or "vizier." Since Shebna was corrupt, God told Isaiah that Eliakim was to be installed as master of the house instead (Isa 22:20–21). The language used to signify the transfer of authority from Shebna to Eliakim is God placing the key of the house of David on Eliakim's shoulder, and when Eliakim opens no one shall shut and when he shuts no one shall open (Isa 22:22). Hans Wildberger explains the significance of Isaiah 22:22: "In those days, the keys were so large that they could be placed on a shoulder. The power of the keys, which is given to Eliakim at this point, apparently goes

---

[29]   Ibid., 54.

far beyond the literal meaning; it means the overall responsibility and authority for the dynasty of the Davidic family, their possessions, and all their affairs."[30] The similarity of Matthew 16:19 with Isaiah 22:22 is obvious. Eliakim had the duty of governance in the house of David bestowed upon him by God, and Peter had the duty of governance in the Church bestowed upon him by Christ. The authority that Peter is given by Christ in Matthew 16:18 is indicated by whatever Peter binds being also bound in heaven and whatever Peter looses being also loosed in heaven.[31] This terminology of binding and loosing was already in the Jewish milieu. It described a judge binding or loosing the accused from their charges or a person being expelled or readmitted to the synagogue.[32] Peter is indeed "over the house," to use the ancient biblical expression. One example of the duty of being over the house that successors of Peter fulfilled was deciding which books reflected the faith of the early Church and were suitable for admission into the canon of the New Testament. Roman primacy canonized the New Testament.[33]

A peculiarity in the description of Eliakim's investiture for office in Isaiah 22:21 is the two garments with which he is to be vested, the tunic and the girdle. These are the garments normally associated with priests. Every priest wore a tunic, mentioned many times, (e.g., Exod 28:4, 40; 29:5; 39:27; Lev 8:7; Ezra 2:69; Neh 7:69, which is 7:70 in some English translations). Apart from Isaiah 22:21, the girdle is mentioned elsewhere in the Old Testament only in connection with priests (Exod 28:4, 39, 40; 29:9; 39:29; Lev 8:7, 13; 16:4). Even though the Old Testament priesthood was transfigured in Christ and shared by Christ with the apostles, as we will see in John 17:17, there is another link between Eliakim and Peter. Christ bestows the keys on Peter using the language employed in Isaiah to bestow the keys on Eliakim, whose investiture was peculiarly described in priestly language. But the priestly connections in Matthew 16:18-19 do not end

---

[30] Hans Wildberger, *Isaiah 13–27*, A Continental Commentary (Minneapolis, MN: Fortress Press, 1997), 399.

[31] Ratzinger suggests that, because of the parallel between binding and loosing in Matthew 16:18 and forgiving and retaining sins in John 20:23, the power to bind and loose is the authority to forgive sins (*Called to Communion*, 64).

[32] Andreas J. Köstenberger, *John*, Baker Exegetical Commentary on the New Testament (Grand Rapids, MI: Baker Academic, 2004), 575–576.

[33] Ratzinger, *Called to Communion*, 70.

there. Michael Barber has shown that imagery of keys is associated with priests in later Jewish texts.[34] So it could be said that we have two subtle priestly associations in Christ bestowing the keys on Peter, Eliakim's investiture described in priestly terms and key imagery later associated with priests. Another interesting connection is that Eliakim is told he will be a father to the inhabitants of Jerusalem (Isa 22:21) and the successor of Peter has the title "Our Holy Father."

Even though Paul had a public row with Peter (Gal 2:11–14), the words used by Paul during the discord indicate Peter's primacy: "how can you compel the Gentiles to live like Jews?" Though Paul strongly disagreed with Peter, it was Peter who had the keys and the authority to bind and loose. Paul's respect for Peter's primacy is even more striking when he reports that Christ appeared first to Cephas and then to the Twelve (1 Cor 15:5). Another noteworthy observation on 1 Corinthians 15:5 is that Paul does not call Peter by the Greek translation of his name, *Petros*, but by the Greek transliteration, *Cephas* (Κηφᾶς), of the original Aramaic *Kēpā'* (Rock), which Christ had bestowed on Peter. For Paul, Peter was the rock on which the Church was held together.

In Matthew 18, Jesus gives a discourse on Church leadership. Jesus repeats the charge of Matthew 16:18 again in 18:18, that whatever is bound on earth shall be bound in heaven and whatever is loosed on earth shall be loosed in heaven. In its context in Matthew 18 on Church leadership, this means not just Peter, but all Church leaders, have been given divine authority. However this is given preeminently to Peter in 16:18, so when Church leaders bind and loose, it is to be done in union with Peter. It also means by corollary, that when Peter binds and looses, he is to do so in union with all Church leaders. Peter and the apostles are to act collegially. We talk nowadays of the College of Bishops when referring to that sense of unity.

Simon, strengthen your brothers (Luke 22:32)

It is only in Luke's account of the Last Supper that we find Jesus' prayer for the twelve apostles facing a future trial and Jesus' prediction of Peter's restoration again afterwards and Peter strengthening the apostles (Luke 22:31–32). Jesus makes a prediction for the

---

[34] Michael Barber, "Jesus as the Davidic Temple Builder and Peter's Priestly Role in Matthew 16:16–19," *JBL* 132 (2013): 945–947.

apostles and a prediction for Peter, but in some translations it may not be apparent whether Jesus is addressing all the apostles or only Peter, so I offer this version here: "Simon, Simon, Satan demanded to have you [plural = apostles] to sift like wheat, but I have prayed for you [singular = Peter] that your faith may not fail, and when you [singular = Peter] have returned, strengthen your brothers." That test of the apostles' faith foretold by Jesus began when Jesus was arrested in Gethsemane. Luke, always gentle on the weakness of the apostles, does not mention how the apostles reacted to Jesus' arrest, but Mark never hides their weakness and bluntly says all the apostles abandoned Jesus and fled (Mark 14:40). It was the test of their faith by Satan that Luke 22:31-32 foresaw. Three times Peter denied he knew Jesus by the fire in the courtyard of the high priest (Luke 22:54-62). Jesus had already prayed for Peter that his faith might not fail, and that, when recovered, Peter would strengthen the others. The Greek word in Luke 22:32 to describe Peter's future recovery or repentance, *epistrephō* (ἐπιστρέφω), signifies turning around again to the original place. Once Peter has returned again, he will have the responsibility of strengthening the brothers' faith. The Greek word for Peter's obligation to fortify the brothers, *stērizō* (στηρίζω), means Peter is to fix their faith so that it will be immovable. It is the same word, *stērizō*, that Luke employs to describe Jesus' determination to face his Passion in Jerusalem in 9:51. Jesus fixed himself firmly to face his Passion in Jerusalem, and after Peter's faith is restored, he must firmly fix the faith of the apostles. Many times in the Acts of the Apostles we see Peter firmly fixing the faith of the apostles, and Peter commences this act of strengthening their faith immediately after Jesus' Ascension, when he replaced Judas (Acts 1:15-26). It is noteworthy that Jesus calls the apostles "brothers" in Luke 22:32. While Peter has primacy, they are all brothers in communion, in a college. Jesus gave the primacy to Peter in a dramatic way in Matthew 16:18-19, and this is reflected here also in Luke 22:31-32 in a less dramatic way. Peter is the rock and has the keys to bind and loose, and he is the one to strengthen the brothers' faith. It is Peter's role in faith formation that is stressed here in Luke. Since Peter is the one who will have the role of strengthening, and therefore also of guarding the faith, he has the duty of preventing and healing schisms that would damage the faith. Regrettably, anyone not in full union with Peter's successor is not in full union with the Church.[35] Under Peter and under his successors, the faith is to be nourished, protected, and guarded.

Simon, do you love me? (John 21:15–17)

The encounter between Jesus and the apostles takes place by the shore of the lake, but a little detail has significance, the lakeside charcoal fire (John 21:9). The last time a charcoal fire was burning in John's Gospel was in the courtyard of the high priest as Peter denied he knew Jesus (John 18:18). Now Jesus, after his Resurrection, by a different charcoal fire in 21:9, asks Peter three times if he loves him. Peter had denied Jesus three times by a charcoal fire, and now three times by a charcoal fire Peter is given the opportunity to profess his love for Jesus. This is his repentance, his turning back again to where he was, to recall the Greek verb *epistrephō* (ἐπιστρέφω) of Luke 22:32. The lack of faith by the first charcoal fire is restored by what takes place beside the second charcoal fire. As Jesus asks Peter the first and second time if he loves him, using *agapas* (ἀγαπᾷς), Peter responds that he does love Jesus, but with a different verb, *philo* (φιλῶ). The third time, Jesus asks Peter using the same verb Peter himself used, *phileis* (φιλεῖς). Since the early centuries, it has been debated whether there is significance to Peter responding with a different love verb and for the third question Jesus using the same love verb as Peter. While the majority opinion has swayed to and fro over the centuries, the common opinion now is that, since these two love verbs are used interchangeably in this Gospel, there is no special significance to their use here in 21:15–17. Keener has done a study of their interchangeability in John, showing that they are both used even to describe the Father loving Jesus.[36] If one were to try to make the case that there is a difference in these two love verbs in John, which would be that *agapas* is stronger than *pheileis*, that would lead to the conclusion here in 21:15–17 that, when Jesus could not get a suitable loving response from Peter, Jesus lowered the bar to the inferior type of love that Peter was capable of offering Christ, but that does not seem to fit. There are also different Greek words used for "sheep" and

---

[35] Joseph Ratzinger, "Primacy, Episcopacy, and Apostolic Succession," in Karl Rahner and Joseph Ratzinger, *The Episcopate and the Primacy* (New York: Herder and Herder, 1962), 39.

[36] Craig S. Keener, *The Gospel of John: A Commentary* (Grand Rapids, MI: Baker Academic, 2012), 1:324–325.

"you know" in these verses, and surely if one were to argue for significance in the different love verbs, one would also have to see significance in the different words for sheep and knowing. That would muddle the objective of the passage. Instead, it seems the emphasis is on the loving relationship between Christ and Peter, which in turn is to energize Peter to look after Christ's flock. Peter is asked to demonstrate his love for Jesus by his care for the flock.

Immediately following the three questions in John 21:15–17, Peter is told where his love for Christ and for Christ's flock will take him, to crucifixion like Jesus (21:18–19). The future action of stretching out his hands (21:18) is what Peter will do on a cross when crucified upside down in Rome during Nero's persecutions. Jesus is the good shepherd who lays down his life for his sheep (John 10:15). Jesus asked Peter to shepherd his flock, and like Jesus, Peter too will lay down his life for the flock.

It is sometimes suggested that the primacy of Peter is a cause of tension in John's Gospel between Peter and the beloved disciple. While Peter is occasionally reliant on the beloved disciple for information or access to the high priest's courtyard (e.g., Peter asks the beloved disciple to find out who is the betrayer in 13:23–24; the beloved disciple got Peter invited into the high priest's courtyard in 18:16; and the beloved disciple recognized Jesus when they were fishing and told Peter in 21:7), it is unjustified to read into this that tension existed between the beloved disciple and Peter. The beloved disciple knew his place in relation to Peter, and this is most evident at Jesus' Resurrection. Both Peter and John ran to Christ's tomb, and the beloved disciple reached it first but did not go in and only went in after Peter entered before him (20:4–8). There is no ambiguity in John's Gospel about Peter's position: he has charge of the sheep.

In Matthew 16, Peter is told by Christ he is the rock on which Christ will build the Church, he has the keys like the master of a royal house, and whatever he binds and looses, heaven does likewise. In Luke 22:32, Peter is told by Christ that he must strengthen the apostles. Here in John 21, he is told three times to feed the flock. The spiritual nourishment of Christ's flock is Peter's responsibility. Here again, the primacy of Peter is seen, but expressed differently. In each of the three passages we have examined, Matthew 16:18–19, Luke 22:32, and John 21:15–17, Peter is given primacy by Christ. That is more evident in Matthew 16, but also present in Luke 22 and John 21.

Succession

While the primacy of Peter is affirmed by the New Testament, the Petrine succession cannot be directly deduced from any passage of the New Testament, although from the beginning the bishops of Rome were recorded as successors.[37] Nonetheless, we can infer Petrine succession in Scripture. Eliakim succeeded Shebna as master of the king's house in Isaiah 22. That office of master of the king's house was not just for Eliakim. The office existed prior to Shebna and continued after Eliakim. Apart from Shebna, the names of three of his predecessors are recorded in Scripture: Ahishar in 1 Kings 4:6 during the reign of Solomon, Arza in 1 Kings 16:9 during the reign of Asa, and Jotham in 2 Kings 15:5 during the reign of his father, Azariah (also known as Uzziah in many biblical books). Scripture mentions two of the corresponding officials in the courts of the northern kings: Obadiah during the reign of Ahab in 1 Kings 18:3, and an unnamed official in 2 Kings 10:5. It would be even more helpful had Scripture given us the names of viziers after Eliakim (many believe his removal is foretold by Isa 22:25), but this lack does not negate the point that Eliakim was invested into an office that was not just for him, or that the keys given to him would be given to his successor. When bestowing the primacy on Peter, Christ's deliberate paralleling of the language of Isaiah 22:22 for the appointment of Eliakim as vizier in succession to Shebna could be taken to indicate Christ's intention that Peter be succeeded by another who would have primacy (the keys) and by another after him and so on, since Eliakim himself would be succeeded by another vizier.

We can offer other suggestions that Christ intended Peter would have successors in his ministry of primacy, and the concept of succession was certainly well known at the time of Jesus, because the scribes and Pharisees regarded themselves as successors to Moses' teaching authority (Matt 23:2; see John 9:28). Peter is the rock, and the rock will remain, while the Church will grow and spread during the ensuing decades and centuries. A rock is not an image of temporality but of permanence and endurance. Immediately after telling Peter that he is the rock, Christ proclaimed that the gates of

---

[37] The need to clearly enunciate succession arose only during the problems caused in the second century by Gnosticism (see Ratzinger, "Primacy, Episcopacy, and Apostolic Succession," 46).

death would not prevail against the Church (16:18). Even if individual Church members will be martyred, the Church itself will not die. This promise suggests a long time span, and coming immediately after the declaration of Peter as the rock, adds more weight to the suggestion that Peter as rock is an image of permanence including successors. In Isaiah 51:1–2, Abraham is described as the rock from which the Jews came. Abraham, the father of the Jewish people, received promises of many descendants and land from God (Gen 15:5; 17:8), and those promises held good for the patriarch after him, his son Isaac (Gen 26:3–4), and for the patriarch after him, his son Jacob (Gen 28:13–14). In a similar way, I would suggest Christ's promise of primacy to Peter was not only for Peter but also for those who would succeed him. Christ's charge of primacy surely makes most sense when seen as a promise for not just Peter but also for his successors. The duty and responsibility bestowed on Peter was one that could not die with Peter's martyrdom, but continued on the shoulder of his successors, as the Church is ever in need of unity and governance.

The most recent thorough studies of the Scriptural and extra-biblical evidence on Peter are by Markus Bockmuehl. In the conclusion to his second book on Peter, he states:

> the remembered Peter's profile in the second and subsequent centuries includes a recognition that his Petrine ministry was entrusted to a continuing succession of ecclesial shepherds.[38]

He continues later:

> the principle of a continuation of the Petrine ministry *as such* seems clear in the memory of the man, beginning perhaps with classic "Petrine primacy" texts such as Matt. 16:17–19; Luke 22:31–32; and John 21:15–17. All three texts imply a post-Easter continuation of Peter's task that seems intrinsically permanent in nature and not tied to the identity of the one apostle.[39]

---

[38]   Markus Bockmuehl, *Simon Peter in Scripture and Memory: The New Testament Apostle in the Early Church* (Grand Rapids, MI: Baker Academic, 2012), 182.

[39]   Ibid., 183.

It seems only logical that when Christ established Peter's primacy, it was needed to stabilize the Church, not just in the first years after Christ but also during subsequent centuries.

The lack of mention of Peter in Paul's letter to the Romans has been used in confessional arguments against Peter ever having gone to Rome. It makes most sense to see no mention of Peter as signifying that Peter was not in Rome when Paul wrote his letter to the Christians of Rome in the 50s. Many documents of the late first century and early second century affirm Peter's martyrdom, and some of them specifically state he was martyred in Rome.[40] Acts 12 recounts the first widespread persecution against Church leaders in Jerusalem. Upon his release from prison, Acts 12:17 reports, Peter went to another place. There is no certainty where that place is. It could be Rome, but before going to Rome Peter is known to have ministered in Antioch (according to Eusebius' *Ecclesiastical History* 3.36) and the locations in 1 Peter 1:1 are said to have been visited by Peter. It is difficult to know how many years Peter had come to Rome before his martyrdom at the hands of Nero or whether he left Rome temporarily to minister elsewhere during his ministry in Rome before returning again. Bockmuehl, in his first book on Peter, concluding his investigation into early Christian literature on Peter in Rome, writes, "The first two Christian centuries underscore the remarkable uniqueness of Petrine memory in Rome. There are simply no competing localities for Peter's tomb, during this period or indeed later, East or West, orthodox or heretical, Jewish, pagan or Christian."[41] The early successors of Peter in Rome are mentioned by Irenaeus in *Against the Heresies* (3.3.3).[42] The first list of bishops of Rome was drawn up by Hegesippus around AD 150.[43]

---

[40]   Ibid., 102.

[41]   Markus Bockmuehl, *The Remembered Peter in Ancient Reception and Modern Debate*, WUNT 262 (Tübingen: Mohr Siebeck, 2010), 131.

[42]   *The Apostolic Fathers with Justin Martyr and Irenaeus*, ed. Alexander Roberts, James Donaldson, and A. Cleveland Coxe, The Ante-Nicene Fathers 1 (Buffalo, NY: Christian Literature Company, 1885), 416.

[43]   This is referenced in Hegesippus, "Fragments from His Five Books of Commentaries on the Acts of the Church," in *Fathers of the Third and Fourth Centuries: The Twelve Patriarchs, Excerpts and Epistles, the Clementina, Apocrypha, Decretals, Memoirs of Edessa and Syriac Documents, Remains of the First Ages*, ed. Alexander Roberts, James Donaldson, and A. Cleveland Coxe, trans. B. P. Pratten, The Ante-Nicene Fathers 8 (Buffalo, NY: Christian Literature Company, 1886), 764.

Peter was to serve his brothers by being a bond of unity in the Church. This important duty is evident in the most beautiful title given to Peter's successor, "Our Holy Father." The father is the one who unites the family, and "Our Holy Father," the successor of Peter, unites the whole Church. The role of Peter's successor as servant of the servants of God is to constantly forge unity in the Church. Christ, in his foresight, saw the Church's need for a unifier, and so Ratzinger states, "The Roman primacy is not an invention of the popes, but an essential element of ecclesial unity that goes back to the Lord and was developed faithfully in the nascent Church."[44] Of course, no man who is given the responsibility of succeeding Peter can, by his own human strength, fulfill the task, and history reveals the weaknesses of the men so entrusted. But above all, the Roman primacy reminds us of God's guidance and presence with his Church.

First Experimental Mission of the Twelve

Each of the Synoptics tells us that Jesus sent the twelve apostles out on what could perhaps be described as a temporary mission a short time after he chose them (Matt 10:5–15; Mark 6:7–13; Luke 9:1–6). Those preparing for priesthood now usually spend two months during the summer vacation from seminary every year in a parish and a half day every week during the school year in a parish or other apostolic activity. The mission of the Twelve appears to be a similar learning experience for them except that they already ministered with the power of Jesus during this mission. For a reason that will become clear when we look at Luke 10 in the next section, I want to point out the structure of the narrative in Mark 6 and Luke 9. For simplicity I reduce it to a tri-partite structure:

a) Jesus assembles the Twelve and instructs them, and they begin the mission (Mark 6:7–13; Luke 9:1–6),
b) an interlude follows (Mark 6:14–29; Luke 9:7–9), and
c) the return of the Twelve is related (Mark 6:30; Luke 9:10).

In Matthew, the instruction of the Twelve follows immediately after Jesus chose them in 10:1–4 and there is no clear reference to their

---

44   Ratzinger, *Called to Communion*, 72.

departure, no interlude while they are out on mission, and no report about their return. John lacks a report of this apostolic mission. Because of the similarity between Mark's and Luke's account, we will examine them first.

Mark 6:7–13

After the Twelve are gathered, Jesus gives them authority over unclean spirits and instructions concerning what not to bring with them. They are to be dependent on the generosity of those who listen to their preaching, so they are to take only a staff, sandals, and a tunic with them (Mark 6:8–9). Ultimately, they are dependent on God's providence for their mission, just as the Israelites were dependent on God while wandering in the desert.[45] Jesus also warns them in advance that their preaching will be rejected by some, in which case they are to shake off the dust from their feet as a witness, probably a witness to judgment (Mark 6:11).

The brief description of their successful mission in 6:12–13 reports their preaching and healing and reveals that their model for ministry was Jesus, who also preached and healed. Jesus began his ministry urging repentance (1:15), and the Twelve also urged repentance (6:12). Jesus expelled demons (Mark 1:25–26, 34, 39; 3:22), and they also expelled many demons (6:13). Jesus healed many sick (Mark 1:34; 3:10; 5:34; 6:5), and they healed many sick (6:13). Their preaching and actions mimicked the preaching and actions of Jesus. In effect, Jesus was now carrying on his ministry through the Twelve. The mission of the Twelve performing the same actions as Jesus would support the view that each one acted as an agent of Jesus, reflecting the Jewish understanding of agency we examined. That is why whoever received them received Jesus and whoever rejected them rejected Jesus (Matt 10:40; Mark 9:37; Luke 10:16; John 13:20). Jesus ministered through them where they ministered.

There is a novelty in their ministry in 6:13 in that they anointed many sick people with oil and healed them. Nowhere was it stated in this Gospel or the others that Jesus anointed people with oil. Since their ministry is an extension of the ministry of Jesus and replicates

---

[45] Marcus sees many parallels between God's providential care of the Twelve on their mission and his providential care of the Israelites during their desert wandering (*Mark 1–8*, 389–390).

the ministry of Jesus, could we not suggest that this act of anointing with oil was surely carried out at the command of Jesus? Might we also ask whether Jesus himself may have anointed with oil even though it is not recorded by the evangelists? Anointing with oil had many uses at that time: it was used for cosmetic purposes, for sports, and for medicinal reasons (e.g., Isa 1:6; Luke 10:34). But since oil is mentioned here in connection with healing, on a mission commanded by Jesus, it suggests that what is at stake in this anointing is more than its well-known contemporary uses. In James 5:14, we read that the sick are to be anointed by the presbyters with oil *in the name of the Lord*. It is not just anointing with oil, but anointing with oil in the name of the Lord. When the apostles anointed with oil, they were acting as the agents of Jesus, and surely the anointing was not just any ordinary anointing, and it was continued in the ministry of Church, as we see in James 5:14.

Luke 9:1–6

Luke's account parallels Mark's closely, but there are minor differences (e.g., in Mark the Twelve healed by anointing with oil, but Luke 9:1 specifically says they were given the power and authority to cure diseases). As in Mark, they are portrayed as doing what they saw Jesus himself doing. Joseph Fitzmyer summarizes the pericope in this way, "The meaning of the passage is not difficult to discern. One now sees the purpose behind the choosing of the Twelve in 6:13: they are to be given a share in Jesus' own mission of preaching the kingdom of God."[46]

Matthew 10:5–15

Jesus' instructions to the Twelve for their mission in Matthew 10:5–15 are part of a larger discourse taking up chapter 10 of Matthew, often called the Missionary Discourse. In Matthew's account, Jesus tells the apostles not to minister to the Gentiles and Samaritans, but only to the lost sheep of Israel (10:5–6). This command is only for this particular mission, because Jesus will send them to all the nations at the end of the Gospel (Matt 28:18–20). For this particular mission, the Jews are to be the privileged recipients of the message.

---

[46]   Fitzmyer, *The Gospel According to Luke I-IX*, 752.

When Paul preached, he also preached to the Jews first and then to the Gentiles, as we see many times in Acts (e.g., Acts 13:46; 18:6). The priority of Jews as recipients of the preaching of the kingdom is also alluded to in Romans 1:16. There is more detail in Matthew, by comparison with Mark and Luke, about not taking provisions for their mission and relying instead on those who receive their ministry to fund their mission. Their healing ministry is also described in more detail. As in Mark and Luke, the apostles are to do what they have already seen Jesus do. The dust-shaking sign (10:14), when read with the pronouncement by Jesus of lighter judgment for Sodom and Gomorrah (10:15), is a judgment. It is a warning about the gravity of rejecting God and his message, even when it is delivered through mere mortals acting as the agents of Jesus.

Concluding this brief examination of the mission of the apostles, it is clear that they did what Jesus did in his ministry, preaching, healing, and exorcising. Their ministry was an extension of the ministry of Jesus. They acted with the power and authority of Jesus, and where they ministered, it was really Jesus who ministered through them.

The Seventy(-two) (Luke 10:1–20)

Luke is the only evangelist to relate the mission of the seventy (-two). He depicts it similarly to the mission of the Twelve in his previous chapter in some respects, including a comparable tri-partite structure, though the narrative of the mission of the seventy(-two) is longer than the mission of the Twelve:

a) instruction from Jesus (Luke 9:1–6; Luke 10:1–12),
b) interlude (Luke 9:7–9; Luke 10:13–16), and
c) return of the missionaries (Luke 9:10; Luke 10:17–20).

Following so quickly after the mission of the Twelve and having the same structure would seem to indicate that Luke wants us to see this mission in relation to the mission of the Twelve.

Before we examine the mission, a difficulty to be confronted is whether the text of Luke has seventy or seventy-two missionaries, a problem not always evident in English translations of 10:1, 17. The

Greek manuscripts are fairly evenly divided between seventy and seventy-two missionaries, so one way to do deference to both numbers is "seventy(-two)." The number seventy(-two) is often taken to be symbolic. Firstly, just as the Twelve symbolize the twelve tribes of Israel, the seventy(-two) could symbolize all the nations of the earth, based on Genesis 10, which lists seventy/seventy-two nations in the world (seventy in the Hebrew text of Genesis 10, and seventy-two in the Septuagint text of Genesis 10, which might explain why some ancient scribes wrote seventy-two instead of seventy in their Greek copies of Luke 10). Secondly, the number could also be recalling the seventy elders whom God allowed to assist Moses (Num 11:16–17, 24–25) after he complained to the Lord about the burden of leadership (Num 11:14). Those seventy elders received the spirit in the Tent of Meeting but two others outside the tent also received the spirit and prophesied, which brought the total number to seventy-two (Num 11:26). The fluctuation in the manuscripts of Luke 10 between seventy and seventy-two could be also explained by ancient copyists being influenced by either the seventy or seventy-two of Numbers 11.

Symbolizing the mission to the Gentiles and recalling the seventy-two elders of Numbers can both be held as valid for Luke's intentions. But for this study, the connection with Numbers 11 is noteworthy. Moses needed help for his task of leading the people, and he was granted seventy-two elders. Jesus had already sent out the Twelve on their mission in Luke 9, and now a short time afterwards, he sends the seventy(-two) out on a similar mission. Just as the seventy-two aided Moses, the mission of the seventy(-two) in Luke 10 could be seen as aiding and assisting the prior mission of the Twelve in Luke 9. Even if the mission of the seventy(-two) is symbolic of the Church's future mission to the Gentiles (because of the number of the nations of the world in Genesis 10), their mission can still be seen as supporting the apostles' prior mission.

The similarity of structure and content between the missions of the Twelve and the seventy(-two) begs the question of whether Luke used the mission of the Twelve as his foundation when writing the narrative of the mission of the seventy(-two). Darrell Bock says, "The interchangeability of elements from each mission shows their inherent relationship."[47] The similar elements in both missions include the

---

[47]   Darrell L. Bock, *Luke*, vol. 2, *9:51–24:53*, Baker Exegetical Commentary on the New Testament (Grand Rapids, MI: Baker Books, 1996), 1006.

directives on what not to take with them, to rely on the generosity of those who receive their preaching, to preach, to heal, and to expect rejection. However, similar structure and content do not mean the narrative is ahistorical.[48] It seems to me that Luke deliberately wanted those resemblances to be perceived, since they are very evident. What does Luke want to convey by these likenesses?

Clearly the seventy(-two) are important missionaries who have received power and authority from the Lord to preach, exorcise, and heal in his name. The verb Luke uses for their appointment by Jesus in 10:1 is *anadeiknymi* (ἀναδείκνυμι). It occurs in only one other place in the New Testament, in Acts 1:24 for the appointment of Matthias in place of Judas. In Acts 1:24, those assembled ask God to reveal (*anadeiknymi*) to them whom God has already chosen to replace Judas. The use of the same verb for the institution of the seventy(-two) by Christ and the revelation of God's choice for Judas' replacement suggests the seventy(-two) have no small significance in the divine plan. There is another verb frequently used in the New Testament to appoint someone to office, *kathistēmi* (καθίστημι), which Luke uses in Acts 6:3 for the Twelve appointing the seven deacons. Instead here in Luke 10:1, the verb is the same one also used to reveal Judas' replacement. The appointment of the seventy(-two) in 10:1 is of some considerable weight.

Though there is similarity between the mission of the Twelve and that of the seventy(-two), there are some minor but significant differences. Luke's narrative of the mission of the seventy(-two) is longer than that of the mission of the Twelve, yet Luke gives primary importance to the mission of the Twelve. This is only to be expected, since Jesus called the Twelve out of all the disciples for special formation after a night in prayer in 6:12–13. From the literary point of view, it seems fair to say the mission of the Twelve has more importance, considering that in 9:1–2, Jesus gave the Twelve *power and authority over all demons and to cure diseases* and then sent them to preach the kingdom of God and to heal, while the seventy(-two) were merely

---

48   Taking it that Matthew formed his narrative of the mission of the Twelve by combining the mission of the Twelve in Mark and Q and Luke formed his two missions out of the same material in Mark and Q, this speaks only about the text of Luke, rather than the historicity of the mission. In similar fashion, Luke used 1 Sam 1–2 as a literary frame for the composition of Luke 1–2, even though he is often thought to have relied on Mary the mother of Jesus as a source for those chapters.

instructed to heal the sick (10:9). In fact, it is only when the seventy (-two) return that we learn they had been given powers similar to the Twelve by Christ when they reported that even the demons obeyed them (10:17). Then Christ confirms he had given them authority over serpents, scorpions, and all the power of the enemy (10:19). While the Twelve and seventy(-two) were given the same power and authority, it was already highlighted at the beginning of the mission of the Twelve, not afterwards, as in the mission of the seventy(-two), suggesting the greater importance of the mission of the Twelve.

Another interesting difference between the missions of the Twelve and the seventy(-two) is that the seventy(-two) were sent to the places where Jesus himself was about to visit (10:1). The Twelve were not given geographical instructions (with the exception of the account in Matthew), whereas the mission of the seventy(-two) is preparatory for Christ's forthcoming mission in the same areas. Both missions have the authority of Christ but, the power and authority of the mission of the Twelve, as well as its lack of geographical constraint (with the exception of Matthew), accentuates the greater importance of the mission of the Twelve.

The seventy(-two), like the Twelve, have been chosen by the Lord. We could even suggest they emanate from Jesus' prayer, because in 10:2 Jesus asks them to pray to the Lord of the harvest for laborers. It is the same request for prayer to the Lord of the harvest that Jesus makes before calling the Twelve in Matthew 9:37–38, again giving significance to the choice of the seventy(-two). The mission of the seventy(-two) was an extension of the mission of the Twelve in that they too had been commissioned, given similar powers to the Twelve and sent on mission. Luke wrote the Gospel already with the intention of writing Acts,[49] and in Acts, not only do the apostles continue the ministry of Jesus, but as we will see in the next chapter, presbyters assist the apostles in that ministry. To me it seems the significance of the seventy(-two) is that Luke intends us to see them anticipating the ministry of the presbyters assisting the apostles in Acts. This explains some features of the choosing of the seventy(-two) pointed out above: the similar structure and content to the mission of the Twelve, having the same power and authority as the Twelve (though downplayed initially), and their appointment designated with the same

---

[49]   Thomas J. Lane, *Luke and the Gentile Mission: Gospel Anticipates Acts*, European University Studies Series XXIII/571 (Frankfurt am Main: Peter Lang Press, 1996), 84.

verb, *anadeiknymi,* used for God revealing Matthias as his choice to replace Judas. Just as seventy-two assisted Moses in his mission (Num 11), the seventy(-two) foreshadow the presbyters who will assist the Church's mission, as we will see in the next chapter. J. T. Forestell puts it like this: "By constructing this second commission out of 'Q' material Luke wants to show that the work of the Twelve is being carried on in his day by a larger group, and that this development is according to the intention of Jesus."[50]

Who are the seventy(-two)? Unlike the lists of the Twelve, Scripture gives us no list of the seventy(-two), and they are never mentioned again in Luke or in Luke's second volume, Acts. Eusebius gives a brief list of some possible names, though it contains errors, such as including Cephas in the seventy(-two), because Eusebius' source distinguished between Peter and Cephas, probably not wanting to admit to a public row between Peter and Paul in Galatians 2:11.[51] The two disciples on the road to Emmaus, one of whom is Cleopas, are sometimes considered very likely to be among the seventy(-two) (Luke 24:13, 18), as are also the two candidates proposed to replace Judas, Joseph Barsabbas and Matthias (Acts 1:23). If Nathanael (John 1:45; 21:2) is not one of the Twelve, he may have been one of the seventy(-two). Barnabas, who makes his first appearance in Acts 4:36 and accompanied Paul on mission later (Acts 13:2), may have been included. If James of Jerusalem (Acts 15:13) is not the same person as James the apostle and son of Alphaeus ("James the Less"), he too is likely to have been one of the seventy(-two). We can presume that the seventy(-two) were among the one hundred and twenty gathered after Jesus' Ascension in the upper room (Acts 1:15), and among the five hundred who saw Jesus risen from the dead on one occasion (1 Cor 15:6).

---

[50] J. Terence Forestell, *As Ministers of Christ: The Christological Dimension of Ministry in the New Testament: An Exegetical and Theological Study* (New York: Paulist Press, 1991), 43.

[51] Eusebius of Caesaria, *Historia ecclesiastica* 1.12.2, in *Eusebius: Church History, Life of Constantine the Great, and Oration in Praise of Constantine,* trans. Arthur Cushman McGiffert, ed. Philip Schaff and Henry Wace, A Select Library of the Nicene and Post-Nicene Fathers of the Christian Church, 2nd ser., vol. 1 (New York: Christian Literature Company, 1890), 99. Another problem in Eusebius is his listing Thaddaeus among the seventy(-two), because normally he is considered to be the same person as "Judas the son of James" in Luke 6:10, but called Thaddaeus by Matthew and Mark to avoid confusion with Judas Iscariot.

That the seventy(-two) may be seen as foreshadowing the presbyters has not gone unnoticed by theologians in the history of the
Church. St. Bede—who has often been called the last of the Church
Fathers[52]—noted, "The number of the twelve apostles marked the
beginning of the episcopal rank. It is also apparent that the seventy-
two disciples, who were also sent out by the Lord to preach the word,
signify in their selection the lesser rank of the priesthood that is now
called the presbyterate."[53] Bede's interpretation of the seventy (-two)
anticipating priests was accepted by St. Thomas Aquinas, who sees
the seventy(-two) anticipating both diocesan and religious priests,
and in another work Thomas again sees the seventy(-two) anticipating priests (*Summa Theologica* II-II q.188, a.4, ad 5; see also II-II,
q.184, a.6, ad 1).[54] With St. Bede in mind, Cornelius à Lapide refers
to Church Fathers seeing bishops as successors of the apostles and
he links priests with the seventy (-two).[55] Finally, the mission of the
seventy(-two) was interpreted by Pope St. John Paul II to anticipate
the establishment of the presbyterate with priests as co-workers with
the order of bishops, successors to the twelve apostles:

> This also means that they [the seventy(-two)] participate
> with the Twelve in the redemptive work of the one Priest of
> the new covenant, Christ, who wanted to confer on them too

[52] Arthur G. Holder, "Bede and the Tradition of Patristic Exegesis," *AThR*
72 (1990): 401. In the Carolingian ecclesiastical councils, Bede is treated
similarly to the traditional four great Doctors of the Church—Gregory the
Great, Jerome, Augustine, and Ambrose—and seen as an authority; see
Joyce Hill, "Carolingian Perspectives on the Authority of Bede," in Scott
DeGregorio, *Innovation and Tradition in the Writings of the Venerable Bede*
(Morgantown, WV: West Virginia University Press, 2006) 235–236. Joshua
A. Westgaard says, "Bede's writings ranked with the works of the Latin
Fathers in importance in a typical twelfth-century book collection"; see
Westgaard "Bede and the Continent in the Carolingian Age and Beyond,"
in Scott DeGregorio, *The Cambridge Companion to Bede* (Cambridge, UK:
Cambridge University Press, 2010), 202,

[53] Arthur A. Just, *Luke*, Ancient Christian Commentary on Scripture, New
Testament 3 (Downers Grove, IL: InterVarsity Press, 2005), 171.

[54] Thomas Aquinas, *The Religious State: The Episcopate and the Priestly Office*, ed. John Procter (St. Louis, MO/London: B. Herder/Sands & Co., 1903),
137.

[55] Cornelius à Lapide, *The Great Commentary of Cornelius à Lapide: S. Luke's
Gospel*, trans. Thomas W. Mossman, 4th ed., vol. 4 (Edinburgh: John Grant,
1908), 243–244.

a mission and powers like those of the Twelve. The establishment of the presbyterate, therefore, does not only answer one of the practical necessities of the bishops, who feel the need for coworkers, but derives from an explicit intention of Christ.[56]

Consecration of the Twelve during the Last Supper

The Last Supper in John's Gospel differs from the Synoptics in that it begins with the foot washing in John 13, followed by Jesus giving a long discourse concluding at the end of John 17. The Synoptics leave us in no doubt that the twelve apostles were at table with Jesus during the Last Supper: Matthew 26:20 says Jesus sat at table with the Twelve; Mark 14:17–18 refers to the Twelve at table with Jesus; Luke 22:14 says Jesus sat at table and the apostles were with him; and Luke had already made it clear in 6:13 that the apostles were the Twelve. Instead, John refers to the *disciples* being present at the Last Supper (John 13:5, 22, 23, 35; 15:8; 16:17, 29). We saw that the Twelve were introduced in John 6:67 out of nowhere, which I take means John expected the reader/listener to already know all about the Twelve. I would suggest a similar idea is at play in John saying the disciples were with Jesus during the Last Supper: John expected his readers to already know it was the Twelve who were at table with Jesus because each of the Synoptics had clearly stated this. Additionally, in the text of John, there are small clues that John intends us to understand that it was the Twelve. In the central section of the High Priestly Prayer, there is a reference to Judas (17:12) that parallels a previous reference to Judas in the context of the Twelve (6:70). Also during the Last Supper, John uses the verb *eklegomai* (ἐκλέγομαι) for Christ choosing the disciples (13:18; 15:16, 19) and the only other use of that verb in John is in 6:70 for choosing the Twelve. Finally, the names mentioned during the Last Supper are only the Twelve: Peter (13:6, 8, 9, 24, 36, 37), Philip (14:8, 9), Thomas (14:5), Judas Iscariot (13:2, 26, 29), and the other Judas (14:22).

---

[56]   Pope John Paul II, Wednesday Audience of March 31, 1993, in *Priesthood in the Third Millennium: Addresses of Pope John Paul II 1993,* compiled by James P. Socias (Princeton, NJ/Chicago: Scepter Publishers/Midwest Theological Forum, 1994), 20.

Washing of the Feet (John 13)

It was common in Palestine and elsewhere to wash at least one's feet when entering a house from the street,[57] and the Pharisees practiced ritual washing of their hands before meals (Matt 15:1–2; Mark 7:3; Luke 11:38). But the washing during the Last Supper is entirely different. It has been interpreted in many ways. Naturally, it has been given a moralizing interpretation, since that is Jesus' own interpretation: as Jesus served, so also should his followers (John 13:13–15). In that sense, Jesus washing the apostles' feet is acting out the teaching he gives during the Last Supper in Luke 22:25–27 and elsewhere in Matthew 20:25–27 and Mark 10:42–45. It could be seen prefiguring Jesus' Passion, since Jesus "laid down" his garments and "took" them up again, just as in John 10:17, the Father loves Jesus because Jesus lays down his life and takes it up again. Jesus' statement in 13:8 that if he does not wash Peter, Peter can have no part in him has given rise to seeing sacramental symbolism in the foot washing, as Church Fathers such as Augustine and Cyprian saw the foot washing symbolizing washing away sins in the Sacrament of Reconciliation before celebrating the Eucharist.[58] It has also been seen as a symbol of Baptism.[59]

André Feuillet, in *The Priesthood of Christ and His Ministers*, offers new views that he admits are a working hypothesis and worth only as much as the arguments that back up the hypothesis.[60] Jesus' assertion that if Peter does not allow himself to be washed by Jesus, he can have no share with Jesus (John 13:8) is a Hebraic formula always referring to the Levites having no share or inheritance with the remainder of Israel because Yahweh alone is their inheritance (Deut 10:9; 12:12; 14:27, 29; 18:1–2; Num 18:20). When Christ uses this formula in John 13:8, it suggests that Christ alone is Peter's possession or inheritance because soon he will be consecrated by Christ (John

---

57   Keener, *The Gospel of John*, 903–904.

58   Cornelius à Lapide, *The Great Commentary of Cornelius à Lapide: S. John's Gospel—Chaps. 12 to 21 and Epistles 1, 2, and 3*, trans. Thomas W. Mossman, 4th ed., vol. 6 (Edinburgh: John Grant, 1908), 50–52.

59   Raymond E. Brown, *The Gospel According to John (XIII–XXI): Introduction, Translation, and Notes*, Anchor Yale Bible 29A (New Haven, CT/London: Yale University Press, 2008), 566–567.

60   André Feuillet, *The Priesthood of Christ and His Ministers* (Garden City, NY: Doubleday, 1975), 162–165.

17:17). Preparation for the ordination rite of priests in the Old Covenant involved ritual cleansing (Exod 29:4; Lev 8:6). Feuillet states, "It is permissible to think that the washing of the feet represents a transposition of the ritual bath that prepared Levitical priests for their consecration."[61] Feuillet believes the washing of the feet is a symbolic preparation for the consecration of the apostles in John 17.[62] His argument would be stronger if the Levitical priests washed only their feet prior to their ordination in Exodus 29:4 and Leviticus 8:6, but it is universally agreed that Exodus 29:4 and Leviticus 8:6 mean they immersed themselves. If the foot washing had this secondary symbolism of preparing for the apostles' priestly consecration in John 17, as Feuillet proposes, this would give a whole new meaning to what Christ said to Peter, "What I am doing you do not know now, you will understand later" (John 13:7).

The Apostles Are Consecrated in Truth as Priests of the New Covenant (John 17:17–19)

Before the apostles' consecration in John 17:17, Jesus says to his Father, "I have given them your word" (17:14). The apostles have spent three years being formed in the seminary of Jesus in Galilee and Jerusalem. During this time, Jesus gave them his word. It was the time "to be with him" (Mark 3:14) after being chosen as his apostles. During this time, they became friends of Jesus (John 15:15) and were sent out on temporary mission with the power and authority of Jesus to preach, heal, and exorcise. Now, after three years of intense formation with Jesus, it is the time for their consecration for mission.

Consecrate Them in the Truth (John 17:17)

Jesus petitions the Father in 17:17 to consecrate the disciples in truth. The Father is the source of their consecration. Their sanctification originates from the Father. Earlier, in 17:11, Jesus addressed his Father as "holy Father." Holy is the English translation of the Greek *hagios* (ἅγιος) from the same root as "consecrate" in 17:17, *hagiazō* (ἁγιάζω). So Jesus is asking his Father who is holy, *hagios*, to give some of his holiness to the apostles also, to also make them *hagios*.

---

61   Ibid., 164.

62   Ibid.

In the Septuagint, *hagiazō* is the usual translation of *qāḏăš* (קָדַשׁ) in Hebrew for the consecration of priests in Exodus 28:41, 29:21, and 30:30, and in Leviticus 8:12, 30. Obviously it is significant that John 17:17 has the same word, *hagiazō*, for the consecration of the apostles during the Last Supper as was used for the ordination of priests in the Old Covenant. Also, *hagiazō* (consecrate) in John 17:17 has additional significance, since the Levitical high priest's turban had a gold plate in front engraved with the words "Consecrated to God," *Hagiasma Kyriou* (Ἁγίασμα Κυρίου; see Exod 28:36 in the LXX). The high priest's turban acknowledged him as consecrated to God, and Christ consecrated his apostles.

Ratzinger sums up consecration as, "handing over a reality—a person or even a thing—to God, especially through appropriation for worship. This can take the form of consecration for sacrifice (cf. Exod 13:2; Deut 15:19); or, on the other hand, it can mean priestly consecration (cf. Exod 28:41), the designation of a man for God and for divine worship."[63] When Jesus petitions the Father to consecrate the apostles in truth, he is entreating that they be removed from the profane, to use the sense of *qāḏăš*, and set apart for God.

There is yet further significance we can draw out of the consecration of the apostles in 17:17. In John 10:36 we read that the Father consecrated Jesus, and this consecration is described using the same verb, *hagiazō* (ἁγιάζω). The Father consecrated Jesus for his mission in the world, and now Jesus asks the Father to also make the apostles holy, *hagios*, for their mission. Even before this consecration, Jesus said they were not of the world (17:14, 16). Now they are removed from the ordinary to live in God's truth, not for themselves, but to be sent back to the world again when Jesus sends them (17:18). Ratzinger writes of this dual sense of separation and mission combined in consecration:

> Something that is consecrated is raised into a new sphere that is no longer under human control. But this setting apart also includes the essential dynamic of "existing for." Precisely because it is entirely given over to God, this reality is now there for the world, for men, it speaks for them and exists for their

---

63   Joseph Ratzinger, *Jesus of Nazareth. Holy Week: From the Entrance into Jerusalem to the Resurrection*, trans. Philip J. Whitmore (San Francisco: Ignatius Press, 2011), 86.

healing. We may also say: setting apart and mission form a single whole. . . . Consecration means that God is exercising a total claim over this man, 'setting him apart' for himself, yet at the same time sending him out for the nations.[64]

This duality of being for God and for the world was articulated by Jesus already: he chose and appointed them and they are to bear fruit (John 15:16).

They are to be consecrated *in the truth*. What is truth? In John 1:14, Jesus incarnate is full of grace and *truth*. In John 1:17, the law was given through Moses but grace and *truth* through Jesus. In John 14:6, Jesus is identified as the way, *the truth*, and the life. Based on this, consecration in truth means that the apostles are to be consecrated in Jesus. We have seen Feuillet propose a link between the Levitical priests' immersion prior to ordination and Jesus washing the feet of the apostles. Ratzinger instead links the immersion of the Levitical priests with consecration in truth in John 17:17. The Levitical priests, following bathing, were consecrated when they were anointed and vested in sacred robes. In 17:17, Christ asks the Father to consecrate the disciples in truth. Ratzinger describes this truth as

the bath that purifies them; the truth is the robe and the anointing they need. This purifying and sanctifying "truth" is ultimately Christ himself. They must be immersed in him; they must, so to speak, be "newly robed" in him, and thus they come to share in his consecration, in his priestly commission, in his sacrifice.[65]

Their consecration is not just putting them at the service of the truth, but rather they are penetrated and interiorly transformed by the truth.[66] Jesus is asking the Father to make them like him, prolongations, as it were, of himself.[67] After their consecration, there is not just one Jesus, but twelve men who are extensions of Jesus, like Jesus.

---

[64]   Ibid.

[65]   Ibid., 89–90.

[66]   Marie-Joseph Lagrange, Évangile selon Saint Jean (Paris: J. Gabalda, 1925), 448.

[67]   Feuillet, *Priesthood of Christ and His Ministers*, 140.

The power and authority that Christ gave them for their temporary mission earlier is now a permanent reality.

How does their assimilation into Christ come about? They will be conformed to Christ by the action of the Holy Spirit. John 17:17 does not refer to the action of the Holy Spirit in their consecration, but earlier in the discourse, Jesus said, "When he comes, the Spirit of truth, he will lead you into all truth" (16:13). It is through the Spirit that the Twelve are consecrated in truth. Jesus told the Samaritan woman that the new worship of the New Covenant would be worship in spirit and truth (John 4:23–24). After their consecration in truth, the apostles are empowered by Jesus to lead that worship in spirit and truth. Jesus himself was consecrated by the Father (10:36). So when Jesus consecrates the apostles, he is drawing them into the unity between the Father and himself.

Pope Benedict XVI interprets the sanctification in truth of the apostles in John 17:17 as their priestly ordination:

> "Sanctify them in truth": this is the true prayer of consecration for the Apostles. The Lord prays that God himself draw them towards him, into his holiness. He prays that God take them away from themselves to make them his own property, so that, starting from him, they can carry out the priestly ministry for the world.[68]

More specifically, Ratzinger sees John 17:17 and the sanctification in truth of the apostles as the institution of the New Covenant priesthood:

> If the disciples' sanctification in the truth is ultimately about sharing in Jesus' priestly mission, then we may recognize in these words of John's Gospel the institution of the priesthood of the Apostles, the institution of the New Testament priesthood, which at the deepest level is service to the truth.[69]

---

[68]   Pope Benedict XVI, Chrism Mass Homily of April 9, 2009 (http://w2.vatican.va/content/benedict-xvi/en/homilies/2009/documents/hf_ben-xvi_hom_20090409_messa-crismale.html).

[69]   Ratzinger, *Jesus of Nazareth. Holy Week*, 90.

In summary, Jesus, high priest of the New Covenant consecrated by the Father, asked the Father to consecrate the apostles in truth, in Jesus himself, so that they might share in his priesthood and be sent into the world as his priests.

Sent into the World (John 17:18)

Christ says to his Father in prayer that he has sent the disciples on mission (John 17:18). The verb "sent" is in the past tense, but there was no mission of the Twelve in this Gospel as in the Synoptics, unless we include their brief mission to the Samaritans in 4:38. Raymond Brown believes the past tense is from the viewpoint of the evangelist as author and refers to the future mission of 20:21–22.[70] The Father sent Christ into the world (10:36), and in 17:18 Christ mentions sending the disciples into the world. The relationship between the Father and Jesus is now replicated in the relationship between Jesus and his disciples. The apostles' ministry is the prolongation of the ministry of Jesus, and as Christ said in the Synoptics, those who receive them receive Christ and receive the Father who sent Christ (Matt 10:40; Luke 10:16). We have seen that consecration involves a dual aspect, being given over to God but also for the world. Being set aside for God is to the fore in 17:17, while serving the world is highlighted in 17:18.

The Apostles' Consecration Emanates from Jesus' Self-Consecration (John 17:19)

Christ consecrates himself on behalf of the apostles so that they also may be consecrated in truth. The consecration of Jesus is the prerequisite for the apostles' consecration, which proceeds from the consecration of Jesus. What might be this self-consecration of Jesus, since Jesus was already consecrated by the Father in his incarnation (John 10:36)? It is a consecration "for them," for the apostles (17:19), and in the wider sense for all disciples. Brown sees Christ's self-consecration to be Christ as a priest offering himself for the disciples and points to three verses where Christ dies "for" others: in 10:11, the good shepherd lays down his life for his sheep; in 11:51, Jesus dies for the nation; and in 15:13, Jesus lays down his life for his

---

[70]   Raymond Brown, *The Gospel According to John (XIII–XXI)*, 762.

friends.[71] Viewed in this way, Christ's consecration in 17:19 anticipates Calvary. Christ's self-consecration on behalf of the disciples is
a commitment to his self-sacrificial death on Calvary. Calvary was
Christ's total self-giving of himself to his Father, and in that sense
it was his consecration. Commenting on Hebrews 5:9, we saw this
as Christ's priesthood attaining its perfect fulfillment. It was a self-
giving also for the world, so it was a consecration in the dual sense, to
God and for the world. Christ's self-sacrificial priestly consecration
to his Father on Calvary was the prerequisite for the consecration of
the apostles; without Christ's consecration on Calvary there would
be no consecration of the apostles. The consecration of the apostles
announced here will derive its power and effectiveness from Christ's
consecration on Calvary. The ministry of the apostles will emanate
from Christ's consecration on Calvary. The apostles have nothing of
their own to offer; everything they will offer to people in their future
ministry will come from Christ on Calvary.[72]

Do This in Memory of Me

In the Synoptic Gospels there is nothing comparable to John 17:17–
19, where Christ prayed to the Father to consecrate the Twelve. But
when Christ charged the apostles, "Do this in memory of me" (Luke
22:19; 1 Cor 11:24), Christ gave them the authority to offer the Eucharist. Aidan Nichols writes, "Later tradition will hold, plausibly
enough, that the consecration of the Twelve for their ministry . . .
was fundamentally given in the command to celebrate the Eucharist,
made as this was in anticipation of the Lord's glorious death."[73] The
institution of the Eucharist is recorded by the Synoptics during the
Last Supper and in 1 Corinthians 11:23–26, and a theology of the
Eucharist is given in John 6. Based on Nichols' statement that the
consecration of the Twelve is inherent in the command to celebrate

---

[71]   Ibid., 766–767.

[72]   Systematic theologians say the defining moment in the ordination of the
Twelve was certainly during the Last Supper, but Christ empowered the
Twelve before the Last Supper in their temporary mission and afterwards
to forgive sins, so Christ sharing his priesthood with the apostles was not
totally limited to the Last Supper. See, e.g., Gerald O'Collins and Michael
Keenan Jones, *Jesus Our Priest: A Christian Approach to the Priesthood of
Christ* (Oxford, UK: Oxford University Press, 2010), 280.

[73]   Nichols, *Holy Order*, 12.

the Eucharist, could we not also say that the institution of the priest-hood is given us in "Do this in memory of me" in Luke 22:19, and a theology of the priesthood in John 17:17–19? The celebration of the Passover was looking back remembering the first Passover from Egypt, but Jesus' command to "do this in memory of me" is looking forward to future celebrations in which it will be Jesus himself who will be remembered. The apostles were commanded to share bread and wine to remember Jesus, and as they do so, these celebrations will be in spirit and truth (John 4:23–24) because they have been consecrated in truth (John 17:17–19).

The Authority to Forgive Sins (John 20:19–23)

The Resurrection appearance of Jesus in John 20:19–23 took place on the evening of the day of Jesus' Resurrection (20:19). The disciples had locked themselves in out of fear (20:19). Once again John states, "the disciples" are present, just as during the Last Supper, and again we need to decipher who is present. In John 20:24, we read that Thomas, one of the Twelve, was not with them when Jesus appeared. That reference to "the Twelve" is significant and could be read as an indication that we are to understand the others present are also from the Twelve. Also helpful for deciphering who the disciples are is to note that they are commissioned/sent by Jesus during this apparition (20:21) and that, in Matthew 28:19 and Mark 16:15, it is the apostles who are commissioned and sent. We will return to this in more detail in the next section. Just as earlier John expected us to know that the "disciples" present at the Last Supper were the apostles, likewise here I would suggest John expects us to know that it is the apostles who are commissioned and sent by Jesus.

Following their commissioning/sending in 20:21, Jesus breathed on the apostles saying, "Receive the Holy Spirit" (20:22). This is not the Johannine equivalent of Luke's Pentecost, as has sometimes been erroneously suggested. This is a bestowal of the Spirit on the apostles for the specific ministry of forgiving sins (20:23). As Feuil-let notes, the Greek verb John uses for Jesus breathing on the apos-tles, *emphysaō* (ἐμφυσάω), is utilized in the Septuagint when God breathed the breath of life into the first man in Genesis 2:7, when he breathed a living spirit into man in Wisdom 15:11, and when Ezekiel was asked to call on the Spirit to breathe upon the slain in the valley of bones that they might live in Ezekiel 37:9.[74] We could also add 1 Kings 17:21 (3 Kings 17:21 in the Greek), where Elijah breathed three times on the child, praying for his resurrection. Charles Barrett saw the implication of these parallels in this way: "That John intended to depict an event of significance parallel to that of the first creation of man cannot be doubted; this was the beginning of the new creation."[75] This reception of the Spirit was to empower the apostles with the authority to forgive sins (20:23), just as the reception of the spirit at Pentecost would empower the apostles to begin their ministry. After the reception of the Holy Spirit in John 20:23, the apostles have the authority to bind or loose from sins. As noted above, the terminology of binding and loosing was already in Judaism depicting a judge binding or loosing the accused from their charges or a person being expelled or readmitted to the synagogue.[76] Similarly, having sins bound or loosed presupposes that the apostles listen to the sins and then decide to bind or loose. Catholics naturally see this passage as the scriptural foundation for the Sacrament of Reconciliation. Other Christians reject this. It is unfair to charge that Catholics are forcing the text to say what it does not contain. The text clearly states that Jesus gave to men empowered with the Holy Spirit the authority to forgive sins. Since God empowered men consecrated in truth to offer the Eucharist in memory of him and to baptize all nations, why would it be strange that they could not also be empowered by the Spirit to forgive sins in the name of God?

Commissioned to Preach, Teach, and Baptize

Before his Ascension, the risen Christ commissioned the apostles to preach, teach, and baptize all nations. This is often called the "Final Commission" or "Great Commission." The contexts in the Gospels are varied. The commissioning of the eleven in Mark 16:14–16 occurs in the part of the Gospel (16:9–20) considered by most to be a later addition appended to give the Gospel a neater conclusion than the

---

[74]   Feuillet, *Priesthood of Christ and His Ministers*, 169.

[75]   Charles K. Barrett, *Gospel According to St John: An Introduction with Commentary and Notes on the Greek Text*, 2nd ed. (London: SPCK, 1978), 570.

[76]   Köstenberger, *John*, 575–576.

abrupt original ending of 16:8. The impression is given that the commission occurs in Jerusalem on the evening of the day of the Resurrection and the apostles have not yet left for Galilee in compliance with the instruction of 16:7. Christ appeared to the eleven as they were at table (Mark 16:14), chastising them for not believing reports of his Resurrection, and commissioned them to preach the Gospel to the whole world (16:15). Those who believe and are baptized will be saved (16:16), and signs will accompany believers (16:17–18).

In Matthew, the commissioning of the eleven takes place after they have gone to Galilee (Matt 28:16–20). In Matthew 28:19, as in Mark, the apostles are sent on mission to the whole world. When the apostles were sent out on temporary mission earlier, they were forbidden to go to the Gentiles (Matt 10:5), but now they are commanded to go to all nations, making them disciples. In Mark 16:16, Baptism was only mentioned, but in Matthew 28:19 there is an explicit command from Jesus to baptize all nations in the name of the Father and the Son and the Holy Spirit and a promise to be with them until the end of time. It is the most precise expression of the Trinity in the New Testament, but others can also be found in 1 Corinthians 12:4–6, 2 Corinthians 13:14, and 1 Peter 1:2.

John 20:21 has the shortest commission, given to the apostles on the evening of Jesus' Resurrection: "as the Father has sent me, I also send you." It is embedded in Jesus bestowing authority on the apostles to forgive sins on the evening of the Resurrection (John 20:21–23). Just as the apostles' consecration comes from the Father at the request of Jesus (John 17:17), so also their mission comes from the Father through Jesus. The entire Gospel is recounting Jesus' mission, and now as Jesus was about to depart before his Ascension he bestowed the continuation of his mission on the apostles.

Matthew, Mark, and John have the commissioning of the apostles in common. Luke is the exception. Jesus appears after the two disciples return again from Emmaus (24:36–49), and unlike in Matthew, Mark, and John, those present include not only the eleven but also "those who were with them" (24:33). Those others include at least the two disciples returned from Emmaus (24:33), and we could speculate that the seventy(-two) or many of them were also present. Christ showed them his Calvary victory wounds and ate food, proving he rose in his body. Then he explained that everything written about him in the Old Testament had to be fulfilled, everything in the Law of Moses, the Prophets, and the Psalms. Those Scriptures foretold that the Christ would suffer and rise from the dead on the third day (24:46) and that repentance for forgiveness of sins would be preached in his name to all nations, beginning from Jerusalem (24:47). Yet, unlike in the other Gospels, there is no commissioning of those present to carry out this preaching, but Christ says they are witnesses of these things (24:48) and they are to remain in the city until empowered (with the Holy Spirit) from on high (24:49). In Matthew and Mark, the *apostles* were commissioned to preach and baptize. In Luke, there is no direct imperative to preach or baptize, but *all disciples* are called to witness. Preaching and witnessing are different roles assigned to different disciples: all disciples are called to witness to Jesus, but the apostles are called to preach and baptize. This differentiation reflects the different calling to the priesthood of the faithful and the ministerial priesthood, the priesthood of the faithful that everyone shares by virtue of Baptism and the ministerial priesthood of those ordained in the Sacrament of Holy Orders.[77]

---

[77] Why in Acts 1, when only the apostles are present, does Jesus say they shall be his witnesses in Jerusalem, Judea and Samaria, and to the ends of the earth (Acts 1:8) rather than commission them with words similar to his words in Matthew, Mark, and John? The command to witness is generic and therefore already understood in all the commissioning accounts. In the commissioning of the apostles in Matthew, Mark, and John, it is specified how that witnessing is to take place. The witnessing in Acts 1 is closely connected with the Holy Spirit they will receive at Pentecost: they are to wait in Jerusalem for the promise of the Father (1:4); they will be baptized with the Holy Spirit (1:5); and they will receive power at the coming of the Holy Spirit upon them (1:8). So in practice, the witnessing of the apostles after the gift of the Holy Spirit bore fruit in many baptisms (Acts 2:41), fulfilling the words of Jesus to the apostles in the commissioning accounts in Matthew 28:19 and Mark 16:16. But there seem to be other factors at play here in Acts 1. The same word "witness" (*martys*; μάρτυς), on Jesus' lips in both Acts 1:8 and Luke 24:48, serves to link the scenes closely together even though so many other elements are different. Thus, repeating the command to witness in Acts 1 serves the unity of Luke-Acts. The account of the risen Jesus in Acts and the closing account of the risen Jesus in the Gospel serve as a hinge between the Gospel and Acts, made all the stronger by repeating the command to witness. Additionally, the command to witness here in Acts has a further purpose, because it is tied with the structure of Acts: they will witness in Jerusalem (until the end of Acts 7), in Judea and Samaria (Acts 8–12), and to the end of the earth (Acts 13–28). So, although only the apostles are present at the beginning of Acts 1 and are commanded to witness, it seems to me that it remains significant that Matthew, Mark,

The Apostles Continue Jesus' Ministry after Pentecost

Reconstitution of the Twelve Apostles before Pentecost

The New Testament makes no attempt to conceal the scandal of Judas betraying Jesus or his manner of death. Repeatedly it refers to Judas who betrayed Jesus—for example, Judas is introduced in each of the lists of the Twelve in the Synoptics as Jesus' betrayer (Matt 10:4; Mark 3:19; Luke 6:16). After Judas' death, it fell to Peter to choose a replacement (Acts 1:15–26). Judas' replacement had to have three characteristics according to Acts 1:21–22:

1. He had to be a man. Luke uses the word *anēr* (ἀνήρ) in Acts 1:21, which generally means a male, rather than *anthrōpos* (ἄνθρωπος), which can mean someone of either sex.[78]
2. He had to have been present with the other apostles all the time from the Baptism of Jesus until his Ascension.
3. He had to have seen Jesus risen from the dead.

Matthias was the candidate chosen and added to the eleven apostles (Acts 1:26). Acts does not mention choosing a successor for the apostle James when he was martyred during the decade after Pentecost (Acts 12:2), but Peter had to replace Judas before Pentecost. There had to be twelve apostles at Pentecost because Jesus' choice of twelve apostles is fulfilling Jewish hopes for the restoration of the twelve tribes, albeit in a totally unexpected manner, as we saw earlier in this chapter. Matthew 19:28 and Luke 22:30 confirm this when Jesus promises the Twelve that they will sit on thrones judging the twelve tribes of Israel. It is precisely for this reason that Peter had to replace Judas before Pentecost when the Church inaugurated its mission with its first preaching and baptisms.

---

and John have a commissioning of the apostles, while instead, Luke commands all the disciples at the end of the Gospel to witness, and the apostles at the beginning of Acts to witness.

[78] In a minority of uses, *anēr* (ἀνήρ) means "a person" (see Arndt, Danker, Bauer, *Greek-English Lexicon of the New Testament*, 79).

The Twelve Receive the Holy Spirit at Pentecost

Luke commences his Pentecost account by telling us, "they were all together" (Acts 2:1). We have to deduce from the text who "they" were. We encounter a similar situation in Luke 24:1, where we read that "they went to the tomb" early on Easter Sunday morning, and it is only later, in 24:10, that Luke tells us "they" were the women and names some of them. Opinion is divided on who "they" were in Acts 2:1. Some believe "they" refer to the apostles, Mary the mother of Jesus, and the others mentioned in Acts 1:13–14, or to the 120 (approximately) in Acts 1:15. The 120, however, are not the last group mentioned before Acts 2:1, but rather the apostles are. Just prior to Acts 2:1, the last word in the Greek text of Acts 1 is the word "apostles," when Matthias was added to the list of apostles in 1:26. Acts 2 confirms that those referenced in Acts 2:1 who received the Spirit were the apostles. There was a distinct Galilean accent (Matt 26:73), and it was obvious that those who spoke after receiving the Spirit were Galileans (Acts 2:7). The Twelve are highlighted twice in Acts 2 immediately after the Pentecost event: Peter stood with the eleven and addressed the people (Acts 2:14), and after Peter's sermon, the people asked him and the other apostles what they ought to do (Acts 2:37). Regardless of whether "they" in Acts 2:1 included only the reconstituted Twelve, which makes sense exegetically, based on the evidence above, or a larger group, Acts 2 makes it clear that the twelve apostles were the leaders of the Church immediately after the Pentecost event. Two further references to the apostles in Acts 2 add further weight to this: the first Christians devoted themselves to the apostles' teaching (Acts 2:42), and the apostles worked many miracles (Acts 2:43). The apostles are now the leaders of the Church. The apostles received the Holy Spirit (Acts 2:4), and Peter, standing with the other eleven apostles, inaugurated their ministry with his sermon in Acts 2:14–36, defending them against the false accusation of being intoxicated and proving from the Scriptures that Jesus is the Messiah.

The Apostles' Ministry after Pentecost

The twelve apostles' ministry got off to a vibrant start on the day of Pentecost itself after Peter's sermon, when three thousand were baptized (Acts 2:41). After Pentecost, we see the apostles ministering in unison (e.g., Acts 5:12). Their success earned them the jealousy of the Sadducees, who had them arrested and imprisoned (Acts 5:17–18). After being released from prison by the angel, the apostles preached in the temple, were arrested again and warned by the Sanhedrin, were released again, and continued to preach daily about Jesus (Acts 5:19–42; a repeat of what happened to Peter and John earlier, in Acts 3–4). The Twelve prayed and laid hands on the seven new deacons (Acts 6:1–6), and in unity with James of Jerusalem, they decided not to require circumcision of Gentiles before Baptism (Acts 15).

A key to understanding the ministry of the apostles is given us in Acts 1:1. Luke begins his second volume, the Acts of the Apostles, recalling his first volume, the Gospel. He tells us he wrote his first volume about all that Jesus *began to do and teach* until his Ascension (Acts 1:1). It is important to see that Luke specifies the Gospel was not about what Jesus did and taught, but about what Jesus *began* to do and teach. This means that, after Jesus' Ascension, Jesus continued to do and teach as he had before his Ascension. This significant difference is unfortunately not evident in all translations of Luke's Greek. Luke's second volume, Acts, is therefore really the story of what Jesus *continued to do and teach* through the ministry of his apostles acting in his name. In Acts, Jesus ministers through his apostles and the others who will assist them in their ministry.

The parallels of miracles between Jesus in the Gospel and Peter in Acts confirm that Jesus continues to do in Acts through his apostles what he began to do himself in the Gospel:[79]

- A lame man is healed by Jesus (Luke 5:17–26), and a lame man is healed by Peter using the name of Jesus (Acts 3:1–10).
- Jesus disputes with religious leaders (Luke 5:29–6:11), and Peter disputes with religious leaders (Acts 4:1–22).
- Luke 6:17–19 contains a summary of Jesus' miracles on the plain, and Acts 5:12–16 contains a summary of the miracles of Peter and the apostles in Jerusalem.
- A centurion sends to Jesus to come to his servant (Luke 7:1–10), and a centurion sends to Peter to visit him (Acts 10).
- A widow's son is raised to life by Jesus and "sat up" (Luke 7:11–17), and Tabitha is raised to life by Peter and "sat up" (Acts 9:36–43).

---

[79]   Lane, *Luke and the Gentile Mission*, 69.

- A Pharisee thinks badly of Jesus for allowing himself to be touched by a certain kind of woman (Luke 7:36–50), and Peter is criticized by the circumcision party for associating with the uncircumcised (Acts 11:1–18).

These parallels attest that Peter did indeed carry out his mission to look after Christ's flock (John 21:15–17). What Jesus began to do during his earthly ministry, he continued to do through the ministry of the apostles. As Ratzinger writes:

> What is important for us in this context is Jesus' creation of the new figure of the Twelve, which after the Resurrection then passes over into the office of the apostles—of those who have been sent. Jesus confers his power upon the apostles and thereby makes their office strictly parallel to his own mission.[80]

Jesus, the high priest, shared his priesthood with the apostles who continued his mission and ministry.

Christ's Intention to Form a New Priesthood of the New Covenant

The Gospel texts surveyed in this chapter clearly show that Christ had a specific intention in choosing the Twelve. Mark says Jesus created twelve. Luke unambiguously states that Jesus called the Twelve out of all the disciples. Peter was given a special position by Christ over the apostles. Jesus sent the Twelve out on temporary mission to preach, heal and exorcise as Jesus did. The seventy(-two) also preached, healed, and exorcised as Jesus did. During the Last Supper, Jesus asked the Father to consecrate the Twelve. Their consecration empowered them to lead the new worship of the New Covenant in spirit and truth. After his Resurrection, Jesus bestowed on the apostles the authority to forgive sins and commissioned them to preach to the ends of the earth and baptize. Christ never used the word "priest" of the apostles because, before the consciousness of the apostles'

---

[80]   Ratzinger, *Called to Communion*, 113.

sharing in the priesthood of Christ could arise, it was necessary for the early Christians to understand that Jesus himself was a priest and that his death was his self-sacrificial priestly offering. It would be some time after Jesus' death before Christians would think of the ministers of the New Covenant, the apostles and their co-workers, in priestly terms. But even though the understanding of what Christ did and what he bestowed on his apostles would crystallize only over time, it was already obvious during the earthly ministry of Jesus that something new was happening. Jesus chose the apostles so that they would continue his ministry; what Jesus began to do during his ministry, his apostles continued after him.

Resonances in Catholic Liturgy

At the end of the first chapter we examined the Old Testament references in the Prayer of Ordination that follows the laying of hands on a bishop, priests, and deacons when they are ordained. The New Testament reference in the Prayer of Ordination for bishops asks God to pour out on the bishop-elect "that power which is from you, the governing Spirit, whom you gave to your beloved Son, Jesus Christ, the Spirit whom he bestowed upon the holy Apostles, who established the Church."[81] In Preface II of Apostles, preceding the Eucharistic Prayer, again there is a reference to the Church founded on the apostles, "you have built your Church to stand firm on apostolic foundations."[82]

Twice during Eucharistic Prayer I, we ask to benefit from the prayers of the "blessed Apostles and Martyrs," and the names of those whose intercession we invoke are listed. The first listing includes eleven apostles and is followed by other martyrs, concluding by asking that, through their merits and prayers, in all things we may

---

[81]   Congregatio de Cultu Divino et Disciplina Sacramentorum, Vox Clara Committee, *The Roman Pontifical* (Vatican City: Vox Clara Committee, 2012), 34.

[82]   *Roman Missal, Renewed by Decree of the Most Holy Second Ecumenical Council of the Vatican, Promulgated by Authority of Pope Paul VI and Revised at the Direction of Pope John Paul II*, 3rd typical ed. (Washington, DC: United States Conference of Catholic Bishops, 2011), 596.

be defended by God's protecting help.[83] The second list includes Matthias (who replaced Judas), has his name followed by many martyrs, and concludes by asking that we be admitted into their company in heaven.[84] See the end of Appendix 5.

The primacy of Peter is remembered in the collect for the Votive Mass of St. Peter, with reference to keys, as well as to binding and loosing: "O God, who gave the keys of the Kingdom of Heaven to your blessed Apostle Peter and handed over to him the pontifical office of binding and loosing, grant, we pray, that through the help of his intercession we may be set free from the bonds of our sins."[85] The Mass for the Pope describes the role of Peter's successor in authority and fostering communion: "O God, who in your providential design willed that your Church be built upon blessed Peter, whom you set over the other Apostles, look with favor, we pray, on N. our Pope and grant that he, whom you have made Peter's successor, may be for your people a visible source and foundation of unity in faith and of communion."[86] These two collects, each in its own distinctive way, echo the primacy of Peter and succession. The collect for the Memorial of St. Leo the Great refers to God who never allows the gates of hell "to prevail against your Church, firmly founded on the apostolic rock."[87]

We examined the mission of the seventy(-two) in Luke 10 and saw they received similar power and authority to the apostles and performed the same ministry as Jesus, and I suggested they foreshadow the presbyters in Acts. The Prayer of Ordination for a priest immediately following the laying on of hands by the bishop says, in reference to the apostles, "You provided them also with companions to proclaim and carry out the work of salvation throughout the whole world."[88] In that excerpt, the Prayer of Ordination does not explicitly refer to the seventy (-two) of Luke 10, but it is logical to so understand it in view of its earlier reference to the seventy wise men assisting Moses and Aaron (see end of chapter 1). We could therefore say the Ordination Prayer for priests sees the seventy elders assisting Moses and Aaron and the

---

[83]   Ibid., 636.

[84]   Ibid., 642.

[85]   Ibid., 1362.

[86]   Ibid., 1243.

[87]   Ibid., 991.

[88]   Ibid., 78, 94.

seventy(-two) assisting the apostles as anticipating the presbyterate. The prayer recited by the ordaining bishop continues, "And now we beseech you, Lord, in our weakness, to grant us these helpers that we need to exercise the Priesthood that comes from the Apostles," and describes the priests as "next in rank to the office of Bishop" and petitions that "they be worthy co-workers" with the order of bishops.[89] The unity of priests with their bishop is similarly seen in one of the questions put by the bishop to his priests during the Chrism Mass, in its reference to Christ bestowing his priesthood on the apostles during the Last Supper: "on the anniversary of that day when Christ our Lord conferred his priesthood on his Apostles and on us."[90] In all these examples we see the language of the Scriptures becoming part of the liturgical texts.

---

[89]   *Roman Pontifical*, 79, 95.
[90]   *Roman Missal*, 291.

CHAPTER 4

APOSTLES, OVERSEERS, PRESBYTERS, AND DEACONS IN THE EARLY CHURCH

WE HAVE SEEN IN THE PREVIOUS CHAPTER how Christ prepared the twelve apostles to continue his ministry. Jesus called them out of the disciples to be the twelve apostles. For them it was a second calling after their initial call to be his disciples. Christ gave Peter primacy over the Twelve and sent them on a mission with his same powers. They preached, worked miracles, and exorcised demons as Jesus did. Their ministry was an extension of Jesus' ministry. Jesus, high priest of the New Covenant, asked the Father during the Last Supper to consecrate the apostles in truth. Jesus is the truth (John 1:14, 17; 16:6), so their consecration by the Father is consecration in Jesus himself so that they might share in his priesthood and be sent into the world as his priests (John 17:17). Jesus gave them the authority to offer the Eucharist ("Do this in memory of me") and the authority to forgive sins in the name of God and commissioned them to preach, teach, and baptize. When Jesus ascended to heaven, he left the apostles to continue his ministry. To use the language of Acts 1:1, what Jesus "began to do" during his earthly ministry, he continued to do through his apostles, which we read in Luke's second volume, the Acts of the Apostles. After Pentecost, they continued the ministry of Jesus the high priest of the New Covenant.

The number of converts to Christianity grew and grew after Pente-cost, so the apostles needed assistance for their ministry. This chapter takes up from the previous chapter by examining briefly the many others—overseers, presbyters, deacons, and St. Paul—who assisted the apostles in carrying on the ministry of Jesus. The New Testament refers to these assistants, particularly in Jerusalem, as "presbyters," which corresponds to the Hebrew word for "elders" in Judaism. Clem-ent of Rome tells us the apostles appointed presbyters, and he gives the impression some of them were still alive as he wrote. The apostles also chose deacons to assist them. The word *episkopos* (ἐπίσκοπος), "overseer," (from which our word "bishop" is indirectly derived) be-gan to be used in Gentile Christianity for its leaders. The designations "overseer" and "presbyter" were used interchangeably for some time before the overseer became the leader of the presbyters. Much of this chapter will concentrate on Paul, who termed himself an "apostle," the apostle to the Gentiles. Acts 13:1–3 is at least a blessing bestowed on Paul and Barnabas for ministry, but is much more likely their con-secration for ministry. If we can talk of the apostles as priests, can we not also talk of Paul as a priest? Paul's writings display what could be described as his "priestly" consciousness. Every new mission in the early Church preserved its link with the apostles in Jerusalem, and Paul also preserved that link and unity with the Church in Jerusalem by reporting back after each of his missionary journeys. Luke tells us Paul appointed leaders in every church, and Paul's letters confirm that there were leaders in his churches, though there is fluidity in their designations at first. The Pastoral Letters show a development in that by the time they were written, Church leadership was "the overseer" and presbyters and deacons. This is anticipating the post New Testa-ment development of the threefold rank with which we are familiar: a bishop, priests, and deacons, with the bishop leading a college of presbyters in a local church, assisted by deacons. The Pastoral Let-ters give more attention to Church leaders than any other book of the New Testament, as they list the necessary qualities in an overseer, in presbyters, and in deacons. Mission is transferred by the laying on of hands: the apostles laid hands on the seven new deacons, and Paul laid hands on Timothy. Either explicitly or implicitly, the laying on of hands is usually stated to also confer the Holy Spirit. The chap-ter concludes with a brief examination of the application of priestly terminology to the New Covenant ministers and the stabilization of three clearly distinguishable ranks, one bishop leading many presbyters and assisted by deacons.

In the pages that follow, it will be seen that it is difficult to draw precise inferences about a maturing ecclesiastical structure in the first century because the writers of the New Testament were not overly concerned with that topic. It would be doing an injustice to the New Testament to force it to say what it does not say with precision. In arriving at conclusions, it is somewhat by way of deductions. As Joseph Ratzinger writes:

> how wrong it is to attempt to draw final conclusions from isolated texts of the New Testament. Neither the New Testament as a whole nor its individual authors follow a strict system of terminology. They grasp a thought from a particular perspective, but they do not systematize it.[1]

Aidan Nichols puts it like this: "The precise stages in the full takeover of universal apostolic authority by the local ministerial leadership cannot now be traced."[2] An error in the opposite direction would be to suggest that, unless something is stated explicitly in Scripture, it did not occur.[3] The New Testament is concerned with ecclesiasti-

---

[1]   Joseph Ratzinger, *Principles of Catholic Theology: Building Stones for a Fundamental Theology*, trans. Mary Frances McCarthy (San Francisco: Ignatius Press, 1987), 276.

[2]   Aidan Nichols, *Holy Order: The Apostolic Ministry from the New Testament to the Second Vatican Council* (Dublin: Veritas Publications, 1990), 30.

[3]   This is the type of interpretation we find in places in Raymond E. Brown, *Priest and Bishop: Biblical Reflections* (Eugene, OR: Wipf and Stock Publishers, 1999). However, even Scripture itself tells us that there is much more that could have been written about Jesus (John 20:30–31), and in Acts 20:35 we have a saying of Jesus that did not appear in the Gospels. By extension, we could apply the same to the rest of the New Testament. Scripture is a product of the Church and intended to be read with the mind of the Church. Scripture arose within a context, the Church, and was intended to be understood within that same context. Also, we cannot overlook the role of oral tradition. Many extra-biblical facts were taken for granted by the biblical writers because they were already being passed on orally. The one grandparent I never knew was my paternal grandfather, who died more than two decades before I was born. But important details of his life from a century ago were passed on to me orally. We cannot exclude the same taking place in the life of the Church and being consigned to writing in succeeding centuries outside of the canon of Scripture.

cal topics but not directly with hierarchical organization. With this limitation, we proceed.

The Apostles Are Assisted by Presbyters, Overseers, and Deacons

The overseers, presbyters, and deacons of the New Testament developed into our threefold rank of today: bishops, priests, and deacons. As the presbyters are the most numerous in the New Testament, and we encounter them frequently in the church in Jerusalem, we commence with the presbyters.

Presbyters

The word "presbyter" is the English transliteration of the Greek adjective *presbyteros* (πρεσβύτερος), meaning "older/elder."[4] The term "presbyter" was most likely imported into Jewish Christian churches because the corresponding Hebrew word, *zāqēn* (זָקֵן), translated as "elder," had already been utilized in Judaism since Moses for the Jewish elders and referred to synagogal governance. Our English word "priest" is an Anglo-Saxon contraction of the Latin *presbyter*, which in turn is derived from the Greek *presbyteros*.

Elders first appear in Judaism when the seventy elders assisted Moses (Num 11:16–17). Some of Moses' spirit was transferred to them (Num 11:24–25), just as some of Moses' spirit was transferred to his successor Joshua by the laying on of hands (Deut 34:9). Jewish elders had an important role in the synagogues and were members of the Sanhedrin. They were very involved in Jesus' Passion. The following are just some of the references we find in the Gospels. In all three Synoptics, Jesus predicts that he will be rejected by the elders, chief priests, and scribes (Matt 16:21; Mark 8:31; Luke 9:22). The elders came with the chief priests and officers of the temple to arrest Jesus in Gethsemane (Matt 26:47; Mark 14:43; Luke 22:52). The elders are mentioned along with the priests and scribes in the trial of Jesus (Matt 26:57; 27:1; Mark 14:53; 15:1). In Acts, the elders are involved

---

[4]   *Presbyteros*, "older," is the comparative of *presbus* (πρέσβυς), "old." The word *presbyteros* is used in this sense in Acts 2:17 and 1 Timothy 5:1 for old men.

in the Sanhedrin questioning Peter (Acts 4:5, 8, 23), in the questioning of Stephen (Acts 6:12), and in the difficulties Paul endured (Acts 23:14; 24:1; 25:15).

As Acts progresses, we see a development as the Greek word *presbyteros* takes on an additional meaning. In some instances it now refers to assistants to the apostles in Jerusalem, not Jewish elders. The context of each usage tells us which meaning is relevant. Some translations continue to render *presbyteros* as "elder" even when referring to leaders in the Christian church, while others translate it as "presbyter" when it means Christian leaders. To avoid confusion, I will translate it as "presbyter" here. Why did Jewish Christianity import the word "presbyter" for its ministers? We can imagine the apostles were conscious of being ministers of the New Covenant, but they would not have used the word "priest" to designate themselves or their assistants. Nowhere does the New Testament employ the word "priest" (*hiereus*; ἱερεύς) or "high priest" (*archiereus*; ἀρχιερεύς) for the ministers of the New Covenant. *Hiereus* could mean only one thing to the writers of the New Testament—the Jewish priesthood and its sacrificial system, which remained in place until the destruction of the temple in Jerusalem in AD 70 by Roman soldiers. Different terminology was needed for ministers of the New Covenant, or as Christ would say, new wine had to be put into new wineskins (Matt 9:17; Mark 2:22; Luke 5:38). Jean Colson suggests the Jewish converts to Christianity during the Church's earliest years might have influenced the decision to use the word "presbyter."[5] Such converts were the large number of Levitical priests who became Christian (Acts 6:7), and Barnabas also was a Levite (Acts 4:36). Since the word "presbyter" was used for leaders of Judaism but not for the priests employed in temple sacrifices, Christians could use it for their leadership and there would be no confusion with Jewish priests. With the passing of time, Christians understood that Christ's death was a priestly sacrifice, as the Letter to the Hebrews confirms. This prepared the way for the application of priestly terminology to New Covenant ministers by Tertullian two centuries later. The change in meaning in the word *presbyteros* (the additional meaning it assumed to denote not only a Jewish elder but also a minister of the New Covenant) is cer-

---

5　Jean Colson, *Ministre de Jésus-Christ ou le Sacerdoce de l'Évangile: étude sur la condition sacerdotale des ministres chrétiens dans l'Église primitive*, Théologie historique 4 (Paris: Beauchesne et ses fils, 1965), 189.

tainly not unique in language. Similar changes in meaning occur in
all languages. Albert Vanhoye gives the example of the French word
"chauffeur," which originally referred to the man who fed the fire in
the steam locomotive (from *chaud* + *faire*, "to make heat") but now
refers to someone who drives a car.[6]

The first use of "presbyter" in Acts signifying a Christian minister is in 11:30 when there was a famine in Jerusalem and the church
in Antioch sent help to the presbyters in Jerusalem through Paul and
Barnabas. The presbyters are frequently mentioned together with the
apostles in the decision made at the Jerusalem Council to allow Gentiles to receive Baptism without prior circumcision (Acts 15:2, 4, 6,
22, 23; 16:4). When Paul concluded his third missionary journey, he
met the presbyters in Jerusalem (Acts 21:18). In these instances we
can see the presbyters are very closely associated with the apostles
and are really assisting them in their ministry. While the New Testament does not explicitly say the apostles chose presbyters for ministry, the letter from Clement, Bishop of Rome, to the Corinthians before the end of the first century assumes that some of the *presbyters
appointed by the apostles* are still living (1 Clem. 44:3).[7] Referring to
this text in Clement, Thomas Herron states that "we have here a clear
statement that the Apostles did in fact appoint presbyters since this
assertion forms such a central part of 1 Clement's argument."[8] Even
if we did not have 1 Clement, it would be logical for us to say that the
presbyters, working so closely with the apostles in Jerusalem, would
have been chosen and appointed to ministry by the apostles, because,
as we will see, every expansion of the church in Acts came under
apostolic approval. Is there anything in the ministry of Jesus that
might have confirmed the apostles in their decision to choose the
presbyters for ministry? Jesus sent out the seventy(-two) in Luke 10
on a mission similar to that of the twelve apostles in Luke 9. The mis-

---

[6]   Albert Vanhoye, *Old Testament Priests and the New Priest: According to the
New Testament* (Persham, MA: St. Bede's, 1986), 276n56.

[7]   That letter was traditionally dated AD 96, but a recent doctoral disserta-
tion by Thomas J. Herron, published as *Clement and the Early Church of
Rome: On the Dating of Clement's First Epistle to the Corinthians*, ed. Scott
Hahn (Steubenville, OH: Emmaus Road Publishing, 2008), argues that the
letter should be dated to AD 70. One of many translations of Clement avail-
able is in Michael William Holmes, *The Apostolic Fathers: Greek Texts and
English Translations*, updated ed. (Grand Rapids, MI: Baker Books, 1999).

[8]   Herron, *Clement and the Early Church of Rome*, 29.

sion of the seventy(-two) was an expansion beyond the Twelve. The apostles replicated that expansion in the life of the Church by appointing presbyters and, I would suggest, found justification for their decision in the very ministry of Jesus when he sent seventy(-two) on a mission similar to that of the Twelve. What happened during the ministry of Jesus is now taking place in the mission of the Church.

Apart from the presbyters in Jerusalem, there are two other uses of "presbyter" in Acts, not in areas of Jewish Christianity but in areas of Gentile Christianity. In 14:23, Luke says Paul appointed presbyters in every church he founded (we will return to this text again when we examine the laying on of hands), and during his third missionary journey, Paul summoned the presbyters from Ephesus to meet him in Miletus (Acts 20:17). Since the term "presbyter" is of Jewish provenance, we might ask why Luke applies it to Paul's mission in these Gentile areas, where the term "overseer" would be expected instead. I would suggest that Luke decided to continue using the term "presbyter" for the sake of consistency and because a presbyter in Jewish Christianity was functionally the equivalent of an overseer in Gentile Christianity. In that sense, there is a certain interchangeability in their use in Acts 14:23 and 20:17, which seems to be confirmed when the "presbyters" of 20:17 are called "overseers" in 20:28, where, as Ratzinger says, overseer "is not used as an actual title but is applied to the presbyter as a designation of function."[9] Putting it more strongly, Ratzinger elsewhere writes, "the two terms *presbyter* and *episcopoi* are identified: the offices of Jewish and Gentile Christianity are equated and defined as a single office of apostolic succession."[10] It is also interesting to note that "presbyters" and "overseers" are still used interchangeably in 1 Clement (e.g., in 44:4–5), which also explains why, in 1 Clement 42:4, we read that the apostles appointed overseers and deacons, and two paragraphs later that the apostles appointed presbyters.

The text of Acts 20 is important not only because it shows the functional equivalence of presbyter and overseer in New Testament texts before the Pastoral Letters, but also because it shows these presbyters/overseers had received the gift of the Holy Spirit for their ministry. In the course of Paul's speech to the presbyters of Ephesus at

---

[9] Ratzinger, *Principles of Catholic Theology*, 277.

[10] Joseph Ratzinger, *Called to Communion: Understanding the Church Today*, trans. Adrian Walker (San Francisco: Ignatius Press, 1996), 122.

Miletus, he says *the Holy Spirit made them overseers of the flock* (Acts 20:28). Although they were presumably appointed overseers in Ephesus by Paul himself through the laying on of hands during his previous ministry in Ephesus (Acts 19), the speech on Paul's lips does not attribute the source of their ministry to Paul, but to the Holy Spirit. The Holy Spirit made them overseers of the flock. It all came from the Holy Spirit. As Ratzinger writes, the office of presbyter/overseer is instituted by the Holy Spirit.[11] Since it was Jesus who poured out the Holy Spirit at Pentecost according to Peter in Acts 2:33, could we not also say it was Jesus who poured out the Holy Spirit on the presbyters/overseers of Acts 20?

Moving on from Acts, in James 5:14 presbyters anoint and pray over the sick. A presbyter named John, distinct from the apostle and evangelist John, is the author of the letters 2 John and 3 John and simply refers to himself as "the presbyter" in the first verse of each letter, and is also most likely the redactor of the text of John's Gospel.[12] Peter's mention of presbyters in 1 Peter 5:1 is important for the light it throws on the relation between apostle and presbyter. Peter exhorts the presbyters and counts himself among them, as one of them: he describes himself as a co-presbyter, a fellow presbyter, *sympresbyteros* (συμπρεσβύτερος). This shows that, whatever a presbyter is, an apostle is also. Commenting on this, Ratzinger writes:

> the two offices—apostle and presbyter—are identified with each other. By this formula, the apostolic office is interpreted as identical with the presbyteral office. This, in my opinion, is the strongest linking of the two offices to be found in the New Testament. In practice, it means a transfer of the theology of apostleship to the presbyterate.[13]

When we arrive at the Pastorals, we have separate instructions for the appointment of presbyters in 1 Timothy 5:17–22 and Titus 1:5–9 and for overseers in 1 Timothy 3:1–7. But even in Titus 1:5–9, the distinction between presbyters and overseers does not yet seem completely fixed. We will return to the Pastorals for fuller treatment later

---

[11] Ratzinger, *Principles of Catholic Theology*, 278.

[12] Joseph Ratzinger, *Jesus of Nazareth: From the Baptism in the Jordan to the Transfiguration* (New York: Doubleday, 2007), 225–227.

[13] Ratzinger, *Principles of Catholic Theology*, 279.

in this chapter.[14] We conclude this section with these apt words of Ratzinger:

> the New Testament has itself established the link between the office of apostle and that of presbyter, so that the constitutive elements of the one belong also to the other. Above all, the presbyter is involved in the mediating ministry of Jesus Christ in the same way that the apostle is; like the apostle, he is the servant of Jesus Christ.[15]

Overseers

We saw that the term "presbyter" became associated with Jewish Christianity after being imported from Judaism. Similarly, the word "overseer" (*episkopos*; ἐπίσκοπος) was already in existence in the Gentile world before it was imported by Gentile Christianity to designate some of its leaders. In the Greco-Roman world, an *episkopos* was someone who had the duty of guardianship over a group of people. The word *episkopos* is a composite word, formed from *epi* + *skopeō* (ἐπί + σκοπέω), meaning "over/on" + "look/contemplate," so usually translated as "overseer." Since our English word "bishop" is derived from the Old English *bisceop*, in turn derived from the Latin *episcopus*, in turn derived from this word *episkopos*, a small number of English translations have opted to translate *episkopos* in the New Testament as "bishop." However, I will continue to translate it here as "overseer" to distinguish from its later usage at the turn of the first century, when it meant one bishop having governance over presbyters and deacons. However, some are of the opinion that the *mebaqqēr* (מבקר)—the overseer in the Rule of the Community in Qumran (1QS 6:12, 20) and in the Damascus Document (4Q266 10 i; 4Q267 9 v, 13), who had the duty of guarding people's faith—also anticipated overseers in the Church.[16]

---

14   Presbyters are mentioned many times in the Book of Revelation from 4:4 onwards, but they are often understood in that context to represent the saints in heaven, the twenty-four priestly classes of Judaism, or the twelve tribes and the twelve apostles.

15   Ratzinger, *Principles of Catholic Theology*, 280.

16   Colson, *Ministre de Jésus-Christ*, 190. L. Coenen, "Bishop, Presbyter, Elder," in *New International Dictionary of New Testament Theology*, ed. Lo-

The earliest occurrence of *episkopos*/"overseer" in the writings of Paul is in Philippians 1:1, where he greets the overseers and deacons. Based on Acts 14:23, where Paul appointed presbyters in every town, and the interchangeability of "presbyters" and "overseers" in Acts 20:17 and 20:28, we can suggest that Paul appointed these overseers (and the deacons) in Philippi. The Pastorals list the qualities necessary in an overseer (1 Tim 3:1–7; Titus 1:7–9). What is significant in the Pastoral Letters is that in them the terms for leaders in both Jewish Christianity (presbyters) and Gentile Christianity (overseers) are spoken of together. As we have seen, Luke does the same with presbyters in Acts 20:17 and "overseers" in 20:28. Another significant development in the Pastorals is that overseer is used in the singular in 1 Timothy 3:2 and Titus 1:7, as opposed to its plural use earlier in Philippians 1:1.

As in Acts 20 and Titus 1, there is interchangeability of "presbyter" and "overseer" in 1 Peter 5:1–2, when Peter exhorts the presbyters in 1 Peter 5:1 and in the next verse when he addresses them as overseers. That may not be evident in all English translations, since the Greek participle *episkopountes* (ἐπισκοποῦντες), "overseeing," is not in a number of Greek manuscripts of 1 Peter 5:2 and is consequently omitted from some English translations. When *presbyters overseeing the flock of God* in the Greek of 1 Peter 5:2 is read together with 1 Peter 2:25, where *Christ is the Overseer*, we perceive that the ministry of overseer is a sharing in the ministry of Christ. To expand this, in 1 Peter 2:25, the straying sheep return to the Shepherd and *Overseer* of souls, and most take the "Shepherd and Overseer" to refer to Christ rather than the Trinity. So, Christ is the *Overseer* of souls, and the presbyters in 1 Peter 5:2 are shepherding and *overseeing* the flock of God, which allows us to say that the ministry of presbyters overseeing is a sharing in the ministry of Christ the Overseer.

When Peter addressed those gathered in the upper room after Jesus' Ascension to choose Judas' replacement, one of the Scripture passages Peter quoted in Acts 1:20 is Psalm 108:8 in the Septuagint (Ps 109:8 in English translations following the Hebrew enumeration), "let another take his office [*episkopē*; ἐπισκοπή]," and Peter saw it applicable to replacing Judas. The word *episkopē* is obviously closely related to *episkopos*, because *episkopē* is the role/office exercised by the

---

thar Coenen, Erich Beyreuther, and Hans Bietenhard (Grand Rapids, MI: Zondervan Publishing House, 1986), 190.

one who is an *episkopos*. To coin a word, we might translate Psalm 108:8 in the Septuagint as "let another take his overseership," or to put it another way, "let another take his episcopacy." According to Peter in Acts, Judas had the office of overseeing, *episkopē*, and consequently the Twelve could also be said to have had the role of overseeing, *episkopē*. While the twelve apostles had a unique role in the foundation of the Church, they were assisted by many others quickly afterwards having the same duty of "overseeing," *episkopē*, who were known as *episkopoi*, "overseers."

We asked if there was anything in the ministry of Jesus that might have confirmed the apostles' decision to appoint presbyters and suggested that Jesus sending out the seventy (-two) could be seen as an expansion beyond the mission of the Twelve that was replicated in the appointment of presbyters. Since overseers in Gentile Christianity appear to have been synonymous with presbyters in Jewish Christianity at first, it follows that the mission of the seventy(-two) would also have been the event in Jesus' ministry that anticipated Paul appointing overseers (Acts 14:23).[17] When overseers and presbyters later became distinct, with one overseer leading a college of presbyters, the apostles were seen anticipating the overseers who became their successors, and the seventy(-two) anticipating the presbyters.

Deacons

In Acts 6:1, two groups of Christians are presented without prior introduction, the Hellenists and the Hebrews. The Hebrews were Aramaic speaking Jews in Jerusalem now converted to Christianity. The Hellenists were Greek speaking Jews who had migrated to Jerusalem from outside Palestine and had by now converted to Christianity. The Hellenists were open-minded about what the Hebrews would have considered essential to salvation, especially the temple, since the Hellenists grew up abroad and came from countries far from the temple. The Hebrews tried to make the Hellenists conform by targeting their most vulnerable, their widows (Acts 6:1). The twelve apostles intervened and asked the Hellenists to pick seven men of their own to *diakonein* (διακονεῖν) tables—to "deacon" (serve) tables

---

17   Alistair Stewart-Sykes argues unconvincingly against overseers and presbyters being synonymous in *The Original Bishops: Office and Order in the First Christian Communities* (Grand Rapids, MI: Baker Academic, 2014).

(Acts 6:2). All seven have Greek names (Acts 6:5). The apostles did not pick the seven deacons themselves; they delegated this task to the community (Acts 6:3), but then prayed and laid hands upon them (Acts 6:6). Somewhat analogously nowadays, many are consulted over many years for their opinion about a candidate for Holy Orders before the man is finally called to receive Holy Orders and ordained by his bishop.

The Greek word for deacon, *diakonos* (διάκονος), does not appear anywhere in Acts 6:1–6, only the verbal form "to deacon"—meaning "to serve"—in 6:2. The word *diakonos* is employed a number of times throughout the New Testament. We have seen fluidity in the use of "presbyter/overseer," and there is fluidity of a different kind in the use of the word *diakonos*. The word is utilized for service and also for Christian ministry. Paul described himself as a *diakonos* many times (e.g., 1 Cor 3:5; 2 Cor 3:6; 11:23) and Timothy is described as a *diakonos* in 1 Timothy 4:6. However, on three occasions (Phil 1:1; 1 Tim 3:8, 12), the word *diakonos* carries the meaning "deacon," or as we might say, the office of deacon. As we will see later, 1 Timothy 3:8–13 lists qualities necessary to be a deacon in Ephesus. Apart from Jerusalem and Ephesus, the only other church said to have deacons is Philippi, in Philippians 1:1. The deacons in Philippians 1:1 were most likely chosen as deacons when Paul ministered in Philippi previously (Acts 16:12–40).

In Acts 6, Luke is concerned to show that this new form of leadership in the Church, the diaconate, is divinely inspired. Luke presented the deacons' appointment/ordination in such a way as to recall the appointment of Moses' successor, Joshua. In Numbers 27:15–23, Moses asked the Lord to appoint a man over the congregation and · the Lord told Moses to lay his hand on Joshua. In Acts 6, the Twelve asked the disciples to choose the seven and they laid hands on them. Everett Ferguson notes, "Luke's linking of the first step in developing an organization for the Church with the first transmission of authority in Israel (an event which also served as the pattern for rabbinic ordination) was a bold claim that Christians were the true heirs of the biblical traditions."[18]

An anomaly in the account further confirms the divine inspiration of this new Church office. They were chosen to "deacon"/serve

---

[18]   Everett Ferguson, "Ordain, Ordination," in *The Anchor Yale Bible Dictionary*, ed. David Noel Freedman (New York: Doubleday, 1996), 5:39.

tables; yet we find some of the seven engaging almost immediately in preaching, performing miracles and exorcisms, and baptizing, although not at first imparting the Holy Spirit. One of the seven, Stephen, after his long sermon in Acts 7 urging his listeners to re-evaluate the temple in the light of Jesus, has his martyrdom presented by Luke in parallel fashion to Jesus' death. False charges were brought against Stephen (Acts 6:13) as against Jesus (Luke 23:2), and before Stephen died as the first Christian martyr, he uttered the same two prayers as Jesus on the Cross. He asked Jesus to receive his spirit (Acts 7:59), just as Jesus asked the Father to receive his spirit (Luke 23:46), and Stephen asked God not to hold the sin of his executioners against them (Acts 7:60), just as Jesus asked the Father not to hold the sin of his crucifiers against them (Luke 23:34). Luke is showing that the manner of Jesus' life has been replicated in Stephen, and this is confirmed in Acts 7:55, where we read that Stephen was full of the Holy Spirit, as Jesus was in Luke 4:1.

Another of the seven deacons, Philip, went to Samaria. Many believed because of his preaching and miracles, and demons were expelled (Acts 8:5-7). However, the new believers in Samaria did not receive the Holy Spirit when baptized by Philip (Acts 8:16), so Peter and John went from Jerusalem and laid hands on them, and then they received the Holy Spirit (Acts 8:17). This was apostolic approval and divine confirmation of Philip's preaching ministry. Subsequently, Philip explained the Scriptures to a eunuch returning to Ethiopia, baptized him, and preached in other towns (8:26–40). There is no mention in the text of Acts that Peter or John had to go and lay hands on the eunuch after his baptism for his reception of the Holy Spirit.[19] The implication is that Philip's preaching had apostolic endorsement after Samaria, and later Luke describes Philip as "Philip the evangelist" (Acts 21:8). I would suggest that, by inference, the ministry and authority of all the deacons is recognized and authorized by the Twelve, indeed originates in a decision of the Twelve, even if there appears to be discrepancy between their original appointment to serve tables and their actual ministry later. L. T. Johnson believes the "disjointedness of the account is therefore the best evidence that Luke's main preoccupation was in establishing this transition of

---

[19]   Interestingly, the Western Text of Acts 8:39 says the Holy Spirit fell upon the eunuch and the angel snatched Philip away.

leadership."[20] It is precisely because of that anomaly in Acts 6–8 that some have suggested the seven were chosen to be presbyters rather than deacons in Acts 6.[21] However, Luke is clear that the seven were chosen to serve tables (Acts 6:2), and the tradition of the Church is that they were deacons. We have seen that, when bishops, priests, and deacons receive the Sacrament of Holy Orders, the Prayer of Ordination after the laying on of hands contains both a New and Old Testament reference, and when deacons are ordained, the Prayer of Ordination gives the seven in Acts 6 as the New Testament reference.[22] In the time of Clement of Rome, before the end of the first century, deacons were involved in both liturgy and acts of charity, and this is confirmed in the second century document the Didache (Did. 15:1–2).[23]

We asked if there was anything in the ministry of Jesus that might have confirmed the apostles' decision to appoint presbyters/overseers and suggested Jesus sending out the seventy(-two). We could similarly ask if there was anything in the ministry of Jesus that would confirm the apostles in their decision to appoint the seven. While it is a bit of a stretch, one proposal that could perhaps be offered is the exorcist in Mark 9:38–40 and Luke 9:49–50 casting out demons using the name of Jesus. There is no agreement as to whether he is a Jewish exorcist or is in some way a follower of Jesus, although not according to the criteria of the apostles.[24] What is significant for us here is that Jesus told the apostles not to forbid this man conducting these exorcisms. His activity was an expansion beyond that of the Twelve. Just a little earlier, the apostles themselves had failed to exorcise a boy (Mark 9:14–29), yet this man who was *not an apostle* successfully exorcized in the name of Jesus. In Acts 6, the apostles dedicate themselves to prayer and ministry of the word of God and the seven, who were *not apostles*, serve

---

[20] Luke Timothy Johnson, *The Acts of the Apostles*, ed. Daniel J. Harrington, Sacra Pagina 5 (Collegeville, MN: The Liturgical Press, 1992), 111.

[21] For a very brief summary, see David Bohr, *The Diocesan Priest: Consecrated and Sent* (Collegeville, MN: Liturgical Press, 2009), 27–28.

[22] Congregatio de Cultu Divino et Disciplina Sacramentorum, Vox Clara Committee, *The Roman Pontifical* (Vatican City: Vox Clara Committee, 2012), 116, 132.

[23] Edward P. Echlin, *The Deacon in the Church: Past and Future* (Staten Island, NY: Alba House, 1971), 14–16.

[24] Robert H. Stein, *Mark*, Baker Exegetical Commentary on the New Testament (Grand Rapids, MI: Baker Academic, 2008), 445.

the widows who had been neglected in the daily distribution of food.

Phoebe is described as a *diakonos* in Romans 16:1, which some Bibles translate as "deaconess" even though it is the masculine *diakonos*. The feminine word *diakonissa* only made its appearance in the third century. Earlier, I pointed out the fluidity in the meaning of *diakonos*, as it can refer to service as well as Christian ministry and on three occasions refers to the office of deacon. The use of *diakonos* in Romans 16:1 is one of the many occasions in the New Testament where *diakonos* does not mean a deacon, but rather someone who serves others. (Phoebe is often thought to be the one who brought Paul's letter to the Romans.) Thus more correctly, Romans 16:1 describes Phoebe as a "servant of the Church." Paul recommends Phoebe to the Romans because of her record serving the church at Cenchreae. The other instances of the word *diakonos* in Romans also carry the meaning of service: the civil ruler is God's servant (Rom 13:4), and Christ became a servant to the circumcised (Rom 15:8).

Earlier Fluidity in the Designations of Church Leaders

There were many leaders in the Church from the beginning, but it took some years before the terminology of their offices became fixed as overseers, presbyters, and deacons. At first there was fluidity in the designations of the early Church leaders, and very often they were simply known by their duty to lead. In Paul's earliest letter, in 1 Thesssalonians 5:12, leaders are simply described as "those who are over you," (*proistamenoi*, προϊστάμένοι, from the verb *proistēmi*, προΐστημι, meaning "rule" or "be head of" or "show concern for"). Some leaders are simply called Paul's fellow workers and laborers, such as Stephanas (1 Cor 16:15–16). Archippus is urged to "fulfil the ministry which you received in the Lord" in Colossians 4:17. Epaphras is a beloved fellow servant with Paul in Colossians 1:7 and a servant of Christ Jesus in Colossians 4:12. In Ephesians 4:11, "pastors-teachers" is a single category of leaders in the Church listed with three others (apostles, prophets, and evangelists). By the time Paul writes his letter to the Philippians, two of the three designations later given to ecclesiastical leaders have made their appearance, as Paul greets the "overseers and deacons" in Philippi (Phil 1:1).

Two persons are described by Paul as apostles in Romans 16:7, the first being Andronicus, but there is confusion over the second.

The latest editions of the most widely accepted critical texts of the New Testament (UBS5, published by the United Bible Society in 2014, and the Nestle-Aland 28th edition of 2012) take the second to be Junias, a male name attested nowhere else, as did earlier editions of these critical texts.[25] Nevertheless, some recent English translations have Junia, a woman's name, who would be Andronicus' wife.[26] Paul refers to Epaphroditus as "apostle" of the Philippians (Phil 2:25), though this is not always evident in English translation. However, the twelve apostles chosen by Jesus were unique (e.g., 1 Cor 15:5–6 tells us Jesus appeared to Cephas and the Twelve and then to more than five hundred).

In the Letter to the Hebrews, the Greek word for leaders is *hēgoumenoi* in Hebrews 13:7, 17, and 24 (from the verb *hēgeomai*, ἡγέομαι, meaning "lead" or "guide"). The leaders speak the word of God in Hebrews 13:7 and keep watch over souls in Hebrews 13:17. Vanhoye believes these *hēgoumenoi* have a special role in the celebration of the Eucharist because their double mention in 13:7, 17 encloses a passage suggesting the Eucharist:[27]

1. 13:10 says only Christians have the right to eat from their own altar.
2. 13:15 refers to the Christian sacrifice as a sacrifice of praise.
3. 13:16 says the Christian sacrifice is an expression of community love.

The Letter to the Hebrews concludes by urging its listeners to greet all their leaders (13:24). Luke employs the same word, *hēgoumenoi*, in Acts 15:22 for the men sent to Antioch from Jerusalem by the apostles and presbyters. All this variety in designations gave way over the first decades of the Church to stability of terminology, leaving us with overseers, presbyters, and deacons.

---

[25] For discussion, see Bruce Manning Metzger, *A Textual Commentary on the Greek New Testament, Second Edition a Companion Volume to the United Bible Societies' Greek New Testament (4th Rev. Ed.)* (London / New York: United Bible Societies, 1994), 475.

[26] For the weakness in a feminist reconstruction of Junia, see Sara Butler, *The Catholic Priesthood and Women: A Guide to the Teaching of the Church* (Chicago: Hillenbrand Books, 2006), 97.

[27] Vanhoye, *Old Testament Priests and the New Priest,* 231.

Coming to the end of our examination of overseers, presbyters, and deacons, it is good to recall that we have biblical and extra-biblical evidence telling us these ecclesiastical leaders were first appointed by the apostles. Clement of Rome, late in the first century, tells us the apostles appointed presbyters/overseers, some of whom were apparently still living as Clement wrote, and he tells us the apostles also appointed deacons. Luke tells us Paul appointed presbyters (who, as we saw, were functionally the equivalent of overseers at that time) in every local church (Acts 14:23).

Paul Called to Be an Apostle

Presbyters, overseers, and deacons assisted the ministry of the twelve apostles but by far the most notable extension of the ministry of the Twelve was Paul. Paul had his life turned upside down as he neared Damascus when he met the Lord in a light from heaven (Acts 9:1-9). After he arrived in Damascus, he was baptized (9:18) and witnessed to Christ in synagogues after his Baptism (9:20, 22). However, his conversion must have seemed too good to be true and aroused suspicions, so for his safety he had to escape Damascus, lowered over the wall in a basket (Acts 9:23-24; 2 Cor 11:33). Three years later Paul went to Jerusalem, but only for two weeks (Gal 1:18-24; Acts 9:26-30). Significantly, Luke describes Paul as a disciple (Acts 9:26), but the disciples in Jerusalem did not believe Paul had become a disciple, so Barnabas introduced him to the apostles in Jerusalem (Acts 9:27), at least to Peter and James the brother of the Lord, according to Galatians 1:18-19. Luke gives the impression that Paul enjoyed full community with the church in Jerusalem, "going in and out" among them (Acts 9:28). However, for a reason Luke does not make clear, the Hellenists disagreed with Paul's preaching, and as in Damascus, he had to escape Jerusalem for his personal safety (9:29-30). The Christians in Jerusalem sent him home to his native Tarsus (Acts 9:30). Paul gives the impression that during this time he witnessed to Christ in Syria and Cilicia (Gal 1:21). Probably about a decade later, Barnabas went to Tarsus to find him and bring him to Antioch to help the growing church there (Acts 11:25-26) before they set out on mission from Antioch in Acts 13.

Before we examine Paul's reemergence in Acts 13, a word on the church in Jerusalem maintaining links with new missions is useful context. Persecution of the church in Jerusalem after the martyrdom of the deacon Stephen drove Christians away from Jerusalem and they witnessed to Christ where they settled (Acts 8:1, 4).[28] The deacon Philip preached Christ in Samaria (Acts 8:4–7). The church in Jerusalem had not planned or given permission for the mission in Samaria; it happened as a result of persecution following the death of Stephen. Although Philip preached successfully and baptized the Samaritans, the Holy Spirit did not come upon them. The church in Jerusalem sent Peter and John to Samaria, and the Samaritans received the Holy Spirit when Peter and John laid hands on them and prayed for them (Acts 8:14–17). In this way, the new mission in Samaria remained under apostolic authority. The reception of the Holy Spirit only at the laying on of hands by the apostles confirms the apostles as God's appointed agents leading the Church.

While the deacon Philip stopped to preach in Samaria following the persecutions after Stephen's death, others went to Antioch and also spoke about Jesus, which brought many to believe (Acts 11:19–21). Instead of the apostles also going to Antioch to make a decision about the mission as in Samaria, the church in Jerusalem sent Barnabas to Antioch (11:22–24). Barnabas was someone whom the apostles obviously could trust. No one else in the New Testament is described like him, a good man full of the Holy Spirit and faith (Acts 11:24). The apostles knew Barnabas would be able to discern whether what was happening at Antioch was of God, and he did, because he rejoiced at what he saw and encouraged the Christians at Antioch (Acts 11:23). Now Antioch, like Samaria, remained under apostolic endorsement and united with the church in Jerusalem.

After each of Paul's missionary journeys, he visited Jerusalem. After the first missionary journey, it is explicitly stated in Acts 15:1–4 that Paul and Barnabas went from Antioch to Jerusalem and reported on the success of their mission. Paul completed his second missionary journey when he landed at Caesarea, and Luke tells us that Paul went up and greeted the church, which I take to be the church in

---

[28] Most believe it was only the Greek speaking Jewish converts to Christianity who were persecuted out of Jerusalem. For the debate, see Craig S. Keener, *Acts: An Exegetical Commentary, vol. 2, 3:1–14:28* (Grand Rapids, MI: Baker Academic, 2013), 1467–1468.

Jerusalem (Acts 18:22). This gave Paul the opportunity to once again report back to the mother church in Jerusalem on the success of his mission. Paul completed his third missionary journey like the second by landing at Caesarea (Acts 21:8–14). Then Luke tells us that Paul went up to Jerusalem (Acts 21:15). Once again, as on the two previous occasions, it afforded Paul an opportunity to report on his successful mission. Just as the apostles themselves, or their representatives, approved of new unplanned missions, so also the new missions begun by the apostle Paul were approved by and united with the church in Jerusalem. The unity of these new missions with the church in Jerusalem was shown in a very tangible way in the collection they made for the poor in Jerusalem (Rom 15:26; 1 Cor 16:1–3; Gal 2:10; and Paul devotes most of 2 Cor 8–9 to the collection).

It is unclear which of Paul's visits to Jerusalem is referenced in Galatians 2:1. It could be his visit to Jerusalem to bring famine relief (Acts 11:30), but most take it to be his visit in Acts 15 after his first missionary journey. James, Cephas, and John were now leading the church in Jerusalem and gave Paul and Barnabas the "right hand of fellowship," allowing them to continue their ministry to the Gentiles. Not only was this important for Church stability, but obviously Paul also judged such unity to be essential. Ratzinger comments on it in this way:

> In giving Paul and Barnabas the right to communio, they were performing an authoritative and binding declaration of ecclesial fellowship—an act which even Paul regarded as indispensable, however much he stressed that he was called directly by the Lord and received direct revelation. For Paul too, the unity of the Church is unthinkable apart from this "continuing in the teaching of the Apostles," i.e., in the Church's apostolic structure.[29]

In each of the above examples, whether it be the mission of a deacon or of Paul, we see the unity of the church maintained by

---

29 Joseph Ratzinger, *Behold The Pierced One: An Approach to a Spiritual Christology*, trans. Graham Harrison (San Francisco: Ignatius Press, 1986), 77–78. See also Ratzinger, *Pilgrim Fellowship of Faith: The Church as Communion*, ed. Stephan Otto Horn and Vinzenz Pfnür, trans. Henry Taylor (San Francisco: Ignatius Press, 2005), 67.

the new mission coming under apostolic oversight, either through a visit of apostles or their delegate or by Paul reporting back to the mother church in Jerusalem after each missionary journey. Paul was no maverick but always ministered in communion with the Church. This is helpful context as we examine Paul being sent on mission in Acts 13.

Is Acts 13:1–3 Paul's Consecration for Ministry?

The apostles were consecrated for ministry during the Last Supper (John 17:17), and the seven deacons were consecrated for ministry by the apostles through prayer and the laying on of hands (Acts 6:6). Was Paul consecrated for ministry, and if so, when? Paul was called to be an apostle by the Lord on the road to Damascus and was baptized a few days later in Damascus (Acts 9:18). Yet, as Stanley Porter observes, Paul's statement in Galatians 1:12 that he did not preach a Gospel from men is not necessarily contradictory with having had hands laid on him.[30] Paul briefly met the apostles in Jerusalem three years after his conversion (Acts 9:26–28), but his witnessing in Jerusalem did not enjoy completely positive results and forced his departure (Acts 9:29–30). The only Scripture text that may refer to Paul being consecrated and approved for ministry by the Church is Acts 13:1–3, where Barnabas is also included. At the very least, it refers to Paul and Barnabas receiving a blessing for their mission. Even if it is only a blessing rather than a consecration, there is no reason to say such a consecration did not occur at some other time not related in Scripture. From what we have seen above, both Paul and Barnabas would certainly want their ministry to be in communion with the Church, and the apostles would also want that.

If Acts 13 is the consecration of Paul and Barnabas for ministry approved by the church in Jerusalem (i.e., approved by the apostles), is there anything in Scripture that might support that? One proposal is by S. Dockx.[31] In a nutshell, his claim is as follows. While Acts 13:1 says there were prophets and teachers in Antioch and lists five names, the text does not specify which of those five were prophets or teach-

---

[30]   Stanley E. Porter, *The Paul of Acts*, WUNT 115 (Tübingen: Mohr Siebeck, 1999), 73.

[31]   S. Dockx, "L'ordination de Barnabé et de Saul d'après Acts 13,1–3," *NRTh* 98 (1976): 238–250.

ers. Elsewhere, the New Testament distinguishes "prophets" from "teachers" (e.g., 1 Cor 12:28; Eph 4:11), as does the Didache, a document dated between AD 70 and the early second century. Didache 13:1–2 refers to prophets and teachers, but Didache 13:3 instructs the Christian community to give the first-fruits to the prophets that previously were given to the Old Covenant high priests. This typological interpretation in the Didache sees the Levitical high priests as types of the prophets in the Christian community. Kurt Niederwimmer notes the novelty in this understanding of the Christian prophets:

> In order to underscore the status of the prophets and to insure that the community recognizes its obligation to care for them, the Didachist parallels the Christian prophets of his own time with the ἀρχιερεῖς [high priests] of the old covenant, thus making the prophets (metaphorically) the "high priests" of Christians. This is a striking formulation, and it has no direct parallels in early Christian literature.[32]

Later, the Didache associates overseers with prophets, and deacons with teachers where it states in 15:1–2 that overseers and deacons perform the services of prophets and teachers. We could add that Ephesians 2:20 and 3:5 link the apostles and prophets. Dockx believes that the five named in Acts 13:1 are teachers and that the prophets are unnamed because, when prophets came from Jerusalem to Antioch, they were anonymous apart from Agabus (11:27–28). For Dockx, the prophets in 13:1 are anonymous leaders of the Christian liturgy who had previously come from Jerusalem.

While this is a hypothesis and not explicit in the text of Acts, is there anything in the text of Acts that might lend support to this theory? We would add the following to Dockx's argument:

1. Reading Acts 13:1–3 in the larger context of Luke-Acts and the Bible gives us some clues that this is no ordinary commissioning but involves a personal transformation of Paul and Barnabas:

---

[32]   Kurt Niederwimmer and Harold W. Attridge, *The Didache: A Commentary*, Hermeneia—a Critical and Historical Commentary on the Bible (Minneapolis, MN: Fortress Press, 1998), 192.

a. As we saw in the previous chapter, the twelve apostles were chosen from the disciples. The twelve apostles were first called to be disciples before they were called a second time to become apostles. Likewise in Acts, Luke describes Paul as a disciple before he designates him as an apostle. In Acts 9:26, Luke describes Paul as a disciple during his visit to Jerusalem after his conversion. Subsequent to Acts 13:1–3, Luke twice designates Paul and Barnabas as apostles (Acts 14:4, 14), which is significant because Luke was careful to reserve the title "apostle" for the Twelve.

b. Surely it is also no coincidence that it is only six verses after Acts 13:1–3 that Luke changes Saul's name to Paul (Acts 13:9), the timing of which must be significant. Elsewhere a new name indicates a new mission from God, as Abram becomes Abraham (Gen 17:5), Sarai becomes Sarah (Gen 17:15), Jacob is renamed Israel (Gen 32:28; 35:10), and Hoshea is renamed Joshua (Num 13:16).

2. Acts 13:2 tells us the church in Antioch was worshipping. The verb for this worship is *leitourgeō* (λειτουργέω). There are only two other occurrences of this verb in the New Testament: in Romans 15:27, where it means non-liturgical serving, and in Hebrews 10:11, where it means priestly service performed by Levitical priests. The cognate noun *leitourgia* (λειτουργία) refers to priestly ministry in Luke 1:23 (Zechariah's worship as priest), in Hebrews 8:6 (Christ's priestly ministry), and in Hebrews 9:21 (referring to vessels used in priestly liturgy). So, the word group from *leitourgeō* refers to priestly service very often, but also sometimes to non-liturgical service. Since the context of Acts 13:2 is religious (worshipping the Lord), could we not infer that the word *leitourgeō* there lends further support to Dockx' understanding the prophets as leaders of the Christian liturgy who had come from Jerusalem? They laid hands on Barnabas and Saul, who were two of the five teachers in 13:1, consecrating them for mission. If that proposal is correct, Paul and Barnabas were teachers in the church in

Antioch (which is supported by Acts 11:26) until their consecration in Acts 13:3 and then set out on mission.[33]

3. Everything in Paul's ministry was always in a spirit of com-
    munion with the Church and faithful to what he himself
    had received, so Paul would also want the laying of hands
    on himself in Acts 13 to have been in communion with the
    Church. Preserving unity with the apostolic church would
    also have been very important for Barnabas:

    a. From the first moment that Paul became a Christian,
        ministry choices were being made for him by Christ
        and communicated to him through the Church. Luke
        tells us that, at the time of Paul's conversion, Jesus
        told Paul he would be informed in Damascus what
        to do (Acts 9:6). Although he experienced a dramatic
        conversion, just like everyone else he also underwent
        Baptism (Acts 9:18). Paul made it very clear in Gala-
        tians 2:9 that his ministry to the Gentiles had apos-
        tolic approval: James, Peter, and John, the pillars of
        the church in Jerusalem, gave him the right hand of
        friendship and agreed that Paul should go to the Gen-
        tiles and they to the circumcised. Paul was careful in
        his teaching to be in communion with the Church (in
        1 Cor 11:23, he told the Corinthians he taught them
        what he had received from the Lord, which is best
        taken in the sense of "a tradition going back to the
        Lord himself,"[34] and in 1 Cor 15: 3–5, he told the Cor-
        inthians he handed on to them *what he himself had
        received* in teaching about the death, burial, and Res-
        urrection of Christ). Everything in Paul's ministry
        was always in a spirit of communion with the Church
        and its leadership, and we could expect that he would
        want the laying of hands on himself in Acts 13 to also
        have been in communion with the Church leadership
        in Jerusalem.

---

[33] The reference in Acts 11:26 to Paul and Barnabas spending a year teaching
      in Antioch refers to the year before they took the famine relief to Jerusa-
      lem in Acts 11:30. They would have spent a number of years teaching in
      Antioch before setting out on mission in Acts 13:1 (see Keener, *Acts*, 1847).

[34] George T. Montague, *First Corinthians*, Catholic Commentary on Sacred
      Scripture (Grand Rapids, MI: Baker Academic, 2011), 195.

b. Barnabas was associated with the apostles since Acts 4:36 and would have known that, while the church chose seven deacons (Acts 6:3), this choice was confirmed by the apostles laying hands on them (Acts 6:6). When Paul and Barnabas were set apart in Acts 13:1–3, we could expect that an apostolic link would have been very important in the mind of Barnabas also.

c. When Paul and Barnabas returned to Jerusalem after their first missionary journey (Acts 15:1–4), they were welcomed by the church and related what God did through them when ministering to the Gentiles (Acts 15:12). Not only did they relate the success of their ministry, but their account also influenced the decision made by James, leader of the church in Jerusalem, to decide that Gentiles would not have to be circumcised before being baptized (Acts 15:19). In this way, Acts 15 shows that the mission of Paul and Barnabas in Acts 13–14, following their consecration in 13:1–3, was in communion with and approved by the church in Jerusalem.

4. While Luke does not explicitly say that the Holy Spirit was given to Paul and Barnabas by the laying on of hands in Acts 13:3, the text comes as close as possible to suggesting it. The Holy Spirit directed that Paul and Barnabas be set aside for mission (Acts 13:2), Paul and Barnabas were sent by the Holy Spirit (Acts 13:4), and Paul was filled with the Holy Spirit (Acts 13:9). The reception of the Holy Spirit confirms this was more than just a simple blessing, and elsewhere on some occasions the reception of the Holy Spirit was linked with apostolic presence or approval (e.g., the Samaritans received the Holy Spirit when Peter and John laid hands on them in Acts 8:17, and the Holy Spirit fell on the household of Cornelius while Peter was preaching in Acts 10:44–45, which is recalled again in 11:1–5).

5. When comparing the consecration of Paul and Barnabas in Acts 13:1–3 with that of others, we see a parallel action of prayer and fasting preceding the consecration, prayer and laying on of hands during the consecration, and the action

of the Holy Spirit, all suggesting we should indeed see what happens to Paul and Barnabas in Acts 13 as a consecration.

  a. Luke tells us Paul and Barnabas appointed presbyters in every church, entrusting them to the Lord with *prayer and fasting* (Acts 14:23), and we will examine this verse more fully later when discussing the laying on of hands. When Paul and Barnabas themselves were sent on mission in Acts 13:1–3, *prayer and fasting* preceded hands being laid on them. We have a parallel: prayer and fasting accompanies the appointment of presbyters and of Paul and Barnabas as they begin their new ministry.

  b. Acts 13:3 refers to two actions as part of the commissioning, *praying* and *the laying on of hands*. When Timothy was consecrated for ministry, there were two actions, prophetic utterances and laying of hands (1 Tim 1:18; 4:14; 2 Tim 1:6, though only 1 Tim 4:14 contains the reference to simultaneous prophetic ut terances and laying on of hands). We could see the prophetic utterances over Timothy as parallel to the praying in Acts 13:3. Taking the prophetic utterances and laying on of hands in 1 Timothy 1:18 and 4:14 and 2 Timothy 1:6 as Timothy's consecration for mission, we can see a parallel in the praying and laying of hands on Paul and Barnabas sending them off on mission.

  c. In Acts 20:28, Paul tells the presbyters it is the *Holy Spirit* who made them overseers, and in Acts 13:2 we read that it was the *Holy Spirit* who chose Paul and Barnabas. There is a parallel action of the Holy Spirit in the appointment of both Paul and Barnabas and in that of presbyters/overseers. Paul and Barnabas undertook a mission, just as the presbyters/overseers took on the duty of overseeing.

6. When Peter left Jerusalem (Acts 12:17), Luke does not tell us where he went, but we know he spent some time in Antioch. Barnabas brought Paul to Antioch (Acts 11:25–26), and Peter and Paul were in Antioch at the same time (Gal 2:11), though it is not clear for how long. Traditionally, Peter has been seen

as the first *episkopos* of Antioch and is said to have appointed Euodius as *episkopos* there to replace himself, and Ignatius after him.[35] Undoubtedly, Peter's influence remained after his departure, though he had likely left Antioch at least a few years if not more before the events of Acts 13. With this in mind we could say that what happened in Acts 13 would have had the approval of Peter's successor in Antioch, was therefore under apostolic approval and in communion with the Church, and was in some way the fruit of Peter's own ministry there prior to his departure for Rome.

Taking all of the above together, it does seem to lend support to the proposal that Acts 13:1–3 was not only a blessing, but rather was the consecration of Paul and Barnabas for mission with apostolic approval. We have seen that in John 17:17 the apostles were consecrated during the Last Supper for their future ministry, and if the above proposal has merit, Acts 13:1–3 is the consecration of Paul and Barnabas for their future ministry.

Paul a New Covenant Minister

The question is sometimes asked in Catholic circles, "Was Paul a priest?" The word "priest" is never applied to Paul by the New Testament, and Paul never called himself a priest, but rather emphasized that he was an apostle. Yet he also compared his ministry to the priestly ministry of the Levitical priests. The twelve apostles likewise are not called priests by the New Testament, but in Catholic circles we talk of them as priests. Here I suggest an approach to answering this question on the priesthood of Paul.

Paul's Consciousness of His Vocation—An Apostle

To begin to answer the question posed above, we have to commence with what Paul says about himself and affirms time after time. He regarded himself as an apostle just as the apostles in Jerusalem. He

---

[35] Markus Bockmuehl, *Simon Peter in Scripture and Memory: The New Testament Apostle in the Early Church* (Grand Rapids, MI: Baker Academic, 2012), 39–40.

employed the word "apostle" to describe himself in the introduction to almost all his letters because he regarded himself as an apostle called by God:[36] "Paul, a servant of Jesus Christ, called an apostle" (Rom 1:1); "Paul, called an apostle of Christ Jesus through the will of God" (1 Cor 1:1); "Paul, an apostle of Christ Jesus through the will of God" (2 Cor 1:1); "Paul, an apostle not from men or through men but through Jesus Christ" (Gal 1:1), "Paul, an apostle of Christ Jesus through the will of God" (Eph 1:1); "Paul, an apostle of Christ Jesus through the will of God" (Col 1:1); "Paul an apostle of Christ Jesus through the will of God" (2 Tim 1:1); and "Paul, a servant of God and apostle of Jesus Christ" (Titus 1:1). Paul emphasizes his apostleship not only at the beginning of his letters but also during his letters: "I am an apostle to the Gentiles" (Rom 11:13); "Am I not an apostle? Have I not seen Jesus our Lord?" (1 Cor 9:1); and "I am the least of the apostles, I am not fit to be called an apostle" (1 Cor 15:9). See also 1 Thessalonians 2:6, 1 Timothy 2:7, and 2 Timothy 1:11. It was Christ who sent Paul (1 Cor 1:17), and the link with apostleship is clearer in the Greek, where the verb translated as "send" is *apostellō* (ἀποστέλλω). In Galatians 1:17, he regards himself as an apostle like the others, "those who were apostles before me." Paul confidently repeats his claim to be an apostle because he received the Gospel through a revelation of Jesus Christ (Gal 1:12), though he also learned of the death, burial, and Resurrection of Jesus from the Church (1 Cor 15:3–5). Paul leaves us in no doubt that he was an apostle. Bonaventure Kloppenburg states that, for Paul, his "constant preoccupation—it is almost an obsession—is simply to base his rights as an Apostle on a mandate from the Lord."[37]

Paul's Consciousness of His Vocation—Priestly Consciousness

Not only is Paul insistent on being an apostle called by God, but in a small number of passages (which we will examine in canonical order) we see hints of Paul's awareness of being a minister of the New

---

[36] Here I do not enter into the debate about the so-called genuine or pseudo-Pauline letters, since even if some letters were written by Paul's disciples after him, it is obvious that these introductions are in the same style as Paul, but I will treat this debate very briefly later in this chapter.

[37] Bonaventure Kloppenburg, *The Priest: Living Instrument and Minister of Christ, The Eternal Priest* (Chicago: Franciscan Herald Press, 1974), 51.

Covenant, a minister with priestly qualities, a priestly minister of the New Covenant.

Paul's Priestly Service of the Gospel (Rom 15:16)

In Romans 15:16, Paul uses language that compares his ministry to the Gentiles with that of a Jewish priest in the temple. Paul describes himself as a *leitourgos* (λειτουργός), a minister of Christ to the Gentiles in the priestly service, *hierourgounta* (ἱερουργοῦντα), of the Gospel. The word *leitourgos* is not in itself confined to priesthood or worship, but it is prone to being applied in that way, and its context here in Romans 15:16 gives it such a cultic meaning.[38] The word *hierourgounta* (ἱερουργοῦντα) is obviously from the same root as *hiereus* (ἱερεύς), priest. Nevertheless, Vanhoye notes that the verb *hierourgeo* does not necessarily refer to priestly activity, and taken by itself does not clarify whether Paul compares himself to a Levitical priest offering sacrifice, a Levite assisting the priest, or the layman bringing the offering, but in this context, it must be priestly, because it refers to the Gentiles giving an offering to Paul and then Paul, as God's *leitourgos*, offering the oblation of the pagans to God.[39] Joseph Fitzmyer sees Paul comparing himself to a Jewish priest: "In his mission to the Gentiles Paul sees his function to be like that of a Jewish priest dedicated to the service of God in his Temple."[40] Jean Galot goes further than Vanhoye and Fitzmyer and describes as superficial the view that would hold these verses as a figure of speech for Paul's ministry, and he regards these verses as a demonstration of Paul's awareness "that in the act of carrying out his apostolic mission he exercises a priesthood that is real and genuine."[41] Paul is using terminology that compares his ministry to that of Jewish priesthood, but showing that his ministry is of a different order, since he is a *leitourgos* of Christ. Paul does not merely compare himself with a Jewish priest; he realizes that he is a *leitourgos* and exercising priesthood coming from Christ.

---

[38] Vanhoye, *Old Testament Priests and the New Priest*, 268.

[39] Ibid., 269.

[40] Joseph A. Fitzmyer, *Romans: A New Translation with Introduction and Commentary*, Anchor Yale Bible 33 (New Haven, CT/London: Yale University Press, 2008), 711.

[41] Jean Galot, *Theology of the Priesthood* (San Francisco: Ignatius Press, 1985), 96.

Servants of Christ and Stewards of the Mysteries of God
(1 Cor 4:1)

In 1 Corinthians 4:1 Paul writes that he and the other Christian missionaries are servants of Christ. Here Paul does not use the word *diakonos*, but rather *hypēretēs* (ὑπηρέτης). Originally it referred to the rower on the lower deck of a ship, but it gradually took on other meanings, including servant.[42] It expresses Paul's dependence on Christ, his relation with Christ, and his acting as agent on behalf of Christ.

Paul then describes himself and his fellow apostles as stewards of the mysteries of God. The Greek word *oikonomos* (οἰκονόμος), translated as "steward," is a composite word from *oikos* + *nemō* ("house" + "distribute/allot/dispense"), meaning the one who distributes to a house, the one who administers the house, and so the administrator. Paul is acknowledging that he has responsibility over the mysteries of God as their administrator who is himself under God, as Christ's servant. Paul has been entrusted with the responsibility of administration, *oikonomia* (οἰκονομία). In 1 Corinthians 9:16–17, *oikonomia* is laid on Paul to preach the Gospel. In Ephesians 3:2, it refers to Paul's responsibility of stewardship of God's grace for the Ephesians. In Colossians 1:25, Paul describes himself as a *diakonos* of the Church according to the *oikonomia* God gave him. Usually *oikonomia* in Colossians 1:25 is translated with terminology reflecting administration or stewardship, but the Revised Standard Version translates the *oikonomia* given to Paul by God there as "divine office." In Titus 1:7, this link between being an *oikonomos* and having office on behalf of God in the Church is clear when an overseer (*episkopos*) is described as an *oikonomos*. While this is explicit in Titus 1:7, would it not be in order to see Paul's use of *oikonomos* in 1 Corinthians 4:1 as already moving in that direction and implying office in the Church on God's behalf?

The Greek word *mystērion* (μυστήριον), "mystery," in 1 Corinthians 4:1 became fixed as the term for "sacrament" in the fourth century,[43] though it was used in this way earlier. It was translated

---

42 Ceslas Spicq, "ὑπηρέτης," in Ceslas Spicq and James D. Ernest, *Theological Lexicon of the New Testament* (Peabody, MA: Hendrickson Publishers, 1994), 3:398–402.

43 Günther Bornkamm, "Μυστήριον," in *Theological Dictionary of the New Testament*, ed. Gerhard Kittel, Geoffrey W. Bromiley, and Gerhard Friedrich (Grand Rapids, MI: Eerdmans, 1964), 4:826.

in Latin as "*sacramentum*," whence comes our English word "sacrament." Here in 1 Corinthians 4:1, we could see the word *mystērion* referring to God's revelation, as Paul reflects on his responsibility as administrator for the revelation of God. Paul is the *oikonomos* of God's *mystērion*. It shows Paul's awareness of holding a position in the Church that places him in a relationship with God and the people and as God's representative to the people whom he serves.

Christian Apostolate Compared to Priesthood (1 Cor 9:13–14)

We saw Paul using terminology in Romans 15:16 comparing his ministry to that of the Jewish priests. Correspondingly, in 1 Corinthians 9:13–14, Paul says ministers of the Gospel should get their living from the Gospel just as those who serve in the Jewish temple get their living from the temple. Numbers 18:8–19 and Deuteronomy 18:3 specify how Jewish priests were to be recompensed for their service. Alluding to those texts, in 1 Corinthians 9:13–14 Paul draws a correspondence between the Old Covenant ministers and the New Covenant ministers as follows:

Old Covenant	
Those employed in the temple	receiving from those sacrificial offerings
Those serving at the altar (of the temple)	receiving their food from the temple
New Covenant	
those proclaiming the Gospel	living by the Gospel

In Paul's opinion, the ministers of the Gospel should receive their livelihood from their proclamation of the Gospel just as the Jewish priests of the Old Covenant received their livelihood from offering sacrifices in the temple (1 Cor 9:14). For Vanhoye, "Paul is therefore likening the Christian apostolate to a priesthood."[44]

---

44   Vanhoye, *Old Testament Priests and the New Priest*, 268.

In the Person of Christ (2 Cor 2:10)

In 2 Corinthians 2:10, Paul says, what he forgave he has forgiven *en prosōpō Christou* (ἐν προσώπῳ Χριστοῦ). The Greek word *prosōpon* (πρόσωπον) can mean "face" or "presence" (i.e., the entire person). Paul's statement could have either of two meanings here:

- Paul forgave sins in the face of Christ, meaning before the face of Christ, with the approval of Christ.
- Paul forgave sins in the person of Christ, meaning as Christ's representative.

If we take the first option, the weaker of the two possibilities, it at least means that Paul forgave sins with the approval of Christ. The second option is stronger: when Paul forgave sins, he did so in the person of Christ, as Christ's agent, in the place of Christ himself.[45] When this is read in conjunction with all the other texts examined here indicating Paul holding office in the New Covenant and acting on behalf of God/ Christ, it does not seem out of place to opt for the stronger of the two meanings, that he forgave sins *en prosōpō Christou*, in the person of Christ, in the place of Christ himself. When Paul forgave sins, Christ forgave sins through him. The apostles' binding and loosing of sins (John 20:22–23) continued in the ministry of Paul and continues today in the Sacrament of Reconciliation.

Minister of the New Covenant (2 Cor 3:6)

In 2 Corinthians 3:6, in the midst of one of the two texts that could be described as "Paul's sharpest contrast between the two Testaments"[46] (2 Cor 3:4–18; Gal 4:21–31), Paul declares, "God has qualified us to be *diakonous* (διακόνους) of the New Covenant, not in written letters but in the Spirit, for the letter kills but the Spirit gives life" (2 Cor 3:6). The word *diakonos* (διάκονος) refers to the office of deacon in 1 Timothy 3:8,12 and Philippians 1:1, but it usually refers to serv-

---

[45] St. Thomas Aquinas observed that Catholic priests acted in the person of Christ when celebrating the Eucharist; see Gerald O'Collins and Michael Keenan Jones, *Jesus Our Priest: A Christian Approach to the Priesthood of Christ* (Oxford, UK: Oxford University Press, 2010), 114.

[46] Joseph Ratzinger, *Many Religions—One Covenant: Israel, the Church, and the World*, trans. Graham Harrison (San Francisco: Ignatius Press, 1999), 52–53.

ing others, acting as an agent or intermediary. In that latter sense, Paul often describes himself as a *diakonos* of God or the Gospel or the Church (e.g., 1 Cor 3:5; 2 Cor 6:4; Eph 3:7; Col 1:23, 25). In the context here in 2 Corinthians 3:6, contrasting the two testaments, Paul's description of himself as servant of the New Covenant shows his awareness of holding office from God in the New Covenant. Here in 2 Corinthians 3:6, his role is variously translated as "minister" or "administrator." Paul is among those who are the servants (*diakonous*) of the New Covenant; he is one of God's agents of the New Covenant. He includes himself with the other ministers of the New Covenant in this act of service—"God has qualified *us*"—and the other *diakonous* of the New Covenant are surely, in the first place, the apostles. In describing himself as a *diakonos*/servant of the New Covenant, Paul distinguishes between Moses, who gave the Old Covenant in stone, and Christ, who bestows the New Covenant in the Spirit (1 Cor 3:7–9), between the ministers of the Old and New Covenants, and between the Jewish priesthood and the Christian ministers, of whom Paul is one. Ratzinger sees Paul's statement in 2 Corinthians 3:6 in this way:

> The Pauline epistles thus corroborate and define more precisely what we had inferred from the Gospels: the christologically founded office of "ministers of the New Covenant" (2 Cor 3:6), which as such has to be understood sacramentally. They show us the apostle as the bearer of a Christ-given authority vis-à-vis the community. The apostle's position vis-à-vis the community continues that of Christ vis-à-vis the world and the Church. In other words, it carries forward that dialogical structure that pertains to the essence of revelation.[47]

The Jewish priests were administrators of a written covenant, but the New Covenant *diakonous*/servants, including Paul, hold office as ministers of a covenant written in Spirit.

Ministering on behalf of Christ (2 Cor 5:20; Eph 6:20)
We have seen that when Paul forgives, Christ forgives through him (2 Cor 2:10). Paul returns again to the reconciliation of man and God

---

[47] Ratzinger, *Called to Communion*, 119–120.

three chapters later, in 2 Corinthians 5:10. The Father reconciled the world to himself through Christ and gave Paul and the other apostles the ministry of making known that reconciliation (2 Cor 5:18). In 2 Corinthians 5:20, Paul acts on behalf of Christ and he describes his ministry with the verb *presbeuomen* (πρεσβεύομεν). Almost every Bible translates this as "we are ambassadors for Christ." An ambassador represents someone else, and Paul sees himself as an ambassador extending the reconciliation of Christ. That verb, *presbeuomen* (πρεσβεύομεν), translated as "we are ambassadors," is from the same root as *presbyteros* (πρεσβύτερος), which we have already seen in Acts took on the meaning of a Christian minister. While the context of *presbeuomen* here in 2 Corinthians 5:20 does indeed refer to ambassadorial duty on behalf of Christ, we might ask whether Paul deliberately used *presbeuomen*, cognate with the word "presbyter," to suggest he is a Christian minister/presbyter with meaning similar to what we saw in Acts? Surely this cannot be ruled out, since in this text Paul is referring to ministering on behalf of Christ. He would certainly have known the presbyters in Jerusalem from his visits there. Therefore, instead of translating *presbeuomen* as "we are ambassadors," might we not translate it as "we are ministers" or, to invent a verb, "we presbyter"? There is a link between 2 Corinthians 5:20 and the ministry of the Old Covenant high priest, as Ratzinger notes: "By calling apostleship a ministry of 'reconciliation,' he brings it very close to the ministry of the high priest in the Old Testament, whose most important duty was the liturgy of the Feast of the Atonement."[48] Paul says that he ministers or "presbyters" (to coin a word) on behalf of Christ, suggesting a New Covenant priestly duty of reconciliation on behalf of Christ.

Again in Ephesians 6:20, we have the verb, now in the singular, *presbeuō*, the only other occurrence of the verb in the New Testament. In Ephesians 6:20, Paul is an ambassador, to use the customary translations, but now an ambassador in chains, since he is seemingly writing from prison. Since I suggest translating *presbeuomen* in 2 Corinthians 5:20 as "we are ministers," in Ephesians 6:20 I would suggest we might translate *presbeuō* as "I minister." Paul is ministering in chains, or again being inventive because of the use of "presbyter" in Acts, "I presbyter."

---

48   Ratzinger, *Principles of Catholic Theology*, 275.

Other Texts on Paul's Consciousness of His Vocation and Mission

In many other places in his letters, Paul displays consciousness of his special divine calling and mission. He is aware that he has been set apart (*aphōrismenos* ἀφωρισμένος) for the Gospel of God (Rom 1:1). This Greek verb describing this act of being separated for the Gospel, *aphorizō* (ἀφορίζω), appears again in Galatians 1:15, where Paul says he was set apart before he was born. This verb is also used by Luke in Acts 13:2 for the Holy Spirit asking for Paul and Barnabas to be set apart for the work to which they were called.

Paul's consciousness of his vocation appears in many other texts. In 1 Corinthians 3:9, Paul describes himself as God's fellow worker. In Galatians 2:7–8, Paul displays the same sense of mission to the Gentiles as Peter has to the Jews: the Lord worked through Paul for the Gentiles as he did through Peter for the circumcised. Paul is conscious of imparting Christ's teaching: he gives instructions through the Lord Jesus (1 Thes 4:2); he commands in the name of the Lord Jesus (2 Thes 3:6); and he appeals in the name of the Lord Jesus (1 Cor 1:10). He strongly defends the divine origin of his ministry in 2 Corinthians 2:17: others sell God's word, but Paul declares "with pure motive, from God; before God in Christ, we speak."

As we continue to address the question posed above "Was Paul a priest?" we say at the very least that Paul compared himself to Jewish Levitical priests in Romans 15:16. He regarded himself as an intermediary between God and those whom he served, an administrator of God's mysteries (1 Cor 4:1). Just as the Levites were compensated for their service to the temple, likewise those who serve the New Covenant should also be compensated (1 Cor 9:13–14). As Christ's representative, he forgives sins (2 Cor 2:10) and "presbyters" on behalf of Christ (2 Cor 5:20). Putting it all together, we see that not only does Paul regard himself as an apostle, but more than that, he has a ministry bestowed on him by God that makes him God's official mediator between God and his people. We could say he comes as close as he possibly can to speaking of his ministry in priestly terms without actually using such terminology.

Applying Priestly Language to the Apostles and Paul

Now we come to the final part of our answer to the question "Was Paul a priest?" The question is not raised directly in the New Testament. The question is thinking in terms of later theology and under-standing, in terms of our theology and understanding. As we have seen, Paul's favorite term to describe himself is "apostle." If we were to say Paul was a priest based on the evidence furnished in the pages above, we would also have to say at the same time that we are apply-ing our categories to Paul. Is there any justification for doing this? Can we say Paul was a priest? We would argue that applying this language to Paul is simply making explicit what was already present in Paul's ministry even if he or the New Testament did not make it explicit. As mentioned earlier, the word "cross" does not occur once in Paul's letter to the Romans even though the letter is permeated with Paul's theology of the Cross.[49] If that holds true for the word "cross" in Romans, we could similarly say that Paul's ministry is im-bued with his priestly consciousness even if he does not describe his ministry as priesthood.

It is sometimes said that the biblical authors retroverted or retro-jected a later Christological understanding into an earlier time (e.g., the titles employed by the angels to describe Jesus to the shepherds in Luke 2:11—Savior, Christ/Messiah, and Lord—are said to reflect Resurrection Christology).[50] If Luke portrays the infant Jesus as Sav-ior, Messiah, and Lord even though it is only after Jesus' Resurrec-tion that the full import of those titles was understood, could we not similarly speak of Paul as a priest even if the Church arrived at this theological understanding later?

In Catholic theology, it is said that the twelve apostles were or-dained priests by Christ during the Last Supper when Christ insti-tuted the priesthood—for example, on John 17:17, Ratzinger writes, "we may recognize in these words of John's Gospel the institution of the priesthood of the Apostles."[51] If we talk of the twelve apostles as priests, then we could also say that Paul was a priest, whether his priestly consecration occurred at the time described in Acts 13:1–3

---

49   Ratzinger, *Called to Communion*, 59.

50   Raymond E. Brown, *The Birth of the Messiah: A Commentary on the Infan-cy Narratives in the Gospels of Matthew and Luke*, new updated ed., Anchor Bible Reference Library (New York/London: Yale University Press, 1993), 29–32. See also Raymond E. Brown, *An Adult Christ at Christmas: Essays on the Three Biblical Christmas Stories, Matthew 2 and Luke 2* (Collegeville, MN: Liturgical Press, 1988), 16.

51   Joseph Ratzinger, *Jesus of Nazareth. Holy Week*, 90.

or at some other time. However, we need to be clear that we are using the terminology of our time and that, at the time of Paul and the apostles, they would not have applied priestly terminology to themselves.

Leaders in the Churches Founded by Paul

Earlier, I mentioned that it is difficult to draw precise inferences from the New Testament about the maturing ecclesiastical structure in the first century and that we arrive at conclusions by way of deductions and assumptions from the New Testament. Reading Paul's letters, we see that he wrote his letters to address problems or to give encouragement to the churches he founded. It has often been said that were it not for abuses during the celebration of the Eucharist in Corinth, Paul would not have included his teaching on the Eucharist in 1 Corinthians and there would be endless debates on the place of the Eucharist in Paul's churches. Although Paul's letters are not meant to systematically address ecclesiastical structure, we find useful information in them for the topic of this study.

The first Christians, while continuing to frequent the temple or synagogue for prayer (Acts 2:46; 3:1; 21:26; 22:17), celebrated the Eucharist in their own homes (Acts 2:46). They met as a church in their own homes (Acts 2:46; Rom 16:5; 1 Cor 16:19; Col 4:15; Phlm 2, and it is also implied in Acts 12:12–17, Romans 16:23, and 1 Corinthians 16:15). We do not know how many elders/overseers and deacons were in each house church, but we get the impression that there were multiple. For example, in Acts 20:17 we are told that Paul sent for the presbyters of Ephesus, and in Philippians 1:1 Paul greets the overseers and deacons in Philippi.

Luke tells us in Acts 14:23 that Paul and Barnabas appointed presbyters in every church they founded. While Paul does not explicitly state in any of his letters that he appointed presbyters/overseers when he established a local church (Paul later sent Timothy to Ephesus and Titus to Crete), we have no legitimate reason to deny Luke's statement. It seems obvious that Paul would put leaders in place in order to oversee and take care of the new Christian communities, just as Judaism had its own leaders. Again and again in Paul's letters, we see his concern for the spiritual well-being of the churches he established. He was their spiritual father (1 Cor 4:15; 1 Thes 2:11), and as their spiritual father, he would not have left them without spiritual fatherhood when he moved to preach the Gospel elsewhere. It is the case, as R. Alastair Campbell asserts, that the so-called charismatic church governance (without structured leadership) attributed to Paul and churches founded by him is wishful exegesis.[52] We will look briefly now at individual churches established by Paul to which he wrote letters, and we see that there were leaders in each of those churches.

Overseers and Deacons in Philippi (Phil 1:1)

Paul founded the church in Philippi (Acts 16:11–40). His first converts were Lydia and her household. When Paul wrote his letter to the Philippians, he addressed it to all the Christians in Philippi with their overseers and deacons (Phil 1:1). Most likely one of them is the Epaphroditus mentioned as a fellow worker of Paul in Philippians 2:25. Paul wrote while imprisoned (Phil 1:7, 13, 14, 17) sometime between AD 50 and the early 60s depending on which location one chooses for this incarceration.[53] What is significant is that the very first verse of this letter, addressed to the holy ones in Philippi with their overseers and deacons, confirms Acts 20:28, that already, in just two or at most three decades after Jesus, the title "overseer" is applied to those who minister in Jesus' name.

Caring Leaders in Thessalonica over Them in the Lord (1 Thes 5:12)

Luke reports on Paul founding the Church in Thessalonica in Acts 17:1–9, and Paul's own account is in 1 Thessalonians 1:8–2:12. In 1 Thessalonians 2:7, we see his concern for the church he founded when he describes his care for it like that of a mother for her children

---

[52]   R. Alastair Campbell, *The Elders: Seniority within Earliest Christianity* (London/New York: T&T Clark, 2004), 242.

[53]   Paul was in prison a number of times, so this could be anytime between AD 50 and the early 60s. For a summary of the possible locations and times, see Gerald F. Hawthorn, "Philippians, Letter to the," in *Dictionary of Paul and His Letters*, ed. Gerald F. Hawthorne, Ralph P. Martin, and Daniel G. Reid (Downers Grove, IL: InterVarsity Press, 1993), 709–711.

and, in 2:11, like that of a father. Two of the new Christians in Thessalonica are named in Acts 20:4, Aristarchus and Secundus. While ministering in Athens, Paul was very concerned about the church in Thessalonica, so he sent Timothy to visit Thessalonica (1 Thes 3:1–3). In 1 Thessalonians 5:12, he urged the Christians at Thessalonica to respect their Christian leaders, whom he describes as those who labor among them, who are over them in the Lord, and who admonish them. The verb *proistēmi* (προΐστημι) can mean "care for" or "govern" and, so, designates a caring leadership, and it is combined with presbyters in 1 Timothy 5:17: "the presbyters who lead." The authority of the leaders who care for them comes from the Lord, those who "are over you in the Lord." Their leaders are not merely ministering by human will, but by divine appointment.

Stephanas and Others in Corinth

Paul established the Church in Corinth (Acts 18) and ministered there for a year and a half (Acts 18:11). In his letters, Paul refers a number of times to founding the church in Corinth. Paul planted, Apollos watered, and God gave the growth (1 Cor 3:6). Paul laid a foundation, and another is building upon it (1 Cor 3:10). In those initial days of his preaching in Corinth, Paul fed them with spiritual milk, not solid food (1 Cor 3:2). He did not use lofty language but simply proclaimed Jesus crucified (1 Cor 2:1–5). Paul is their spiritual father and they are his children (1 Cor 4:14–15). Since he is their spiritual father, they are to imitate him (1 Cor 4:16).

When Paul lists the various parts of the Body of Christ in 1 Corinthians 12:28, he lists leadership of various kinds. Among those leaders we can surely include Stephanas, since later in the letter, Paul referred to the household of Stephanus as the first-fruits of Achaia, they served the church, and Paul asked the Corinthians to be subject to such men (1 Cor 16:15–16). Stephanas had been baptized by Paul (1 Cor 1:16), and when Paul was in Ephesus, Stephanas and Fortunatus came from Corinth to Paul, no doubt giving a report to Paul on the state of the church in Corinth (1 Cor 16:17–18). The church in Corinth was gifted not only with charisms, but also with strong leaders like Stephanas. Galot observes, "an opposition between a charismatic and an institutional aspect of the ministry is untenable, since the ministry is itself regarded as a charism."[54] Indeed, in 1 Corinthians 12:28, *kybernēsis* (κυβέρνησις), "leadership," is listed among the charisms.

Presbyters/Overseers in Ephesus

Acts 18:19–21 reports a brief visit by Paul to Ephesus at the end of his second missionary journey, but also a promise to return again if God willed. Paul made that visit during his third missionary journey, reported in Acts 19:1–20:1, and spent two years there (Acts 19:10). Later during this missionary journey, when Paul was on his way back to Jerusalem, he stopped south of Ephesus in Miletus, since he did not have time to stop in Ephesus again (Acts 20:16), and sent to Ephesus for the presbyters (Acts 20:17), whom he later also calls overseers (Acts 20:28).

Leaders in Churches not Founded by Paul

Paul did not found the churches in Colossae (Col 2:1 says that they have not seen his face) or in Rome (Rom 1:13), but when he wrote to those churches, their leadership is manifest. Epaphras is a fellow servant with Paul in Colossians 1:7 and a servant of Christ Jesus in Colossians 4:12, and Archippus also ministers to them (Col 4:17). At the end of his letter to the Romans, Paul sends greetings to many in Rome (Rom 16). Some of them seem to be church leaders, especially Andronicus and Junias, who are notable among the apostles (Rom 16:7).

Paul Regards Church Leadership to Be Divinely Planned

Paul's writings confirm that he regarded Church structure/leadership as coming from God, in contradiction to those who have suggested that charisms rather than ecclesiastical structure were dominant in the churches founded by Paul. The following examples are noteworthy. Epaphras is a diakonos *of Christ* (Col 1:7), Archippus received his ministry *from the Lord* (Col 4:17), and the leaders in Ephesians 4:11 were *given by God*. We could also include here Acts 20:28,

---

54   Galot, *Theology of the Priesthood*, 168.

where Luke reports Paul saying the presbyters were made overseers *by the Holy Spirit*. This shows that, as Ratzinger observes, "the ministerial offices within this Body are represented as gifts of the Pneuma from the glorified Lord."[55] Church structure and organized leadership were as important for Paul as for the apostles in Jerusalem. As J. Terence Forestell states, there is no dichotomy between office and charism in the New Testament.[56]

Pastoral Epistles—Requirements for Overseers, Presbyters, and Deacons

The Pastoral Epistles (1 Tim; 2 Tim; Titus) are so called because they are written to the pastors of individual churches, Timothy and Titus, in contrast to the other letters associated with Paul, which are written to churches, with the exception of the letter to Philemon, though that is also addressed to others besides Philemon. Authoritative early Christians, such as Irenaeus, attributed the Pastoral Letters to Paul. However, differences between the Pastoral Letters and the other letters attributed to Paul, including differences in vocabulary and style, led some scholars, beginning from the nineteenth century onwards, to question the traditional view that the Pastoral Letters had been authored by Paul. Nevertheless, their genuineness continues to be defended, often by scholars using the same evidence as those who deny their authenticity.[57] How this affects our reading of the letters is best summarized as follows:

> Even if they were not written by St. Paul, that would not affect the permanent value of their content, for the fact that

---

[55] Ratzinger, *Principles of Catholic Theology*, 278.

[56] J. Terence Forestell, *As Ministers of Christ: The Christological Dimension of Ministry in the New Testament: An Exegetical and Theological Study* (New York: Paulist Press, 1991), 96. See also Gisbert Greshake, *The Meaning of Christian Priesthood* (Westminster, MD: Christian Classics, 1989), 39–40; Campbell, *The Elders*, 120–126, 139–140, 236–242; and Benjamin L. Merkle, *The Elder and Overseer: One Office in the Early Church* (New York: Peter Lang, 2003), 69–118.

[57] A helpful summary of the arguments concerning authorship can be found in George T. Montague, *First and Second Timothy, Titus*, ed. Peter S. Williamson and Mary Healy, Catholic Commentary on Sacred Scripture (Grand Rapids, MI: Baker Academic, 2008), 15–25.

they are inspired is not in doubt. Pauline authorship does add to their interest because it shows that the hierarchy of church ministers had begun to take shape in the lifetime of the Apostle.[58]

The concern with church ministers in these letters is evident firstly in both addressees, Timothy and Titus, being the leaders of churches, Timothy in Ephesus (1 Tim 1:3) and Titus in Crete (Tit 1:5). These letters contain advice for the church leaders unlike anything in the other New Testament letters. There is instruction for overseers in 1 Timothy 3:1-7 and Titus 1:7-9, instruction for presbyters in 1 Timothy 5:17-22 and Titus 1:5-6, and instruction for deacons in 1 Timothy 3:8-13. Now for the first time, we see overseers, presbyters, and deacons in the same letter. Yet, as we shall see, in one verse in Titus, overseers and presbyters seem to be synonymous (as we saw in Acts 20:17, 28), which suggests the ecclesiastical structure may not yet be as developed as some would propose. Whether these letters are from Paul's last years or from a disciple of Paul faithfully expressing what would be Paul's thinking, one noticeable difference is that Paul wrote about overseers in Philippians 1:1, but in 1 Timothy 3:2 and Titus 1:7, it is "the overseer" (*ton episkopon*; τὸν ἐπίσκοπον). Also, with the exception of 1 Timothy 5:19, it is presbyters, and not one presbyter, who are mentioned (1 Tim 5:17; Tit 1:5). Another noteworthy indication of development in ecclesiastical structure is that all overseers are to teach (1 Tim 3:2; Tit 1:9) but not all presbyters (1 Tim 5:17). These developments anticipate the situation around the turn of the first century, with one overseer presiding over a college of presbyters. The triple subdivision of overseer, presbyters, and deacons that would later become bishop, priests, and deacons seems to be a merging of the presbyters and deacons in Jewish Christianity with the overseers and deacons in Paul's churches.

Overseers (1 Tim 3:1-7)

At first glance it might seem that there are men in Ephesus ambitious to become overseers, as 1 Timothy 3:1 comments on those aspiring to

---

58   Universidad de Navarra, *Saint Paul's Letters to the Thessalonians, and Pastoral Letters*, The Navarre Bible (Dublin/New York: Four Courts Press/ Scepter Publishing, 2005), 60.

the office of overseer. However, stating that it is good or noble to desire to become an overseer may only be to encourage candidates who
are slow to accept the office of overseer because of the responsibility
and difficulties accompanying the duty. The letter says an overseer
must be "irreproachable/faultless" and explains this by listing eleven
qualities necessary in an overseer (1 Tim 3:2–3). Following the list
of eleven qualities in rapid succession, another three are given a little more attention in 3:4–7: the overseer must be able to manage his
own household well, or otherwise he cannot manage the Church well
(3:4–5); he must not have recently converted to Christianity (3:6);
and he must be well respected (3:7). Managing his own household is
a test of the suitability of a candidate to become an overseer because,
until the end of the first century, Christians gathered in each other's
houses to celebrate the Eucharist.[59] Inability to manage one's own
house would obviously render one ineffective in managing the wider
Christian community meeting in a house.

Presbyters (1 Tim 5:17–22; Tit 1:5–9)

Two chapters after the advice for overseers, in 1 Timothy 5:17–22,
Timothy is given advice on presbyters. They are worthy of a double
honor: the first honor is that of being a presbyter and the second is
receiving financial support. Accusations against a presbyter must be
judged as in a Jewish law court (1 Tim 5:19; see Deut 19:15). Timothy is solemnly charged to be faithful to all these Pauline injunctions
(5:21) and not to decide too quickly on the suitability of someone to
join the presbyterate (1 Tim 5:22).

Perhaps in 1 Timothy 5:17 we see an anticipation of the development of monarchical bishops, where there is reference to presbyters who lead well and to presbyters who teach. Although not every
scholar concurs, it looks like already a distinction is emerging in the
duties of presbyters: some devote themselves to administration and
others to preaching and teaching.

Titus also receives advice on overseeing presbyters in Titus 1:5–
9. He is to install presbyters in every town (1:5) and is also given a
list of qualities required in candidates for the presbyterate. A comparison of the necessary qualities in a presbyter in Titus 1:6–9 with

---

[59] See Vincent P. Branick, *The House Church in the Writings of Paul*, Zacchaeus Studies: New Testament (Wilmington, DE: Michael Glazier, 1989).

the qualifications for an overseer in 1 Timothy 3:2–7 reveals almost identical attributes, even if in a different order or utilizing different Greek words. Such lists, often called "virtue lists," were common in ancient literature.[60] However, there is an anomaly in Titus 1:7 halfway through the list of necessary qualities: now the guidance suddenly changes to that for an overseer, suggesting the distinction between overseer and presbyter is not yet completely defined. There is one quality required in both presbyters (1:6) and overseers (1:7): they are to be irreproachable.

Deacons (1 Tim 3:8–13)

Timothy is also given advice on deacons. Just as he is to seriously discern before admitting someone to the presbyterate (1 Tim 5:22), he is also to test candidates for the diaconate to make sure they are suitable (1 Tim 3:10). He is given a list of required qualities in 3:8–13, many of which are similar to those also prescribed for overseers in 3:1–7. There are two additional attributes needed in an overseer omitted in the requirements for deacons, hospitality and the ability to teach. George Montague observers, "Perhaps not much should be made of this omission, as the very function of distributing the Church's goods would demand hospitality, and the ministry of teaching might require a separate delegation by the bishop."[61] Who are the women in 3:11 whose four requisite characteristics are listed? The Greek word *gynē* (γυνή) can mean "wife" or "woman." While no one can be certain, a common suggestion is that these women are the deacons' wives.[62] As in the case of overseers, deacons are to be able to manage their households properly (3:12). Just as later this letter refers to a double honor for presbyters, this pericope on deacons concludes by referring to two things, their good standing and their courage concerning the faith in Christ Jesus. The latter must refer to the deacons speaking about the faith. The word *parrēsia* (παρρησία), denoting courage or confidence in its root meaning, refers to freedom of speech (see comments on Heb 4:16 in chapter 2), so this must refer to the deacons witnessing to Christ or teaching

---

60   William D. Mounce, *Pastoral Epistles*, Word Biblical Commentary 46 (Dallas, TX: Word, 2000), 166–167.

61   Montague, *First and Second Timothy Titus*, 80.

62   Mounce outlines many reasons (*Pastoral Epistles*, 202–205).

about Christ. So, while teaching the faith was omitted in the list of essential qualities in a deacon, it seems to be included at the very end of the pericope.

Developing Church Governance

Compared with the other letters of the New Testament, the Pastorals devote a lot of space to Church governance, revealing the importance of diligent ecclesiastical governance. But Church governance had not yet developed into what we call a monarchical bishop presiding over a college of presbyters and assisted by deacons. Timothy and Titus had been assigned to oversee the churches in Ephesus and Crete. They were to install overseers, presbyters, and deacons after being assured that the candidates were worthy, but apart from Timothy and Titus, we do not yet see the overseers in Ephesus or Crete having this authority. In Titus and Timothy, we could say that we see emerging what will be the practice at the turn of the first century, an overseer/bishop presiding over presbyters.

Moving on from the Pastorals, at the beginning of the Book of Revelation, Christ gives John a message for each *angelos* (ἄγγελος) of the seven churches in Asia (Rev 1:20; 2:1, 8, 12, 18; 3:1, 7, 14). The Greek word *angelos*, translated as "angel," can also mean "messenger," which can be seen in its verbal form *angellō* (ἀγγέλλω) meaning to "announce," "report," or "inform." Some, though not many, consider these "angels" to be the human leaders of each of the seven churches of Asia.[63] However, the word *angelos* occurs sixty-seven times in the Book of Revelation, and on every other occasion it means an angel. Be that as it may, it would seem strange if John were really asked to write to an angel, especially when he can see and talk to angels during his vision on Patmos (Rev 1:9–10), and there is no indication of how those angels would then pass on the message to the church. On the other hand, it makes sense to regard the angel as the *episkopos* of the church who could pass on the message of John's letter in his preaching, which seems to be the meaning of the conclusion of each message to each "angel" advising that he who has an ear should hear what the Spirit says to the churches (2:7, 11, 17, 29; 3:6, 13, 22). While

---

[63]   Among those who are of this opinion are Simon J. Kistemaker and William Hendriksen, *Exposition of the Book of Revelation*, New Testament Commentary 20 (Grand Rapids, MI: Baker Book House, 2001), 102–103.

rare, there are instances of *angelos* in the New Testament meaning a human "messenger" rather than an "angel": the messengers of John the Baptist (Luke 7:24); Jesus' messengers (Luke 9:52); and the messengers Rahab received (James 2:25). John the Baptist himself is understood as the messenger of Malachi 3:1 by Jesus in Matthew 11:10 and Luke 7:27. So these instances in the first three chapters of Revelation would not be the first or only occurrences where the word *angelos* means a human. While there is no agreement on the meaning of the "angels" of the churches of Asia in Revelation 1–3, I nevertheless think it cannot be ruled out that the *angelos* of each of the seven churches in Revelation is its *episkopos*.[64] If that is correct, these angels/messengers are the *episkopoi* of these seven churches, and in Revelation 1–3, we are now seeing a development in church governance that brings us close to the situation at the turn of the first century, when each local church was presided over by a bishop (assisted by priests and deacons).

We are on stronger ground with the supposition that Diotrephes in 3 John 9 may have been the first monarchical bishop, the only one in the New Testament. John the Presbyter, the author of 3 John, wrote to Gaius (3 John 1) and complained about Diotrephes because Diotrephes did not welcome a letter or missionaries John the Presbyter had sent to the church (3 John 9–10). While there is discord between John the Presbyter and Diotrephes over leadership style, it is clear that Diotrephes does exercise real authority over his local church. Many take it that Diotrephes is the first emerging monarchical bishop of the type we see described by Ignatius of Antioch.[65]

Up to now in this chapter, we have looked at select New Testament texts relevant to the growing and expanding Church leadership. Now we turn to texts demonstrating the specific means by which ministry is passed from one minister to another, the laying on of hands.

---

[64] For a listing of all the proposed meanings, see "Excursus 1C: The 'Angels' of the Seven Churches," in David E. Aune, *Revelation 1–5*, Word Biblical Commentary 52A (Dallas, TX: Word, 1998), 108–112.

[65] Raymond E. Brown, *An Introduction to the New Testament* (New York: Doubleday, 1997), 403.

Laying on of Hands

Old Testament

In the Old Testament, the laying on of hands in most instances is someone laying his hands on an animal to indicate this animal is being singled out for sacrifice[66] or that ownership of the animal is being transferred to God.[67] Laying on of hands also indicates blessing (Gen 48:18) and judgment (Lev 24:14). In the latter instance, the laying on of hands is thought to have many meanings, among them removing guilt from those who heard the guilty one's blasphemy and returning it to himself.[68] During Yom Kippur, transfer of sins is implied when the high priest lays both hands on the head of the goat and confesses all the sins of Israel over the goat (Lev 16:21).

There are two instances in the Old Testament where the laying on of hands occurs in a way that anticipates what we see occurring in the Church in the New Testament. In these occurrences it is specified with the verb *sāmak* (סָמַךְ). The first is in Numbers 8:10, where the Levites are set apart for God when the Israelites lay their hands on the Levites. Jacob Milgrom says this rite was conducted only by representatives of the Israelites, rather than by all the Israelites.[69] The connotation, as we gather in Numbers 8:11, 13, is that Israel sacrificed the Levites to the Lord, so once again we have the notion of transfer.

The second example is Joshua succeeding Moses. In Numbers 27:18, God commands Moses to lay his hand on Joshua the son of Nun, and in 27:23 Moses laid his hands on Joshua. It is strange indeed that the text giving the command to impose hands refers to only one hand (Num 27:18), but when the command is fulfilled, Moses imposes both hands (Num 27:23; Deut 34:9). The Septuagint gets around this

---

[66]   Baruch A. Levine, *Leviticus*, The JPS Torah Commentary (Philadelphia, PA: Jewish Publication Society, 1989), 6.

[67]   Adele Berlin, Marc Zvi Brettler, and Michael Fishbane, eds., *The Jewish Study Bible* (New York: Oxford University Press, 2004), 213.

[68]   Jacob Milgrom, *Leviticus 23–27: A New Translation with Introduction and Commentary*, Anchor Yale Bible 3B (New Haven, CT/London: Yale University Press, 2008), 2113.

[69]   Jacob Milgrom, *Numbers*, The JPS Torah Commentary (Philadelphia, PA: Jewish Publication Society, 1990), 62.

anomaly by stating in Numbers 27:18 that God commanded Moses to impose both his hands. Obviously what is important is the meaning of the gesture, indicated by the next verses (27:19–20), where Moses is to "commission" Joshua and invest him with some of his own authority. Deuteronomy 34:9 reports that Joshua was full of the spirit of wisdom because Moses had laid his hands on him.

New Testament

In the New Testament the laying on of hands has additional associations, now also being linked with healing, Baptism, and significantly for this study, bestowal of the Holy Spirit for mission. The significance of the laying on of hands became one of the foundational teachings of the early Church, as Hebrews 6:2 indicates.

We see a number of times in Acts that the Holy Spirit is given through the laying on of hands, and Luke purposefully tells us in Acts 8:18 that the Holy Spirit is given through the apostles laying on hands. Peter and John visited Samaria and laid hands on the Samaritans for them to receive the Holy Spirit (Acts 8:14–17), as they had not received the Holy Spirit when baptized by the deacon Philip. Paul received the Holy Spirit as Ananias laid hands on him at his baptism (Acts 9:17–18). In Ephesus, Paul encountered disciples who had been baptized only with the baptism of John the Baptist, and when he laid hands on them they received the Holy Spirit (Acts 19:1–6).

We also see the laying on of hands on three occasions in Acts without it being explicitly stated that it bestows the Holy Spirit, but in these instances it seems best to assume Luke's intention is that we understand bestowal of the Holy Spirit is implied. One of these instances is Acts 13:1–3, and I have already shown above that in Acts 13 Luke all but says that the Holy Spirit was granted: the Holy Spirit directed that Paul and Barnabas be set aside for mission (Acts 13:2), Paul and Barnabas were sent by the Holy Spirit (Acts 13:4), and Paul was filled with the Holy Spirit (Acts 13:9). Another example of imposition of hands in Acts without an explicit statement of the gift of the Holy Spirit is when the apostles laid hands on the seven deacons in Acts 6:6. Nevertheless, it is best to take it that Luke intends that the seven received the Holy Spirit.

The final example of laying on hands without an explicit mention of the Holy Spirit is Acts 14:23, where Paul and Barnabas appoint presbyters in every church during their first missionary journey. Even before going any further, this is already making an assumption that the laying on of hands is what occurs in 14:23. The word that is usually translated as "appointed" in 14:23 is *cheirotonēsantes* (χειροτονήσαντες). It is a composite word formed by combining *cheir* + *teneō* ("hand" + "stretch"), meaning stretching the hand. In secular Greek, *cheirotoneō* originally meant to "select" or "choose" (by raising one's hand), such as in voting for a candidate for civil office, but it later came to mean choosing someone by any means. Somewhat similarly, in 2 Corinthians 8:19, the only other occurrence of the verb in the New Testament, the churches chose Paul's travelling companion, perhaps Luke (taking it that "we"/"us" in Acts 16:10–17, 20:5–15, 21:1–18, and 27:1–28:16 indicate they are excerpts of Luke's travel diary with Paul). In time, the word *cheirotoneō* took on religious meaning, and Ferguson notes that "Philo and Josephus attest a religious usage of *cheirotoneō* in Hellenistic Judaism in reference to the appointments of God, including his selection of leaders for his people (Philo *Quod Det* 39; Josephus *Ant.* 4 §34, 54, 66)."[70] Analogously, *cheirotoneō* has a sacred sense in Acts 14:23 when Paul and Barnabas appoint presbyters. Paul and Barnabas had hands laid upon themselves at the beginning of their first missionary journey (Acts 13:3), and Paul laid hands on Timothy (1 Tim 4:14; 2 Tim 1:6). Obviously Paul was aware of the importance, we might say the necessity, of the laying on of hands for the gift of the Holy Spirit on someone being sent on mission. It would make sense, therefore, to assume that Acts 14:23 also intends us to understand that *cheirotoneō* was indeed Paul and Barnabas stretching their hands out to lay them on the presbyters they appointed over the new churches. Later, *cheirotoneō* was rendered in Latin with the word *ordinatio*, whence comes our English word "ordination."

Another possible reason suggests itself for *cheirotoneō* meaning the laying on of hands in Acts 14:23. There is wide variation in the proposed timing of the introduction into Judaism of the ordination of rabbis with laying on of hands. Jewish tradition regards rabbinic ordination as going back to Moses, when he chose seventy elders to assist him leading the people—though the biblical text does not mention laying on of hands (Num 11:16–25)—who in turn ordained their successors in an unbroken line until the end of the temple in

---

70   Ferguson, "Ordain, Ordination," 38–39.

AD 70.[71] However, Eduard Lohse tells us, "There is evidence of rabbinic ordination and the names of those ordained from the second half of the first century AD and it is likely that rabbinic ordination went back before this evidence."[72] The Mishnah gives an account of the ordination of elders in Sanhedrin 4:4. So the Judaism in which Paul was an expert before his conversion had rabbinic ordinations with laying on of hands, and most likely long before then. Earlier, we looked at the temple and its liturgies fulfilled in Christ. Might we not suggest that Paul, as a Christian, would have had a transfigured understanding of the laying on of hands and its necessity and therefore laid hands with Barnabas on the new presbyters in Acts 14:23? I would suggest that Hebrews 6:2 supports this, where the laying on of hands is listed as one of the foundational teachings of the Church.

The laying on of hands in Hebrews 6:2 seems to be distinct from Baptism and a subsequent imposition of hands in what later came to be called Confirmation.[73] The spiritual gifts that the readers of Hebrews have already received, including the Holy Spirit (Hebrews 6:4), flow from the foundations in 6:1–2, which included the laying on of hands. It seems that Hebrews 6:1–4 indirectly associates the gift of the Holy Spirit in the lives of the faithful with a laying on of hands distinct from Baptism.

In the Pastorals, the role of the laying on of hands is underlined, as Paul reminds Timothy to recall when Paul laid hands on him for his mission. John Tipei observes that the mediatory role of the laying on of hands is highlighted and human hands "are literally channels of power by which charisms for ministry are transferred from God, the divine source, to those so appointed."[74] In 1 Timothy 4:14, Paul urges Timothy not to neglect the gift he received through prophecy

---

[71]   J. Z. Lauterbach, "Ordination," in *The Jewish Encyclopedia: A Descriptive Record of the History, Religion, Literature, and Customs of the Jewish People from the Earliest Times to the Present Day*, ed. Isidore Singer (New York/London: Funk & Wagnalls, 1905), 9:428.

[72]   Eduard Lohse, "χείρ," in *Theological Dictionary of the New Testament*, ed. Gerhard Kittel, Geoffrey W. Bromiley, and Gerhard Friedrich (Grand Rapids, MI: Eerdmans, 1964), 9:429.

[73]   In the Sacrament of Confirmation the bishop extends his hands over those to receive the sacrament (rather than lays his hands on them) before they are anointed with chrism (see *Roman Pontifical*, 351, 360–361).

[74]   John Fleter Tipei, *The Laying on of Hands in the New Testament: Its Significance, Techniques, and Effects* (Lanham, MD: University Press of America, 2009), 296.

and imposition of hands by the presbyterate.[75] The gift, *charisma* (χάρισμα), is not specified, but the word *charisma* is associated with spiritual gifts bestowed by the Holy Spirit. Timothy received the gift when hands were laid on him and the presbyterate prayed Spirit-inspired utterances. Those prophetic utterances are almost certainly what Paul referred to earlier in 1 Timothy 1:18. Paul does not specifically say in 1 Timothy 4:14 that he was one of the presbyters laying hands on Timothy, but this is clarified in 2 Timothy 1:6, where Paul makes clear that he laid hands on Timothy. Paul expected that Timothy and Titus would, in turn, also lay hands on others: he advised Timothy to be prudent concerning those on whom he imposed hands (1 Tim 5:22) and reminded Titus he was to appoint presbyters in every town (Titus 1:5), which we take to include the laying on of hands.

The Holy Spirit is bestowed when hands are imposed on the designated person. But the Holy Spirit comes from God and not from the one imposing hands, so the Holy Spirit cannot be manipulated (Acts 8:18–24). The laying on of hands became a sign of receiving the Holy Spirit sacramentally and was accompanied by prayer. The individual sacraments have distinct signs of the reception of the Holy Spirit (e.g., the pouring of water during Baptism and anointing with chrism during Confirmation), and each sign is accompanied by its own prayer. In Catholic theology, these are called "form" and "matter," the form being the prayer and matter being an element of nature applied to the body by which God's power is given. In the Sacrament of Holy Orders, the form and matter are the laying on of hands accompanied by the Prayer of Ordination. Already in the Pastorals, we see the essentials of the Sacrament of Holy Orders are in place: the laying on of hands accompanied by prophetic utterances, which I take to be the Prayer of Consecration (1 Tim 4:14; 2 Tim 1:6).

Succession

The concept of succession, inheriting office, can be seen in the Old Testament and Judaism. Succession in a direct line of descent was important for the office of high priest, which is reflected in their genealogies, the longest of which is 1 Chronicles 5:29–41 (6:3–15 in

---

[75]   It is debated whether *dia prophēteias* (διὰ προφητείας) is *dia* + accusative plural ("because of") or *dia* + genitive singular ("through"); for example, see Tipei, *Laying on of Hands*, 263.

some English translations). The high priesthood was passed from father to son until Jason had his brother deposed by the Syrian ruler of Palestine and got himself appointed instead in 175 BC, and this also signaled the end of the high priest serving in office until death. Elsewhere, we see succession in some of Moses' spirit being transferred to the first elders (Num 11:24–25), and some of Moses' spirit was transferred to his successor Joshua by the laying on of hands (Deut 34:9). The concept of succession is also implicit in the Jewish tradition that the elders go back in an unbroken line to the first seventy elders on whom Moses laid his hands.

In the New Testament, there is succession of the word of God in the teaching of the apostles being handed down (1 Cor 15:3–5). But that succession of the word goes hand in hand with a succession of ministry, ministers who serve a mission that continues after their predecessor.[76] The mission of the apostles continued after their deaths in apostolic succession, as did Paul's mission. Apostolic succession is evident in four places in the New Testament: in subtle form in Acts 20, 1 Corinthians 4:17, and 1 Peter 5, and overtly in the Pastorals through the laying on of hands. We will now examine each of these in turn.

In Acts 20:18–35, Paul addresses the presbyters of Ephesus in Miletus. He asks them to take care of the church of God (the flock over which God has made them overseers in 20:28). It is the last time Paul expects to see them (20:38), so this is transferring care of the church at Ephesus to its presbyters. Ratzinger writes of the significance of the speech for our understanding of succession:

> As a whole, the address is basically an outline of the concept of apostolic succession. It is conceived as a kind of testament in which Paul confides the community to the faithful hands of the priests and, in words of exhortation, transfers his responsibility to them. It is apparent from the whole text in the Acts of the Apostles that Luke regards this address as exemplary and intends to represent in it the apostle's relationship to the presbyters. He is attempting to demonstrate

---

[76] For more on the interrelation between succession and the word, see Joseph Ratzinger, "Primacy, Episcopate and Apostolic Succession," in Karl Rahner and Joseph Ratzinger, *The Episcopate and the Primacy* (New York: Herder and Herder, 1962), 46–54.

the bond between the apostolic and postapostolic Church by depicting the transfer of pastoral responsibility from apostle to presbyters, who thus become, in practice, the "successors of the apostles."[77]

Before Paul's meeting with the elders of Ephesus in Miletus, Paul had made two visits to Ephesus, a brief one (Acts 18:19–21) after which Priscilla and Aquila remained there (18:24–26), and a two year stay (Acts 19:1–20). Now in Acts 20, we witness the final transfer of care for the church in Ephesus from the apostle Paul to the presbyters in Ephesus.

In 1 Corinthians 4:17, Paul tells the Corinthians that he sent Timothy to them to remind them of his way of following Christ. The Corinthians are to reproduce in their lives the Christian lifestyle taught to them by Timothy, and Timothy himself had been taught how to follow Christ by Paul (a son to Paul in the Lord, as Paul writes in 4:17). So in this text, we see a line from Paul to Timothy to the Corinthians.

We have seen that Peter identified himself in 1 Peter 5:1 as a *sympresbyteros* (συμπρεσβύτερος), a co-presbyter, a fellow presbyter, so that whatever a presbyter is, Peter is also. Peter, who is both apostle and presbyter, is encouraging presbyters in their ministry. This also indicates the concept of succession because there is a line from Peter to the presbyters in their ministry. Ratzinger sees the link in this way: "this linking of the content of the two offices also ranks as a significant event in the history of the Church: it is, so to say, the consummated act of *successio apostolica*, which also implicitly establishes the idea of succession."[78] Peter sees the presbyters continuing his ministry as Paul sees the presbyters of Ephesus continuing his ministry in Acts 20:28.

In the Pastorals, the concept of succession is linked to the laying on of hands. Paul laid hands on Timothy (1 Tim 4:14), clarified in 2 Timothy 1:6, and urged Timothy to discern carefully concerning those on whom he in turn would lay hands (1 Tim 5:22). Likewise, Paul asked Titus to install presbyters in every town (Titus 1:5). So we have a line of ministry from Paul to Timothy and Titus and then to those on whom they in turn lay hands. By the time of the Pastoral

---

[77]　Ratzinger, *Principles of Catholic Theology*, 278.

[78]　Ratzinger, *Called to Communion*, 124.

Letters, we see that the laying on of hands accompanied by prayerful utterances is key in the transfer of ministry in apostolic succession. The apostles carried on the ministry of Jesus. Many others—overseers, presbyters, and deacons—continued the ministry of the apostles, and thus the ministry of Jesus, after their martyrdom. The story does not end with the Pastorals but has continued down to our day in an unbroken line of apostolic succession in the Catholic Church.[79] Catholic bishops can therefore speak of their episcopal lineage, and a diocese founded by one of the apostles is designated an "apostolic see."[80]

Ministry Received from Christ

In the Levitical priesthood of the Old Covenant, there was one high priest and many priests, but in the New Covenant there is one priest, Christ, who is the one mediator between God and man (1 Tim 2:5). Christ's ministers of the New Covenant—apostles and presbyters/ overseers—share in his one priesthood by receiving their ministry from Christ. The apostles' consecration proceeded from Christ's consecration, as we saw in John 17:19, and they received their commission directly from Christ (Matt 28:16–20; Mark 16:14–16; John 20:19–23). When Peter healed the crippled man, he was very conscious that he did so not with his own power but in the name of Jesus (Acts 3:6; 4:10). Peter exhorts the presbyters in 1 Peter 5 and describes Christ as the *Chief* Shepherd (1 Pet 5:4), so the presbyters are shepherds under Christ the one Chief Shepherd. Earlier, Peter again described Christ as Shepherd but also as *Overseer* (*episkopos*) in 1 Peter 2:25, so the overseers/presbyters over churches are, we might say, under the Chief Overseer, Christ. Since the overseers are ministering

---

[79]   For an important and wide-ranging reconstruction of episcopal succession by diocese/province, see Pius Bonifacius Gams, *Series Episcoporum Ecclesiae Catholicae, quotquot innotuerant a beato Petro Apostolo* (Graz, AT: Akademische Druck- u. Verlagsanstalt, 1957; reprint collection of three separate volumes published 1873–1886). Importantly, even where early historical records for individual sees may be incomplete and strong positive evidence lacking, no contrary evidence is found.

[80]   Ratzinger, "Primacy, Episcopate and Apostolic Succession," 56. In canon law, the term "apostolic see" has a wider meaning; see canon 361 in *Code of Canon Law: New English Translation* (Washington, DC: Canon Law Society of America, 1998), 116.

under the Chief Overseer, Christ, this means their ministry comes from Christ. Paul is very conscious of having received his apostleship and ministry from God and refers to this many times in the course of his letters, especially in the opening verses of most of his letters. The pastors-teachers in Ephesians 4:11 received their ministry from Christ: "he gave some as . . . pastors-teachers." Again and again the New Testament shows that the ministry of those who minister in the name of Christ comes not from themselves, but from Christ himself. Newman sums up the ministerial priesthood in relation to Christ's priesthood in this way:

> Christ's priests have no priesthood but His. They are merely His shadows and organs, they are His outward signs; and what they do, He does; when they baptize, He is baptizing; when they bless, He is blessing. He is in all acts of His Church, and one of its acts is not more truly His act than another, for all are His.[81]

When John Henry Newman prepared his *Lectures on the Doctrine of Justification* for the third time in 1874, he added the following footnote: "It is true that there is *one* Priest and one Sacrifice under the Gospel, but this is because the Priests of the Gospel are one with Christ, not because they are *improperly* called Priests."[82] Priests share in the one priesthood of Christ, their priesthood is Christ's priesthood, and their ministry is an extension of Christ's ministry. This is beautifully expressed in the invitation to the ordination of a priest, which is often worded in this way: "The Diocese of . . . joyfully invites you to the Ordination of . . . to the Priesthood of Jesus Christ through the imposition of hands and invocation of the Holy Spirit by His Excellency, Bishop . . ."

Post New Testament

Clement, bishop of Rome, martyred around the turn of the first century, wrote a letter to the Corinthians because a disturbance

---

[81]   John Henry Newman, *Parochial and Plain Sermons* (London/Oxford/Cambridge, UK: Rivingtons, 1868), 6:242.

[82]   O'Collins and Jones, *Jesus our Priest*, 213.

had broken out in the church in Corinth. The Corinthians had dismissed some of their presbyters/overseers. In the letter, we see that "overseers" and "presbyters" are still used interchangeably (e.g., 1 Clem. 44). Two paragraphs earlier, in 1 Clement 42, Clement writes that God sent Jesus, Jesus sent the apostles, and they appointed their first-fruits, overseers and deacons. Then in paragraph 44, Clement adds that when the apostles appointed these, they instructed that if they died others should succeed them in their ministry. In Clement, we have the first teaching on apostolic succession, and not only that, but he states that the teaching on apostolic succession goes back to the apostles.

About a decade after Clement wrote to the Corinthians, we have a number of letters from Ignatius of Antioch as he faced martyrdom in Rome in AD 107.[83] Overseer and presbyter are no longer interchangeable. The overseer is attached to one local church or city, and there is only one overseer, unlike what we see in Philippians 1:1 during the time of Paul. Now the overseer has authority over the presbyters and, from now on, may be termed a "monarchical bishop," a bishop in the sense that we understand "bishop" today, as presiding over a college of presbyters.[84] Until now, I have translated the Greek *episkopos* as "overseer," but now we can refer to the *episkopos* in Ignatius' letters as "bishop." For the first time, we have three clearly distinguishable ranks, one bishop leading many presbyters and assisted by deacons. This is evident in a number of instances in his letters. "Follow, all of you, the bishop, as Jesus Christ followed the Father; and follow the presbytery as the Apostles. Moreover reverence the deacons as the commandment of God" (Ign. *Smyrn.* 8).[85] "There is one altar, as there is one bishop, together with the presbytery and deacons" (Ign. *Phld.* 4).[86] See more examples in *To the Smyrnaeans* 12; *To the Magnesians* 6; *To the Philadelphians* introduction, 4, 7, and 8; *To Polycarp* 6; and *To the Trallians* 3 and 7. Ignatius writes strongly on the necessity of a

---

[83]   Concerning the debate about the dating of Ignatius' letters, see Jean-Pierre Torrell, *A Priestly People: Baptismal Priesthood and Priestly Ministry* (Mahwah, NJ: Paulist Press, 2013), 65–67.

[84]   On the transition from overseers/presbyters to one bishop presiding over presbyters, see ibid., 79–82.

[85]   J. H. Srawley, *The Epistles of St. Ignatius, Bishop of Antioch*, revised 2nd ed., Early Church Classics 2 (London/Brighton, UK: SPCK, 1910), 40–41.

[86]   Ibid., 23–24.

bishop and priests: "Without these no group can be called a church" (Ign. *Trall.* 3).[87]

The application of priestly language to bishops and priests in the following centuries is sometimes called "sacerdotalization" from the Latin word for "priest," *sacerdos*, which literally means one who offers sacrifice (*sacer* + *dare*). After being first used by Tertullian (*Treatise on Baptism* 17), it was applied irregularly even up to the time of Augustine. "Origen employed the term for presbyters, Cyprian of Carthage applied the term only to bishops, and Augustine applied it to bishops and sometimes to priests."[88] Kloppenburg points out that the "desacerdotalization" of the New Covenant ministers in the New Testament was necessary because of the radical transcendence of the New Covenant and Christ's priesthood and its continuity in his ministers.[89] After the passing of time and arrival at a more appropriate understanding of New Covenant ministers, they could then be termed priests.

The word "ordination" was first imported into Christian usage by Tertullian from its use in Roman law: "Their ordinations, are carelessly administered."[90] When someone was appointed to office in Rome, it was called *ordinatio*. The word is derived from the Latin word *ordo*, meaning "rank"/"order"/"row." The body of senators in Rome was known as the *ordo senatorum*, the rank of senators. The one who holds office in an ordo is the "Ordinary," a word often applied to bishops. The first ordination liturgy that we have is in *The Apostolic Tradition* attributed to a contemporary of Tertullian, St. Hippolytus.[91] So we have the first application of the word "priest" to New Covenant ministers, the importation of the word "ordination" from Roman law, and the first extant ordination liturgy that we possess all occurring around the same time.

---

[87]   Holmes, *The Apostolic Fathers*, 161.

[88]   O'Collins and Jones, *Jesus Our Priest*, 284.

[89]   Kloppenburg, *The Priest: Living Instrument and Minister of Christ*, 66.

[90]   Tertullian, *De praescriptione haereticorum* 41, in *Latin Christianity: Its Founder, Tertullian*, ed. Alexander Roberts, James Donaldson, and A. Cleveland Coxe, trans. Peter Holmes, The Ante-Nicene Fathers 3 (Buffalo, NY: Christian Literature Company, 1885), 263.

[91]   Paul F. Bradshaw, Maxwell E. Johnson, and L. Edward Phillips, *The Apostolic Tradition: A Commentary*, ed. Harold W. Attridge, Hermeneia—a Critical and Historical Commentary on the Bible (Minneapolis, MN: Fortress Press, 2002), 30–62.

All this post New Testament development is the evolving of what is in the New Testament itself. As Nichols states, "The New Testament contains, then, the beginnings of the threefold ministry."[92] As we pointed out earlier, the development of what was already incipient in the New Testament not only applies to the priesthood but also to the understanding of the divinity of Christ clarified by the great Christological councils in subsequent centuries using non-biblical language. The development of the threefold rank of a bishop, priests, and deacons and the sacerdotalization of ministers had already occurred before the last of the Christological councils, the Council of Chalcedon in AD 451, a council whose teachings are accepted by all mainline Protestant churches. By contrast with the time needed for the crystallization of teaching on Christ's divinity, much less time was needed for development of New Testament overseers, presbyters, and deacons into a bishop leading a college of priests and assisted by deacons.

Catholic Liturgical Texts

A Bishop, Priests, and Deacons

When closing two of the previous chapters, we looked at relevant scriptural allusions during ordination liturgies in the *Rites of Ordination of a Bishop, of Priests, and of Deacons* in the *Roman Pontifical*, the book containing the liturgies celebrated only by the bishop. The very wording in the title of these rites, "*a* Bishop . . . Priests . . . Deacons," reflects the theological understanding that the bishop, through episcopal ordination, receives the fullness of orders, while priests share with him in the priesthood of Christ as his co-workers and deacons are ordained to a ministry of service.

Enquiry among the People of God and Recommendation

The twelve apostles asked the disciples to pick out the seven deacons (Acts 6:3). During ordination liturgies today, just moments prior to the ordination of priests and deacons, there is a dialogue between the bishop and a priest that shows the involvement of many people

---

[92] Nichols, *Holy Order*, 31.

in bringing the candidates to readiness for ordination, just as many were involved in choosing the first seven deacons. During the ordination of priesthood candidates, the designated priest says to the bishop, "Most Reverend Father, Holy Mother Church asks you to ordain these, our brothers, to the responsibility of the Priesthood." The bishop asks if the candidates are worthy, and the priest responds that, after enquiry among the people of God and their being recommended by those responsible, they have been found worthy. The bishop then chooses the candidates for the Order of the Priesthood.[93] During the ordination of deacons, the designated priest says to the bishop, "Most Reverend Father, Holy Mother Church asks you to ordain these men, our brothers, to the responsibility of the Diaconate." When asked if they are worthy, the priest responds that they have been found worthy, and the bishop then chooses the candidates for the Order of the Diaconate.[94] Obviously the bishop personally vets the candidates and makes the decision to ordain them long before the liturgy of ordination, but the liturgy reflects the important role that many people besides the bishop play in bringing the candidates to readiness for ordination, as we see in Acts 6:3.

The Presbyterate

We have seen that the word "priest" is derived from the Latin *presbyter*, which is in turn derived from the Greek *presbyteros*. Other derivations are also employed in the liturgy: the word "presbyterate" is employed many times in the course of the *Roman Pontifical*, and in the homily during the ordination liturgy, we hear:

> After mature deliberation, these, our brothers, are now to be ordained to the Priesthood in the Order of the *presbyterate* so as to serve Christ the Teacher, Priest, and Shepherd, by whose ministry his Body, that is, the Church, is built and grows into the People of God, a holy temple.[95]

One of the questions asked of the candidates before ordination is:

---

93   *Roman Pontifical*, 67–68, 88–89.

94   Ibid., 104–105, 126.

95   Ibid., 68 (emphasis mine).

> Do you resolve, with the help of the Holy Spirit, to discharge without fail the office of Priesthood in the *presbyteral* rank, as worthy fellow workers with the Order of Bishops in caring for the Lord's flock?[96]

The word "presbyterate" occurs a number of times in the *Roman Missal* also, for example, in the *General Instruction of the Roman Missal*: "In celebrations that take place with the Bishop presiding, and especially in the celebration of the Eucharist by the Bishop himself with the Presbyterate, the Deacons, and the people taking part, the mystery of the Church is manifest."[97]

Laying on of Hands during Ordination

The essential element in the ordination of a Catholic bishop, priest, or deacon is the laying on of hands by the ordaining bishop followed by the bishop praying the Prayer of Ordination (form and matter, as explained above).

The homily during the ordination of a bishop refers to the bishops as the successors of the apostles through the laying on of hands:

> Moreover, that this office might remain to the end of time, the Apostles chose helpers for themselves. Through the laying on of hands, by which the fullness of the sacrament of Holy Orders is conferred, they handed on to them the gift of the Holy Spirit which they had received from Christ. In that way, the tradition handed down from the beginning through the unbroken succession of Bishops is preserved from generation to generation, and the work of the Savior continues on and grows even to our own times.[98]

The homily also refers to the bishop-elect being admitted into the college of bishops through the laying on of hands, "Gladly and grate-

---

[96] Ibid., 70 (emphasis mine).

[97] *The General Instruction of the Roman Missal*, no. 22, in *Roman Missal, Renewed by Decree of the Most Holy Second Ecumenical Council of the Vatican, Promulgated by Authority of Pope Paul VI and Revised at the Direction of Pope John Paul II*, 3rd typical ed. (Washington, DC: United States Conference of Catholic Bishops, 2011), 25.

[98] *Roman Pontifical*, 24–25, 49.

fully, therefore, welcome our brother whom we, the Bishops, now admit into our college by the laying on of hands."[99] The ordaining bishop lays hands on the bishop-elect, and concelebrating bishops also impose hands silently. Then the ordaining bishop places the Book of the Gospels over the head of the bishop-elect, where it is held by two deacons while the ordaining bishop prays the Prayer of Ordination with the concelebrating bishops beside him.[100]

During the ordination of a priest, after the bishop lays hands in silence on the candidate for priesthood, the concelebrating priests also impose hands silently, following which, the bishop, with the concelebrating priests by his side, prays the Prayer of Ordination.[101]

The homily for the ordination of deacons refers to their consecration by the laying on of hands: "Consecrated by the laying on of hands that comes down to us from the Apostles and bound more closely to the service of the altar, they will perform works of charity in the name of the Bishop or the pastor."[102]

The Preface prayed before the Eucharistic Prayer during the Chrism Mass on Holy Thursday and during the ordination of a bishop, priests, and deacons, entitled *The Priesthood of Christ and the Ministry of Priests*, refers to the laying on of hands: "For Christ . . . chooses men to become sharers in his sacred ministry through the laying on of hands."[103] The *Roman Pontifical* clarifies that "Deacons receive the laying on of hands not for the priesthood but for ministry."[104] Bishops, priests, and deacons are ordained in the Sacrament of Holy Orders, but only bishops and priests share in the ministerial priesthood of Christ.

Prayer of Ordination

We have already looked at the Old and New Testament references in the Prayer of Ordination of a bishop, priests, and deacons in previous chapters, but by way of concluding this chapter, it would be useful to summarize those examples all together here in the following chart:

---

99   Ibid., 25 (for one bishop), 50 (for more than one bishop).
100   Ibid., 31–35, 54–55.
101   Ibid., 74–79, 93–95.
102   Ibid., 105, 127 (for only one deacon).
103   *Roman Missal*, 295, 1140, 1153, 1158, 1164, 1169.
104   *Roman Pontifical*, 15.

Scripture References in the Ordination Prayers

ORDINATION OF A BISHOP

Old Testament reference

The Ordination Prayer for bishops does not specifically refer to Levitical high priests but to God establishing rulers and priests (the latter being Aaron and his descendants) and to not leaving the sanctuary without ministers.[105]

New Testament reference

The prayer asks God to pour out "that power which is from you, the governing Spirit, whom you gave to your beloved Son, Jesus Christ, the Spirit whom he bestowed upon the holy Apostles, who established the Church."[106]

ORDINATION OF PRIESTS

Old Testament reference

The prayer recalls the seventy elders assisting Moses and Aaron (Num 11:16–17): "you chose men next in rank and dignity to accompany them and assist them in their task."[107]

It also recalls Aaron's sons receiving the priesthood, on whom God "poured an abundant share of their father's plenty, that the number of the priests prescribed by the Law might be sufficient for the sacrifices of the tabernacle . . . "[108]

New Testament reference

The prayer addressing God refers to the seventy(-two) as companions to the apostles who also went on a mission similar to that of the apostles: "You provided them [the apostles] also with companions to proclaim and carry out the work of salvation throughout the whole world."[109]

---

[105] Ibid., 34, 54.

[106] Ibid., 34.

[107] Ibid., 78, 94, 160.

[108] Ibid., 78, 94, 160.

[109] Ibid., 78, 94.

ORDINATION OF DEACONS

Old Testament reference	New Testament reference
The Ordination Prayer for deacons, addressing God, refers to the Levites who assisted the priests: "as once you chose the sons of Levi to minister in the former tabernacle, so now you establish three ranks of ministers in their sacred offices to serve in your name."[110]	It references the seven men chosen in Acts 6: "through the inspiration of the Holy Spirit, your Son's Apostles appointed seven men of good repute to assist them in the daily ministry."[111]

In summary, the ordination liturgies manifest that the threefold rank of bishop, priest, and deacon have New Testament origins and are typologically anticipated by the Old Testament.

---

[110]   Ibid., 116, 132, 156.

[111]   Ibid.

CHAPTER 5

PRIESTLY PEOPLE

THE PRIESTLY PEOPLE, although treated here in the last chapter of this study, precede the ministerial priests. Christ had called many disciples before he chose twelve apostles out of them. Similarly, those ordained to the ministerial priesthood in the Sacrament of Holy Orders are called out of the priestly people who are living the Sacrament of Baptism. The two priesthoods are intimately connected, since both are a response to Christ and they are bound together. The ministerial priesthood is serving the priestly people, and the priestly people receive the sacraments from the ministerial priesthood.

In Exodus 19:6, God promised the Israelites would be a royal priesthood and a holy nation if they kept his covenant. However, in Isaiah 61:6, the priestly role of the people was being rekindled by the prophet, so it seems the promise of Exodus 19:6 had not become a reality. In 2 Maccabees 2:17, in a letter from Jerusalem Jews to their brethren in Egypt sharing the good news of the rededication of the temple, there is an allusion to Exodus 19:6, revealing the expectation that it would be fulfilled. In this chapter, we will see it was fulfilled in the Church, where all Christians are priestly. Two books of the

New Testament, the First Letter of Peter and the Book of Revelation, refer to all Christians as priests.

Recalling what we saw in the first chapter, the Septuagint employs different Greek words, with the exception of Isaiah 61:6, to distinguish between the Levitical priests and the priestly understanding of all Israel: *hiereus* (ἱερεύς) for the Levitical priests and *hierateia* (ἱερατεία) for their priestly office, but *hierateuma* (ἱεράτευμα) for the priestly role of the people. Both 1 Peter and the Book of Revelation show that Exodus 19:6 is now fulfilled in all Christians. Significantly, the First Letter of Peter uses the same Greek word found in the Septuagintal version of Exodus 19:6 for the priesthood of the people, *hierateuma* (ἱεράτευμα). However, the Book of Revelation instead uses the Greek word *hiereus* (ἱερεύς)—the word for Levitical priests—for Christians as priests, but there is no room for confusion with the Levitical Old Covenant priesthood and the book indicates that all Christians are called since Baptism to exercise their priesthood.

We will examine five passages where we see the priesthood of all believers: 1 Peter 2:5 and 2:9 and Revelation 1:4–6, 5:9–10, and 20:6. In each of the five texts, we will look at what they teach about believers receiving their priesthood, and secondly how believers exercise their priesthood.

Living Stones in a Priestly House (1 Pet 2:5)

Peter writes to the Christians in Asia Minor (1 Pet 1:1) and invites them to draw near to Christ, the living stone rejected by men but chosen by God (1 Pet 2:4), an allusion to Psalm 118:22. There has long been speculation that his letter contains catechesis for Baptism based on the understanding that the newborn babies longing for pure spiritual milk in 2:2 refers to the newly baptized being born spiritually in Baptism. I will take it that baptismal catechesis is the context for Peter's comments. Disciples are in relationship with Jesus the living stone (2:4). Since Jesus is a living stone, disciples too will become living stones by drawing near to Jesus (2:5). Stones build a house, and so Peter then alludes to Exodus 19:6 to explain what it means to be Christ's spiritual house built of living stones. For Peter, the spiritual house is Christians being a holy priesthood, *hierateuma* (ἱεράτευμα), offering spiritual sacrifices to God through

Jesus (2:5). In the context of baptismal catechesis, Peter is saying that Christ's life is in them since Baptism makes them living stones, a holy priesthood. Commenting on 1 Peter, Joseph Ratzinger observes, "When Christian baptismal catechesis applies to the baptized this word [priesthood] relating to the institution of the Old Covenant, it means that by baptism Christians enter upon the dignity of Israel—that baptism is the new Sinai."[1] The priesthood of the disciples springs from the priesthood of Christ, though 1 Peter does not here describe Christ as priest. It is through Baptism that Christians receive their priesthood from Christ. The promise of Exodus 19:6 that all Israel would be priests is now fulfilled in the Church, and all Christians are priests because of their union with Christ since Baptism. Christian Baptism has become the means whereby Exodus 19:6 is fulfilled in the Church.

How will Christian disciples exercise a priestly ministry? The Levitical priests offered sacrifice (Heb 8:3; 10:11), Christ the high priest sacrificed himself on the Cross, and Peter says the disciples also, Christ's holy priesthood, are to offer spiritual sacrifices acceptable to God through Jesus (1 Pet 2:5). Peter does not explain precisely what he means by these spiritual sacrifices, but commenting on this verse, Pope Benedict XVI said, "And what is this offering which we are called to make, if not to direct our every thought, word and action to the truth of the Gospel and to harness all our energies in the service of God's Kingdom?"[2] In Romans 12:1, Paul asks Christians to offer their bodies, meaning themselves, to Christ as a living sacrifice. Everything Christians do, everything done with their bodies, is to be holy and capable of being offered to the Father as a sacrifice. Christians' daily activities are a means of sanctifying themselves and the world. So, just as Peter reminded Christians of their priesthood in 1 Peter 2:5, Paul does also in Romans 12:1. In summary, Christians receive their priesthood from Christ in Baptism and exercise that priesthood by living their daily lives for the service of God's kingdom.

---

[1] Joseph Ratzinger, *Called to Communion: Understanding the Church Today*, trans. Adrian Walker (San Francisco: Ignatius Press, 1996), 126.

[2] Benedict XVI, Homily at Yankee Stadium, Bronx, New York, April 20, 2008, in *Homilies of His Holiness Benedict XVI (English)*, Logos Verbum (Vatican City: Libreria Editrice Vaticana, 2013).

Royal Priesthood under Jesus the King (1 Pet 2:9)

In 1 Peter 2:5 there was an allusion to Exodus 19:6, but now four verses later, in 1 Peter 2:9, Peter utilizes the exact same phrases as the Greek Septuagintal version of Exodus 19:6, reminding his listeners that they are a *basileion hierateuma* (βασίλειον ἱεράτευμα), a "royal priesthood," and an *ethnos hagion* (ἔθνος ἅγιον), a "holy nation." The other two descriptions of Christians in 2:9 are taken from Isaiah 43:20 ("chosen people") and Isaiah 43:21 ("my people"). In Exodus 19:5–6, God proclaimed the Israelites would be a royal priesthood and a holy nation *if* they would keep his covenant. Here in 1 Peter 2:9, there is no condition attached. Those receiving Peter's letter are now God's royal priesthood and holy nation. The promise of Exodus 19:6 is fulfilled and broadened beyond Judaism to include all the baptized. The description of the Christian priesthood as a *royal* priesthood signifies priesthood in a kingdom, the kingdom inaugurated by Jesus, and Jesus is their king (Jesus reigns in 1 Cor 15:25). Jesus told Nicodemus that birth through water and the Spirit (i.e., Baptism) is necessary to enter that kingdom (John 3:5). When people wanted to make Jesus king, he withdrew (John 6:15). When asked by Pilate if he were the king of the Jews, Jesus answered that his kingship is not of this world (John 18:33, 36). Peter telling the Christians that they are a royal priesthood indicates that they belong to Jesus their king and their priesthood stems from Jesus. Those who disbelieve Jesus stumble (1 Pet 2:7–8), but Jesus is precious to Christians: he has become their cornerstone on which everything is built (1 Pet 2:7).

How will these priestly Christian disciples exercise their priestly ministry, according to 1 Peter 2:9? Peter urges Christians, the royal priesthood, to sing the praises of God (1 Pet 2:9). Christians exercise their priesthood by declaring God's wonderful deeds, by witnessing to what God has done.

Made Priests by Christ (Rev 1:4–6)

John, writing to the seven churches of Asia, tells his listeners that Christ freed them from their sins by his blood and made them a kingdom, priests to God. It is an allusion to Exodus 19:6 but not using the exact Greek phraseology found there in the Septuagint, as did 1 Peter 2:9. In Exodus 19:6, the Israelites are a "royal priesthood," but in Revelation 1:6, they are a "kingdom, priests" to serve God. The word *hierateuma*, "priesthood," is not utilized here in Revelation, but instead the word "priests," *hiereis* (ἱερεῖς). It was implied in 1 Peter that the priesthood of Christians derives from Christ; it is stated unambiguously here in Revelation 1:6—Christ *made us* a kingdom, priests to serve God. Christians are *made priests* by Christ. The previous verse tells Christians they have been freed from their sins by the blood of Jesus, so the implication is that now their priesthood replaces what was formerly sin in them. So it is by the blood of Jesus, by his self-sacrifice on Calvary, that they too are priestly. Reading this in conjunction with 1 Peter, we can say that Christians become priestly through their baptism, in which they share in the graces of Christ's priestly sacrifice on Calvary.

How will these priestly Christian disciples exercise their priestly ministry, according to Revelation 1:6? Ugo Vanni points out the structure of a liturgical dialogue in Revelation 1:4–6.[3] The text of the celebrant is in 1:4b–5a, and the peoples' response in 5b–6. The dialogue is as follows:

> *Celebrant*: Grace to you and peace from him who is and who was and who is coming, and from the seven spirits who are before his throne, and from Jesus Christ the faithful witness, the first-born from the dead, and the ruler of kings on earth.
>
> *Peoples' Response*: Glory and sovereignty for ever and ever to him who loves us and has freed us from our sins by his blood and made us a kingdom, priests to his God and Father. Amen.

The Christians, in their response during this liturgical dialogue, acknowledge that Christ has made them priests. Since Christians are described as priests in such a liturgical dialogue, Albert Vanhoye concludes, "Christian priesthood finds one of its modes of expres-

---

[3]   Ugo Vanni, *Il Sacerdozio nell'Apocalisse e nella Prima Lettera di Pietro: Un impegno che abbraccia tutta la vita del Cristiano in vista del regno di Dio* (Rome: AdP, 2009), 19–22.

sion in liturgical celebrations."[4] Christians exercise their priesthood by participating in the liturgical celebrations of their parish so that ministerial priesthood and priesthood of the faithful together give glory to God.

Made Priests by Christ's Blood (Rev 5:9–10)

In Revelation 5, John sees the scroll with the seven seals in the hand of God, and the only one worthy to open it is Jesus, the slain Lamb. When Jesus takes the scroll, the four creatures and twenty-four presbyters sing a song in 5:9–10 proclaiming the worthiness of Jesus to take the scroll and open it because he was slain and by his blood he ransomed humanity for God from every tribe, tongue, people, and nation and *made them kings and priests, hiereis* (ἱερεῖς). Here, as in Revelation 1:5–6, it is stated unambiguously that Christ is the source of Christians' priesthood—he *made* them priests—and here again it is also stated how, by Christ shedding his blood for us.

How will these Christian disciples exercise their priestly ministry, according to Revelation 5:10? The duty/honor imposed on Christians as a result of their priesthood is to reign on earth (5:10). This is how Christians are to exercise their priesthood, by reigning on earth. In whatever way is appropriate to each one, Christians are to bring Christ's other-worldly kingdom to this world. In that sense, they will reign on earth, but it is a reign that is not without difficulties: the kingdom is accompanied by tribulation and endurance, as Revelation 1:9 states.

Martyrs Shall Be Priests (Rev 20:6)

The final mention of priestly people in Revelation occurs in chapter 20, which may be said to be the most controversial chapter, due to how the thousand years is interpreted. Satan is bound for a thousand years (Rev 20:2), and Christ reigns for a thousand years (Rev 20:4). I think it best to see the binding of Satan occurring at Christ's death on Calvary (in Rev 5:5, the Lion of the tribe of Judah, the Root of

---

[4]   Albert Vanhoye, *Old Testament Priests and the New Priest: According to the New Testament* (Persham, MA: St. Bede's, 1986), 288.

David, has conquered) and to understand the thousand-year reign of Christ corresponding to the entire ministry of the Church, from Christ until his Second Coming. The thousand years is qualitative, not quantitative, indicating the active presence of Christ in history.[5] Those who have been martyred come to life (in the next life), meaning they gain eternal life. They are called priests, *hiereis* (ἱερεῖς), and reign with Christ for a thousand years (Rev 20:4). Therefore, martyrdom for Christ, giving one's body and blood for Christ, is priestly according to Revelation 20:6. Their martyrdom is the first resurrection (Rev 20:5–6). There is no reference to the second resurrection, but if the mention of a "first resurrection" implies a second resurrection, then in the context of Revelation 20, it can be understood as the general resurrection of the dead at the end of time corresponding to the second death, which is eternal punishment (Rev 20:14; 21:8).

How will these Christian martyrs exercise their priestly ministry, according to Revelation 20:6? They do so in the first place by dying as martyrs. In addition, they reign with Christ during the thousand years between their first resurrection at their death and the second resurrection, the general resurrection at the end of time. During their reign they are called priests of God and Christ. From heaven, they intercede for us on earth. This is their priestly task, to pray for us who still live during the thousand years. They exercise their priesthood, interceding for us in heaven, reigning with Christ.

Other Texts Intimating the Priesthood of Christians

The Scripture passages surveyed above in 1 Peter and Revelation are the only ones that explicitly apply the words "priesthood" or "priest" to all Christians, but there are many other Scripture texts that imply the priesthood of Christians. Texts referring to Christians' lives as a sacrifice for God are making use of priestly language, since it is the duty of priests to offer sacrifice. In Philippians 4:18, Paul describes the gifts sent to him from Philippi as a sacrifice pleasing to God. In 2 Corinthians 9:12, Paul uses language that is priestly, though this is not evident in English translations, as he praises the Corinthians for their generosity to the collection for the poor of Jerusalem. He calls

---

5   Albert Vanhoye, Ugo Vanni, and Franco Manzi, *Il sacerdozio della nuova alleanza* (Milan, IT: Àncora, 1999), 96.

their generosity *diakonia tēs leitourgias* (διακονία τῆς λειτουργίας), "service of the liturgy." Paul asks the Romans to offer their bodies as a living sacrifice to God—that is, everything they do is to be worthy of being offered to God (Rom 12:1). Their entire lives are to be a sacrifice holy to God, a living sacrifice, which contrasts with the sacrifices of dead animals offered in the temple. Hebrews 13:15 asks its listeners to always offer a sacrifice of praise to God and specifies that such a sacrifice issues from lips honoring God's name.

Summarizing our findings in 1 Peter and the Book of Revelation, we can say: Christians are priestly since Baptism (1 Pet 2:5); they are a royal priesthood, which means Jesus is their king (1 Pet 2:9); Christ made them priests by this blood (Rev 1:5–6; 5:9–10); and the martyrs are priestly. Christians exercise their priestly ministry by offering their daily lives as spiritual sacrifices (1 Pet 2:5), by singing the praises of God (1 Pet 2:9), by participating in liturgical celebrations (Rev 1:5–6), by reigning on earth (i.e., bringing God's other-worldly kingdom to this world [Rev 5:9–10]), by being martyred for Christ, and by interceding for us in heaven as they reign with Christ in the next life (Rev 20:6). Now finally, the promise of Exodus 19:6 that all God's people would be priestly has become a reality enjoyed by Christians through their baptism.

Priesthood of the Faithful in the Liturgy

During the Rite of Baptism, before the child is anointed with the oil of chrism on the head, part of the priest's prayer recalls Christ as priest and the newly baptized sharing in Christ's priesthood: "As Christ was anointed Priest, Prophet and King, so may you live always as members of his body, sharing everlasting life."[6]

We have seen in Revelation 1:4b–6 a liturgical dialogue between the celebrant and the people, with the people's response acknowledging their priesthood. During the celebration of Mass, the priest alone confects the Eucharist, making Christ present on the altar, but during the Offertory there is a dialogue between priest and people offering the gifts of bread and wine to the Father. The celebrant says,

---

[6]   International Commission on English in the Liturgy, *Rite of Baptism for Children: Approved for Use in the Dioceses of the United States of America* (New York: Catholic Book Publishers, 1977), 49, 70.

"Pray, brethren (brothers and sisters), that *my sacrifice and yours* may be acceptable to God, the almighty Father," and the people respond, "May the Lord accept the sacrifice at your hands for the praise and glory of his name, for our good and the good of all his holy Church."[7] The assembled people exercise their priesthood in this offering (sacrificing) of bread and wine to the Father, "my sacrifice and yours."

The Ritual Mass for the Conferral of Baptism contains the only reference in the liturgy to Christians as "priestly people." The Prayer over the Offerings commences, "O Lord, who have graciously gathered into your *priestly people* those you have conformed to the likeness of your Son."[8] The priestly sacrificial action of the people offering the bread and wine to the Father is evident in a number of other prayers over the offerings. For example, during the Feast of the Baptism of Our Lord, the bread and wine are called "the oblation of your faithful."[9] On the Sixteenth Sunday in Ordinary Time, the prayer asks God to "accept, we pray, this sacrifice from your faithful servants."[10]

In the sense of 1 Peter 2:5 asking Christians to offer their very lives as spiritual sacrifices, part of the Prayer over the Offerings for the Memorial of Saints Andrew Kim Tae-gŏn, Priest, and Paul Chŏng Ha-sang, and Companions, Martyrs, on September 20 contains this petition: "grant that we ourselves may become a sacrifice acceptable to you."[11] Similarly, part of the Prayer over the Offerings on November 24 for the Memorial of Saint Andrew Dũng-Lạc, Priest, and Companions, Martyrs, contains this petition: "that amid the trials of this life we may always be found faithful and may offer ourselves to you as an acceptable sacrifice."[12] Finally, among the Examples of Formularies for the Universal Prayer, there is a petition with a similar sentiment:

---

[7]   *Roman Missal, Renewed by Decree of the Most Holy Second Ecumenical Council of the Vatican, Promulgated by Authority of Pope Paul VI and Revised at the Direction of Pope John Paul II*, 3rd typical ed. (Washington, DC: United States Conference of Catholic Bishops, 2011), 530.

[8]   Ibid., 1126.

[9]   Ibid., 203.

[10] Ibid., 476.

[11] Ibid., 952.

[12] Ibid., 1001.

For ourselves and our own community,
that the Lord may graciously receive us
as a sacrifice acceptable to himself,
let us pray to the Lord.[13]

---

[13]   Ibid., 1461.

CONCLUSION

THE PRIESTHOOD OF CHRIST and of his apostles and their successors and assistants, who share in Christ's priesthood, is the answer to the imperfection in the Levitical priesthood of the Old Covenant. Initially, before the Levitical priesthood, the firstborn son functioned as the priest in the family. The Book of Exodus reports that, at Sinai, God limited the priesthood to the descendants of Aaron in the tribe of Levi, although that is generally understood to be the theological understanding of the time when the writing of the Torah was completed. As the centuries passed, discontent with the priesthood grew, very evident in the prophetic texts and in both biblical and extra-biblical texts hoping for a renewed priesthood. Those hopes for a transformed priesthood were fulfilled in Christ, the high priest of the New Testament. The Old Covenant high priest, priest, and Levite are transfigured in the priesthood of Christ, who is the high priest of the New Covenant, and also anticipate typologically the New Covenant ministers (bishop, priests, and deacons).

Christ was not from the priestly tribe of Levi, but rather from the tribe of Judah. Nevertheless, the New Testament hints in a number of places that Christ is a priest, though of a different type, and this becomes explicit in the Letter to the Hebrews, the only New Testament document to state that Christ is a high priest, which it does again and again. The high priesthood of Christ dominates the Letter to the Hebrews, which describes his self-sacrifice on Calvary as the fulfillment of the Yom Kippur liturgy. On that day, the Levitical high priest would enter the Holy of Holies sprinkling animals' blood to atone for sins, and Hebrews says Christ on Calvary made one single sacrifice and entered God's heavenly temple. The Holy of Holies in the temple had been forbidden to all except the Levitical high priest (on Yom Kippur), but because of Christ's once-for-all-time effective sacrifice, Hebrews says all are now invited to God's heavenly sanctuary and we enter God's sanctuary by celebrating the Eucharist.

The Gospels show Christ having many disciples, but from them he called twelve who became known as the twelve apostles, and Peter was given the responsibility of leading and unifying. All disciples answer a call from Christ, but these twelve answered a second call from Christ. They were formed into a college, depicted by Mark as an act of creation by Christ. They were sent on temporary mission, already replicating the ministry of Jesus by preaching, exorcising, and healing. Luke alone tells us Jesus also sent out seventy(-two) disciples on a mission, which in many ways was similar to that of the Twelve, and so they anticipate the presbyters in Acts who assisted the apostles, later known as priests who would be co-workers with their bishops.

John 17:17–19 gives us what we might describe as the theology of ordination, as Jesus consecrates the apostles in 17:17 (consecration in Christ the truth), sends them on mission in 17:18, and in 17:19, declares their consecration springs from his own consecration to the Father. Jesus commanding the apostles to "do this in memory of me" during the Last Supper (Luke 22:19) is the Synoptic account of the apostles receiving their priesthood from Jesus. In John 20, Jesus gives his apostles the power to forgive sins after bestowing the Holy Spirit upon them. During Jesus' last appearance risen from the dead, he commissioned the apostles to minister in his name to the whole world. The Twelve were reconstituted again before the revelation of the Church to the world at Pentecost, and following Pentecost, they continued Jesus' ministry: what Jesus began to do during his earthly ministry, he continues to do through the apostles after Pentecost.

The New Testament does not employ the word "priest" in reference to the ministers of the New Covenant, since that word denoted the Jewish Levitical priests offering sacrifices in the temple. New terminology was needed. In Jewish Christian churches, the apostles' assistants were known as presbyters—from which our word "priest" is derived—and the apostles also chose deacons to assist them. Acts 13:1–3 is best understood as Paul's and Barnabas' consecration for ministry before they went on mission together. In Paul's Gentile Christian churches, at first there was a variety of terminology describing those who lead and minister in the name of Christ, but eventually we see the term overseer (*episkopos*), from which our word "bishop" is indirectly derived. By the time of the Pastoral Epistles, there is a merging of Jewish and Gentile terminology, and we see an ecclesiastical structure developing that anticipates Church structure around the turn of the first century, with a bishop leading a college of presbyters and assisted by deacons. Also in the Pastoral Letters, we see a more developed form of the concept of succession, with ministry being passed on by the laying on of hands that bestows the Holy Spirit. A century later, close to the time of our oldest extant account of an ordination liturgy (beginning of the third century), Tertullian applies priestly language to overseers. The Church is living and growing and developing. Christ had already given everything to the apostles during his ministry, and what we see in subsequent centuries is the unfolding of what is already present in the New Testament.

The development of ecclesiastical structure that we see in the first centuries of the Church is merely making explicit what we already see present in the New Testament. That unfurling in subsequent centuries is expansion according to the mind of Christ. As we have seen, there is ample New Testament evidence to demonstrate that Christ, the high priest of the New Covenant, shared his priesthood and ministry with the apostles: they continued the ministry of Jesus, and in turn others continued their ministry. As Joseph Ratzinger says:

> we can say in no uncertain terms that by the end of the apostolic era there is a full-blown theology of the priesthood of the New Covenant in the New Testament. This theology

is given in trust to the Church and through the vicissitudes of history remains the basis of the inalienable identity of the priest.[1]

The Catholic Church was founded by Jesus when he chose the apostles and bestowed his priesthood and ministry upon them. The priesthood of the Catholic Church is not an invention after the time of Christ; it is already present in the ministry of Jesus and is the will of God, the will of Christ for us. What Jesus began to do, he continues to do now through his faithful priests ministering in his name, in apostolic succession, in a line that goes back to the apostles and to Jesus himself. This is what we mean when we pray every Sunday in the Nicene Creed, "I believe in one, holy, catholic and apostolic Church."[2] The Catholic Church is apostolic: the Catholic Church, including its priesthood, goes back to the apostles, who in turn received it from Christ. The development of ecclesiastical structure we see in the first centuries of the Church is merely making explicit what we already see present in the New Testament.

No book is complete, and this book on the biblical foundations of Catholic priesthood leaves room for thoughts in the future on the biblical spirituality of Catholic priesthood, such as the priest as a spiritual father, celibacy, and so on. But it seemed best to confine this volume to the biblical foundations of Catholic priesthood, both the ministerial priesthood and the priesthood of the faithful.

The Preface prayed before the Eucharistic Prayer during the ordination of priests and bishops and during the Chrism Mass, entitled *The Priesthood of Christ and the Ministry of Priests*, is a fitting conclusion. It references Jesus as the high priest of the New Covenant and the Father's decree that Christ's priesthood continue in the Church in the priestly people and in the ministerial priests he chooses to share in his sacred ministry through the laying on of hands:

> For by the anointing of the Holy Spirit
> you made your Only Begotten Son

---

[1]   Joseph Ratzinger, *Called to Communion: Understanding the Church Today*, trans. Adrian Walker (San Francisco: Ignatius Press, 1996), 125.

[2]   *Roman Missal, Renewed by Decree of the Most Holy Second Ecumenical Council of the Vatican, Promulgated by Authority of Pope Paul VI and Revised at the Direction of Pope John Paul II*, 3rd typical edition (Washington, DC: United States Conference of Catholic Bishops, 2011), 527.

High Priest of the new and eternal covenant,
and by your wondrous design were pleased to decree
that his one Priesthood should continue in the Church.
For Christ not only adorns with a royal priesthood
the people he has made his own,
but with a brother's kindness he also chooses men
to become sharers in his sacred ministry
through the laying on of hands.[3]

---

[3]   Ibid., 295, 1140, 1153, 1158.

APPENDIX 1

MELCHIZEDEK AND SHEM

THE ONLY FIRSTBORN TO LEGITIMATELY receive his father's blessing in the Genesis narratives is Noah's son, Shem, since Jacob received the blessing instead of Esau, and Jacob blessed his grandson Ephraim instead of his son (Gen 48). Genesis 11:10–32 gives the list of Shem's descendants down to Abram (Abraham). That genealogy gives not only the line of descent but the age of each son when he in turn fathered his firstborn. The Scriptures wish to teach by the longevity of Noah, Shem, and others that this was still a special time, even though the sin of Adam had brought death into the world (Gen 3:19; see Rom 6:23). Genesis 11:11 states that Shem lived five hundred years after the birth of his firstborn, and close reading of Genesis 11 suggests that Abram was born 296 years after the birth of Shem's firstborn and that Shem lived another 210 years after the birth of Abram. This means that, according to Genesis 11, Noah's son Shem and Abram lived contemporaneously. After Noah blessed Shem (Gen 9:26–27), the next person offering a blessing in Genesis is Melchizedek blessing Abram in Genesis 14:18. This explains why, in Jewish tradition from the second century AD, Shem is considered to be the same person as Melchizedek.[1] Obviously this is going beyond the text of Genesis itself, and not all recent scholars would identify Shem with Melchizedek.[2]

The narrative in Genesis describes Melchizedek as a priest of God Most High. He blessed Abram, and Abram in turn tithed to Melchizedek (Gen 14:19–20). What is significant is that this is the first use of the Hebrew word *kohen* (כֹּהֵן), "priest," in the Old Testament. In haggadic tradition of the second century AD, what is important is not the identification of Melchizedek as Shem, but his being singled out as the first priest in Genesis.[3] The significance of Melchizedek as priest is taken up in the New Testament in the Letter to the Hebrews, which sees Christ as a priest after the order of Melchizedek, an order of priesthood superior to that of the Levitical priesthood (Heb 5:10; 6:20; 7:1–28).

---

[1]   Fred L. Horton, *The Melchizedek Tradition* (New York: Cambridge University Press, 1976), 117–118. See also Scott W. Hahn, *Kinship by Covenant: A Canonical Approach to the Fulfillment of God's Saving Promises*, Anchor Bible Reference Library (New Haven, CT/London: Yale University Press, 2009), 97, 133n141, which also lists the identification of Shem as Melchizedek in Christian tradition. See also Louis Ginzberg, Henrietta Szold, and Paul Radin, *Legends of the Jews*, 2nd ed. (Philadelphia, PA: Jewish Publication Society, 2003), 196n102.

[2]   Horton, *The Melchizedek Tradition*, 114. However, Horton's analysis of the blessing given to Shem in Gen 9:26 and the blessing given by Melchizedek to Abram in Gen 14:19 supports the identification of Melchizedek with Shem. For more speculation on Melchizedek, see Oscar Cullmann, *The Christology of the New Testament* (Philadelphia, PA: Westminster Press, 1963), 85.

[3]   Michael D. Johnson, *The Purpose of Biblical Genealogies: With Special Reference to the Setting of the Genealogies of Jesus* (London: Cambridge University Press, 1969), 270–71.

APPENDIX 2

OLD TESTAMENT ORDINATION LITURGY

FOLLOWING GOD'S CHOICE of Aaron and his sons for the priesthood in Exodus 28:1, the remainder of Exodus 28 gives instructions for the priests' and high priest's liturgical garments. All priests wore four garments: underwear (28:42), tunics, sashes, and miters (28:40). The high priest wore four additional items: the ephod (28:5–14), the breastplate of judgment containing the twelve stones with the names of the tribes of Israel (28:15–29), the robe of the ephod that was not allowed to be torn (28:31–35), and a gold plate affixed to the front of the turban with "Holy to the Lord" engraved upon it (Exod 28:36–38).

The rituals in the rite of ordination were as follows. First, the animals for sacrifice and the unleavened bread to be offered were to be gathered. Then Aaron and his sons were brought to the door of the Tent of Meeting so that they could be washed with water. They had to be ritually pure before being ordained. Following the washing, Aaron was vested in the high priest's garments (Exod 29:5–6; Lev 8:7–9). Aaron was then anointed with the anointing oil. Its special manufacture is described in Exodus 30:22–33. Leviticus adds to the sacredness of Aaron's anointing by telling us that it was this same anointing oil that was used to anoint the Tabernacle, the altar, and all the sacred vessels (Lev 8:10–12; see also Exod 30:26–30). The high priests succeeding Aaron were also to be similarly anointed (Lev 21:10). Following Aaron's anointing, his sons were clothed in their priestly vestments (Exod 29:8–9; Lev 8:13).

The next part of the priestly ordination involved the sacrifice of animals. A blood ritual occurred, with Moses putting some of the blood on the right ear, right hand thumb, and big toe of the right foot of Aaron and his sons (Exod 29:20; Lev 8:23–24). Baruch Levine sees this as analogous to what happened at Sinai when blood was cast on the altar representing God as one of the parties of the covenant and the rest of the blood was cast over the people as the other party of the covenant.[1] As well as signifying purification, the daubing of the ears, thumbs, and great toes is often taken to symbolize the priest entirely given over to God: his ears to receive God's command, his hands to perform his sacred duties, and his feet to walk in the paths of God. Just as the sacredness of Aaron's anointing was denoted by his anointing with the same anointing oil used for the Tabernacle, the altar, and the sacred utensils, so also the sacredness of this blood ritual is denoted by the remaining blood being thrown around the altar, thus connecting the priests with the altar (Exod 29:20).[2] As well as animal sacrifices, there was also a "wave" or "elevation" offering, so named because it involved waving or elevating the offering of unleavened bread up in the air to God before burning it on the altar.

Exodus 29:35 instructs that the ordination last seven days, with a sacrifice of a bull every day as atonement (29:36). Some take it that every ritual of the Rite of Ordination was to be repeated each of the seven days. Leviticus 8:33–36 does not describe a daily repetition but states that the priests were not to leave the Tabernacle for seven days. When the seven-day ordination was over, the newly ordained functioned as priests on the eighth day by offering sacrifice (Lev 9).

Hebrew uses two terms to describe ordination, the idiom "fill the hand" and the verb qāḏāš (קָדַשׁ), "consecrate/sanctify/make holy." The idiom "fill the hand" is not evident in English translations, as it is normally translated as "consecrate/ordain" or "install" when not referring to priests, although it is employed almost always to refer to

---

[1]   Baruch A. Levine, *Leviticus*, The JPS Torah Commentary (Philadelphia, PA: Jewish Publication Society, 1989), 53.

[2]   Martin Noth, *A History of Pentateuchal Traditions* (Englewood Cliffs, NJ: Prentice-Hall, 1972), 72.

priestly ordinations (Exod 28:41; 29:9, 29, 35; 32:29; Lev 8:33; 16:32; 21:10; Num 3:3). Opinions differ as to which of the ordination rituals listed above—sacrifices or anointing—the rite refers.[3] While "fill the hand" is a strange idiom to our ears, Nahum Sarna points out that it must have originally referred to placing something in the hand of the one receiving the mandate, and "mandate" is a reasonable word to use for this idiom because it is derived from two Latin words meaning to "give into the hand" (*manus + dare*).[4]

[3]   Jacob Milgrom, *Leviticus 1-16: A New Translation with Introduction and Commentary*, Anchor Yale Bible 3 (New Haven, CT/London: Yale University Press, 2008), 539.

[4]   Nahum M. Sarna, *Exodus*, The JPS Torah Commentary (Philadelphia, PA: Jewish Publication Society, 1991), 185.

APPENDIX 3

QUMRAN ON THE RENEWED PRIESTHOOD

THE RULE OF THE COMMUNITY (1QS) expected three persons at the end of days: a prophet (seen by Albert Vanhoye as reflecting Deuteronomy 18:18)[1] and two anointed ones (messiahs in Hebrew), the priestly messiah of Aaron ruling over religious matters and the messiah descended from David taking charge over temporal matters, with the priestly messiah of Aaron taking precedence over the non-priestly messiah of David (1QS 9:10–11). The idea of two messiahs is following Zechariah and Haggai. In the Rule of the Congregation (1Q28a [1QSa] 2:11–21), when the messiah is begotten, there will be a banquet to which the priest will enter first, followed by the other priests, and finally the messiah of Israel. The priest will bless the first fruits of bread and wine and stretch out his hands toward the bread, and after him the messiah of Israel will stretch out his hand toward the bread. In this text the messiah of Israel is clearly not a priest and Collins takes the priest as the messiah of Aaron who takes precedence during the eschatological banquet.[2] The Damascus Document,

---

[1]   Albert Vanhoye, *Old Testament Priests and the New Priest: According to the New Testament* (Persham, MA: St. Bede's, 1986), 44.

[2]   John J. Collins, *The Scepter and the Star: The Messiahs of the Dead Sea*

which has affinities with Qumran, foresees one Messiah, who would be both priestly and royal at the same time (4Q 266 10:12). In 11Q13 (11QMelch), the time of a future Melchizedek is described in terms of a Jubilee (11QMelch 2:1–9) in which atonement will be made for sins, with Melchizedek carrying out God's judgment and freeing people from evil (11QMelch 2:13, 25). This will also be a special time as the fulfillment of Isaiah 52:7 (11QMelch 2:15-17).

Scrolls and Other Ancient Literature, Anchor Bible Reference Library (New York: Doubleday, 1995), 76.

APPENDIX 4

BROTHERS AND SISTERS OF JESUS

THE BROTHERS AND SISTERS OF JESUS appear in Matthew 12:46, Mark 3:31–32 and 6:3, Luke 8:19–20, John 2:12 and 7:1–10, and Acts 1:14. Catholics say they are not Jesus' siblings but his cousins. Here are some reasons.

1. In Mark 15:40 and Matthew 27:56 there is mention of a Mary who is the mother of James and Joseph. James and Joseph are two of the four named elsewhere in the Gospels as brothers of Jesus. We would expect the evangelists to have clearly stated if she were also the mother of Jesus. So the crucifixion scene suggests that Mary the mother of Jesus is not the mother of the brothers and sisters of Jesus.

2. On the Cross in John, Jesus gives his mother to John to be looked after (John 19:25–27). If Jesus had younger brothers and sisters it would be beyond strange if he asked someone who was not a family member to look after his mother.

3. There is no word in Aramaic or ancient Hebrew for "cousin" so brother and sister were used instead. Examples of

"uncle"/"nephew" being translated as "brother" are the following:

    a. In Genesis 13:8, the Hebrew describes Abraham and Lot as brothers, whereas they are uncle and nephew.

    b. In Genesis 14:14, the Hebrew "brother" refers to kinsman.

    c. We see the same in Genesis 29:11–15 to describe the relationship between Jacob and Laban.

Even though there is a word for cousin in Greek, *anepsios* (ἀνεψιός), when the Hebrew Old Testament was translated into Greek as the Septuagint (LXX) the practice of using the word "brother" continued, since it was the Semitic way of expression. Likewise, following its adoption in the LXX, it continued in the New Testament with the exception of its sole use in Colossians 4:10.

4. When Matthew writes in 1:25 that Joseph did not know Mary "until" she had given birth to Jesus, the use of "until," *heōs hou* (ἕως οὖ) does not imply marital relations after the birth because *heōs hou* in Greek does not always imply resumption of the negated action beyond the time indicated. Other examples of similar usages are 2 Samuel 6:23, where we read that Michal had no children until the day she died. Another usage is in Deuteronomy 34:6, where no one knows where Moses is buried until this day. The use of the word "until" may not be evident in some translations because translators have removed it due to it making for a strange translation. In 1 Corinthians 15:25 Christ must reign until (*achri hou* rather than *heōs hou*) he has put all his enemies under his feet, and obviously his reign continues afterwards.

5. Describing Jesus as Mary's "first-born" in Luke 2:7 does not imply that Jesus had younger brothers. St. Jerome explained it this way: "Every only begotten son is a first-born son, but not every first-born is an only begotten" (*Against Helvidius* 12).[1] It was

---

[1] In *St. Jerome: Letters and Select Works*, trans. W. H. Fremantle, G. Lewis and W. G. Martley, ed. Philip Schaff and Henry Wace, A Select Library of the Nicene and Post-Nicene Fathers of the Christian Church, 2nd ser., vol. 6, (New York: Christian Literature Company, 1893), 339.

the normal way to describe the first baby whether or not other children followed. Exodus 13:2 defines first-born as the first to open the womb. The attitude of the "brothers" of Jesus betrays that they are not younger siblings, since they give advice to Jesus (Mark 3:21; John 7:3–4) and it would not have been normal for younger brothers to advise older brothers.

6. In Mark 6:3, Jesus is described by the people of Nazareth as "the son of Mary," not "a son of Mary."

7. One of the men named as a brother of Jesus (Matt 13:55) is called Joseph. While it was certainly not unknown for sons to be named after their fathers, it was uncommon.[2]

8. In AD 382 or 383, St. Jerome complained about Helvedius (Helvetius) who interpreted Matthew 1:25 and other passages to mean that Mary had other children. Jerome's document shows Helvidius' thinking was novel (*Against Helvidius* 3–8). So, late in the fourth century, it was a novel and new interpretation of Scripture to suggest that Mary had other children. In the early centuries, Mary was always understood to be a virgin. Jerome referred to previous Church Fathers who held his view: Ignatius, Polycarp, Irenæus, and Justin Martyr. Jerome also wrote that nowhere is there evidence that Joseph had previously been married and states, "I claim still more, that Joseph himself on account of Mary was a virgin, so that from a virgin wedlock a virgin son was born. For if as a holy man he does not come under the imputation of fornication, and it is nowhere written that he had another wife, but was the guardian of Mary whom he was supposed to have to wife rather than her husband, the conclusion is that he who was thought worthy to be called father of the Lord, remained a virgin."[3]

---

[2] W. F. Albright and C. S. Mann, *Matthew: Introduction, Translation, and Notes*, Anchor Yale Bible 26 (New Haven, CT: Yale University Press, 2008), 9.

[3] Schaff and Wace, 344.

APPENDIX 5

THE TWELVE APOSTLES

THE APOSTLES ARE LISTED in the Gospels in three groups of four: Peter is first in the first group of four, Philip first in the second group, and James first in the third group of four. The lists are to be found in Matthew 10:2–4, Mark 3:16–18, Luke 6:14–16, and Acts 1:13.

First Group of Four	Peter, Andrew, James, John
Second Group of Four	Philip, Bartholomew, Thomas, Matthew
Third Group of Four	James, Thaddeus/Judas, Simon, Judas replaced by Matthias

Simon is first in all the lists of the twelve apostles. His name is not uncommon in Judaism; it occurs in the form Simeon a number of times in the Old Testament (e.g., Gen 29:33; Exod 1:2). The name

Peter does not appear in any Greek literature prior to the first century; every occurrence of the word in Greek before then always meant "rock" or "stone." However, the Aramaic form of the name, *Kêpā'* (כֵּיפָא), appears as a name as early as the fifth century BC in Jewish communities in Egypt.[1] Mark 3:16 and Luke 6:14 refer to Simon being renamed Peter by Jesus when they list the twelve apostles just after they were chosen, but that does not necessarily mean the name change occurred at that time. At the beginning of John's Gospel, in 1:42, Jesus says Simon will be called Cephas, which is the Greek transliteration of the Aramaic *Kêpā'* (כֵּיפָא), meaning "rock." However, the verb is in the future tense: Simon "will be called." Mark, Luke, and John are not necessarily in conflict with Matthew 16:18, which tells us Jesus bestowed the name on Peter in Caesarea Philippi. A change of name elsewhere in the Bible indicates a new mission from God: Abram becomes Abraham (Gen 17:5); Sarai becomes Sarah (Gen 17:15); Jacob is renamed Israel (Gen 32:28; 35:10), Hoshea is renamed Joshua (Num 13:16); and after Saul is prayed over and goes on his first missionary journey, he is called Paul (Acts 13:9).

The other three apostles in the first group of four are Peter's brother Andrew, and the brothers James and John. While these four are first in all the lists, they are not listed in the same order. Matthew and Luke list the two sets of brothers one after the other, but Mark lists them as Peter, James, John, Andrew, perhaps because Peter, James, and John are the ones often associated with Jesus on special occasions (raising of the dead girl in Mark 5:37; Luke 8:51; Jesus' Transfiguration in Matthew 17:1; Mark 9:2; Luke 9:28; being near Jesus during his agony in Gethsemane in Matthew 26:37; Mark 14:33). Andrew is a Greek name meaning "manly," revealing the Gentile influence in the northern part of Galilee. He was originally a disciple of John the Baptist, and it was he who introduced Peter to Jesus (John 1:41–42). James is *Iakōbos* in Greek (Ἰάκωβος), from the Hebrew *Jacob* (יַעֲקֹב), the father of the twelve tribes who was renamed Israel. Sometimes he is known as James the Great, which conveniently distinguishes him from James the Less. He was the first apostle to be martyred (Acts 12:2). John is the English rendering of the Greek *Iōannēs* (Ἰωάννης), from the Hebrew *Yôḥānān* (יוֹחָנָן), meaning "God-

1   Joseph A. Fitzmyer, "Aramaic Kepha and Peter's Name in the New Testament," in *To Advance the Gospel: New Testament Studies*, 2nd ed. (Grand Rapids, MI: Eerdmans, 1981), 116.

given" or "God has been gracious." God was certainly gracious to John, as traditionally he is taken to be the beloved disciple in his Gospel. Jesus gave James and John the name Boanerges, which Mark 3:17 conveniently translates as "sons of thunder" for his readers unfamiliar with Aramaic. From Luke 9:54, it could be said that this name suited their characters.

The second group of four apostles is Philip, Bartholomew, Thomas, and Matthew. Philip was called by Jesus in John 1:43 and features a number of times afterwards in that Gospel. Bartholomew is English for the Greek *Bartholomaios* (Βαρ-θολομαῖος), which renders the Aramaic "son (= bar) of Talmay" (בַּר תַּלְמַי). Tolmay is a name mentioned six times in the Old Testament. It is debated whether Bartholomew is the Nathanael of John 1:45–51. He is not mentioned in the New Testament apart from the lists of the Twelve. Thomas is Greek for the Aramaic *Teoma* (תְּאוֹמָא), which means "twin," as John 11:16, 20:24, and 21:2 tell us. He features in the Gospel of John a number of times, most famously for his desire to die with Jesus (John 11:16), doubting Jesus' Resurrection (John 20:25), and his profession of faith, "My Lord and my God" (John 20:28). Matthew is English for the Greek *Maththaios* (Μαθθαῖος) and an abbreviation of the Old Testament Mattathias, which means "gift of God" according to Strack Billerbeck.[2] In Mark and Luke, he was a tax collector named Levi when called by Jesus, but he must have either been renamed Matthew or had Matthew as another name. He is the one associated with authorship of the Gospel bearing his name.

The third group of four apostles, after commencing with James the son of Alphaeus, contains two others (Thaddeus or Judas the son of James, and Simon the Cananaean/Zealot) before ending with Judas Iscariot. The first of the third group of four, James the son of Alphaeus, is the brother of the apostle Matthew if Alphaeus is the same one referenced in Mark 2:14 as the father of Levi the tax collector (presuming Levi is Matthew). If so, that means the Twelve included three sets of two brothers. James the son of Alphaeus is sometimes believed to be the same person as James the Less, so called because of Mark 15:40. Since Galatians 1:19 says James the brother of the Lord was an apostle, it has been theorized that he is the same person as

---

2   Hermann Leberecht Strack and Paul Billerbeck, *Kommentar zum Neuen Testament aus Talmud und Midrasch*, vol 1., *Das Evangelium nach Matthäus* (Munich: C.H. Beck, 1963–1965), 1:536.

James the apostle and the son of Alphaeus (i.e., the James the Less). According to this understanding, James the Less is James the brother of the Lord (i.e., the cousin of Jesus). He is a cousin of Jesus, because his mother Mary (wife of Clopas) was the sister of Mary the mother of Jesus mentioned in John 19:25 and is the same Mary mentioned in Mark 15:40 and Matthew 27:56. Based on this understanding, James the Less, brother of the Lord, became the leader of the church in Jerusalem whom we encounter in Acts 15. He is referenced in Mark 6:3; Matthew 13:55; Galatians 1:19 and 2:9; Acts 12:17, 15:13, and 21:18; 1 Corinthians 15:7; James 1:1; and Jude 1. Ancient sources say he was martyred by being stoned to death after being cast down from the pinnacle of the temple not long before AD 70 and was buried near the temple.

Thaddaeus, in the list of the Twelve in Mark and Matthew, is called Judas the son of James in Luke's lists in his Gospel and Acts, and Jude in Eucharistic Prayer I.[3] Presuming that Judas and Thaddaeus are the same person, this means he had two names, the Jewish name Judas, from the Hebrew Judah, and the Greek name Thaddaeus. If that is the case, we could speculate that Mark and Matthew decided to use Thaddaeus to avoid confusion with Judas the traitor. This would not have been an isolated case of having two names; another example is Joseph called Barsabbas, one of the candidates to replace Judas Iscariot (Acts 1:23).

Mark and Matthew call Simon "the Cananaean," not "the Canaanite," *Kananaios* not *Kananitēs* (Καναναῖος not Κανανίτης), the former being derived from the Aramaic word *Qan'ān* (קַנְאָן), meaning "zealot," while the latter means "Canaanite."[4] This is in agreement with Luke, who calls him "the Zealot" in both his lists. The Zealot movement began with a failed Jewish revolt against Roman tax in AD 6 and had as its aims the liberation of Palestine from Roman occupation.[5] Joseph Ratzinger says their Old Testament heroes would

---

3   *Roman Missal, Renewed by Decree of the Most Holy Second Ecumenical Council of the Vatican, Promulgated by Authority of Pope Paul VI and Revised at the Direction of Pope John Paul II*, 3rd typical ed. (Washington, DC: United States Conference of Catholic Bishops, 2011), 636.

4   See William Arndt, Frederick W. Danker, and Walter Bauer, *A Greek-English Lexicon of the New Testament and Other Early Christian Literature*, 3rd ed. (BDAG), rev. and ed. F. W. Danker (Chicago: University of Chicago Press, 2000), 507.

5   Robert H. Stein, *Mark*, Baker Exegetical Commentary on the New Testament (Grand Rapids, MI: Baker Academic, 2008), 173.

have been those who were zealous: Phinehas, who killed an idolatrous Hebrew (Num 25:6–13), Elijah, who killed the prophets of Baal
(1 Kings 18), and Mattathias, the head of the Maccabees who initi-
ated the rebellion against Antiochus, who had tried to extinguish the
faith of Israel (1 Macc 2:17–28).[6] As a Zealot, Simon would have been
a polar opposite to Levi/Matthew, who collected tolls for the Romans.

Finally, the twelfth apostle in the lists is Judas Iscariot, the traitor. There have been many suggestions put forward to explain "Iscariot." A common explanation is that it is a composite word formed
from two Hebrew words, *ish* (man) + *Kerioth* (man from Kerioth),
and Kerioth is a Judean town mentioned in Joshua 15:25. If that explanation is correct, it makes Judas the only one of the Twelve from
Judah, the others being from Galilee. If it does not mean he is from
the town Kerioth, it is sometimes seen as referring to him being one
of the *Sicarii* (a Roman word describing Jewish extremists, meaning
assassins). It is unknown whether the *Sicarii* were affiliated with the
Zealots or a subgroup of the Zealots. If they were, and Judas belonged
to the Sicarii, two of Jesus' twelve apostles belonged to the Zealots.
However, Meinrad Limbeck states the radical *Sicarii* are known only
from AD 52 onwards.[7] Being cognizant of the opposite backgrounds
of some of the Twelve, from working for Rome to plotting against
Rome, leads Ratzinger to observe the tensions that must have existed
between them and the difficulty in initiating into Jesus' new way.[8]

Twice during Eucharistic Prayer I, we ask to benefit from the
prayers of the "blessed Apostles and Martyrs," and the names of
those whose intercession we invoke are listed. The first listing includes the first eleven apostles, with St. Paul inserted after St. Peter,
and is followed by other martyrs, concluding by asking that, through
their merits and prayers, in all things we may be defended by God's
protecting help:

> In communion with those whose memory we venerate,
> especially the glorious ever-Virgin Mary,
> Mother of our God and Lord, Jesus Christ,

---

[6]   Joseph Ratzinger, *Jesus of Nazareth: From the Baptism in the Jordan to the
        Transfiguration* (New York: Doubleday, 2007), 177.

[7]   Meinrad Limbeck, "Ἰσκαριώθ; Ἰσκαριώτης, ου" in *Exegetical Dictionary of
        the New Testament*, ed. Horst Robert Balz and Gerhard Schneider, vol. 2
        (Grand Rapids, MI: Eerdmans, 1990), 201.

[8]   Ratzinger, *Jesus of Nazareth: From the Baptism*, 178.

and blessed Joseph, her Spouse,
your blessed Apostles and Martyrs,
Peter and Paul, Andrew,
(James, John,
Thomas, James, Philip,
Bartholomew, Matthew,
Simon and Jude;
Linus, Cletus, Clement, Sixtus,
Cornelius, Cyprian,
Lawrence, Chrysogonus,
John and Paul,
Cosmas and Damian)
and all your Saints;
we ask that through their merits and prayers,
in all things we may be defended
by your protecting help.[9]

The second list includes Matthias, who replaced Judas, and is followed by many martyrs and concludes by asking that we be admitted into their company in heaven:[10]

To us, also, your servants, who, though sinners,
hope in your abundant mercies,
graciously grant some share
and fellowship with your holy Apostles and Martyrs:
with John the Baptist, Stephen,
Matthias, Barnabas,
(Ignatius, Alexander,
Marcellinus, Peter,
Felicity, Perpetua,
Agatha, Lucy,
Agnes, Cecilia, Anastasia)
and all your Saints.[11]

---

[9]   *Roman Missal*, 636.
[10]   Ibid., 642.
[11]   Ibid.

GLOSSARY

College of Bishops This term refers to the bishops acting together in communion. The "college of apostles" refers to the apostles acting together in communion.

LXX See "Septuagint" below.

Mishnah The Mishnah is a collection of Jewish oral tradition and written documents foundational for Jewish belief, mostly on Jewish law, compiled ca. AD 200 by Rabbi Judah. It contains sixty-two tractates. Just as the books of the Bible are cited by chapter and verse (e.g., "Luke 1:2"), the tractates in the Mishnah are cited by chapter and verse, although with the abbreviation "m." preceding the name of the tractate to indicate the Mishnah (because the same tractate names appear in the Talmuds; see below on the Tamuds). Thus, "m. Sanh. 4:4" is verse 4 of chapter 4 in the tractate on the Sanhedrin in the Mishnah.

Monarchical Bishop This term refers to bishops as we know them now, meaning a bishop leading a college of presbyters and assisted by deacons.

Roman Missal The *Roman Missal* is the book with the texts of the prayers said by the priest during Mass.

Roman Pontifical The *Roman Pontifical* contains the texts of liturgies celebrated by bishops (ordinations, confirmations, etc.).

Septuagint Abbreviated to "LXX," the Septuagint is the Greek translation of the Hebrew Old Testament and also includes seven extra books and other additions not in the Hebrew Old Testament.

Tabernacle The Tabernacle was the tent the Israelites constructed in the desert containing the Holy of Holies with the Ark of the Covenant at God's command in Exodus 25–27. The construction is described in Exodus 36–38 and 40. Sometimes it is called the Tent of Meeting, or the Dwelling.

Talmud The Talmud, put simply, is a commentary on the Mishnah and a collection of the oral tradition of the early rabbis. It comes in two versions: the Palestinian (Jerusalem) Talmud, probably compiled AD 400–450, and the Babylonian Talmud, compiled AD 500–600. The Babylonian Talmud, the more complete of the two, is among the most important texts in rabbinic Judaism. Since the tractates in the Talmuds contain commentary on those of the same name in the Mishnah, as with the use of "m." for Mishnah, citations of the Babylonian Talmud are preceded by "b." and citations of the Jerusalem are preceded by "y." Thus, just as "m. Sanh." is the tractate on the Sanhedrin in the Mishnah, "b. Sanh." is the tractate on the Sanhedrin in the Babylonian Talmud and "y. Sanh." is the same in the Jerusalem Talmud, both commenting on "m. Sanh." Citations of the Jerusalem Talmud usually give chapter:verse (as with the Mishnah) but also include a page number from the folio edition of the work and a letter for the column on the folio page (two columns per side, so A–D). Thus, "y. B. Bat. 10:1, 17C" is verse 1 of chapter 10 of the tractate Baba Batra in the Jerusalem Talmud, which can be found on folio page 17, column C. The Babylonian Talmud is usually cited by only folio page number and a letter for the side of the page (A–B). Thus, "b. Ber. 2A" is side A of folio page 2 in the tractate Berakot in the Babylonian Talmud. For the purposes of this book, chapter:verse is inserted in square brackets within citations of the Babylonian Talmud for correlation with the same text location in the Jeusalem Talmud and the Mishnah.

WORKS CITED

à Lapide, Cornelius. *The Great Commentary of Cornelius à Lapide.* Vol. 6, *S. John's Gospel—Chaps. 12 to 21 and Epistles 1, 2, and 3.* Translated by Thomas W. Mossman. 4th ed. Edinburgh: John Grant, 1908.

———. *The Great Commentary of Cornelius* à *Lapide.* Vol. 4, *S. Luke's Gospel.* Translated by Thomas W. Mossman. 4th ed. Edinburgh: John Grant, 1908.

Albright, W. F., and C. S. Mann. *Matthew: Introduction, Translation, and Notes.* Anchor Yale Bible 26. New Haven, CT/London: Yale University Press, 2008.

Aquinas, Thomas. *The Religious State: The Episcopate and the Priestly Office.* Edited by John Procter. St. Louis, MO/London: B. Herder/Sands & Co., 1903.

Arndt, William, Frederick W. Danker, and Walter Bauer. *A Greek-English Lexicon of the New Testament and Other Early Christian Literature.* 3rd ed. (BDAG). Revised and edited by Frederick W. Danker. Chicago: University of Chicago Press, 2000.

Attridge, Harold W. "How Priestly Is the 'High Priestly Prayer' of John 17?" *Catholic Biblical Quarterly* 75 (2013): 1–15.

———. *The Epistle to the Hebrews: a Commentary on the Epistle to the Hebrews.* Hermeneia—a Critical and Historical Commentary on the Bible. Philadelphia, PA: Fortress Press, 1989.

Aune, David E. *Revelation 1–5.* Word Biblical Commentary 52A. Dallas, TX: Word, 1998.

Barber, Michael. "Jesus as the Davidic Temple Builder and Peter's Priestly Role in Matthew 16:16–19." *Journal of Biblical Literature* 132 (2013): 935–953.

Barkay, Gabriel. *Ketef Hinnom.* Jerusalem: Israel Museum, 1986.

Barrett, Charles K. *Gospel According to St John: An Introduction with Commentary and Notes on the Greek Text.* 2nd ed. London: SPCK, 1978.

Beasley-Murray, George R. *John.* Word Biblical Commentary 36. Dallas, TX: Word, 2002.

Benedict XVI. Homily at Yankee Stadium, Bronx, New York, April 20, 2008. In *Homilies of His Holiness Benedict XVI (English).* Logos Verbum. Vatican City: Libreria Editrice Vaticana, 2013.

Berlin, Adele, Marc Zvi Brettler, and Michael Fishbane, eds. *The Jewish Study Bible.* New York: Oxford University Press, 2004.

Blenkinsopp, Joseph. *Sage, Priest, Prophet: Religious and Intellectual Leadership in Ancient Israel.* Louisville, KY: Westminster John Knox Press, 1995.

Blomberg, Craig. *Matthew.* The New American Commentary 22. Nashville, TN: Broadman & Holman Publishers, 1992.

Bock, Darrell L. *Luke.* Vol. 1, *1:1–9:50.* Baker Exegetical Commentary on the New Testament. Grand Rapids, MI: Baker Academic, 1994.

———. *Luke,* Vol. 2, *9:51–24:53.* Baker Exegetical Commentary on the New Testament. Grand Rapids, MI: Baker Academic, 1996.

Bockmuehl, Markus. *Simon Peter in Scripture and Memory: The New Testament Apostle in the Early Church.* Grand Rapids, MI: Baker Academic, 2012.

———. *The Remembered Peter: In Ancient Reception and Modern Debate.* Wissenschaftliche Untersuchungen zum Neuen Testament 262. Tübingen: Mohr Siebeck, 2010.

Böhler, Dieter. "The Church's Eucharist, the Lord's Supper, Israel's Sacrifice: Reflections on Pope Benedict's Axiom 'Without its coherence with its Old Testament heritage, Christian liturgy simply cannot be understood.'" In *Benedict XVI and the Roman Missal: Proceedings of the Fourth Fota International Liturgical Conference, 2011,* 107–123. Edited by Janet E. Rutherford and James O'Brien. Fota Liturgy Series. Dublin/New York: Four Courts Press/Scepter Publishers, 2013.

Bohr, David. *The Diocesan Priest: Consecrated and Sent.* Collegeville, MN: Liturgical Press, 2009.

Bradshaw, Paul F., Maxwell E. Johnson, and L. Edward Phillips. *The Apostolic Tradition: A Commentary.* Edited by Harold W. Attridge. Hermeneia—a Critical and Historical Commentary on the Bible. Minneapolis, MN: Fortress Press, 2002.

Branick, Vincent P. *The House Church in the Writings of Paul.* Zacchaeus Studies: New Testament. Wilmington, DE: Michael Glazier, 1989.

Brown, Francis, Sammuel Rolles Driver, and Charles Augustus Briggs. *Enhanced Brown-Driver-Briggs Hebrew and English Lexicon.* Oak Harbor, WA: Logos Research Systems, 2000.

Brown, Raymond E. *An Adult Christ at Christmas: Essays on the Three Biblical Christmas Stories, Matthew 2 and Luke 2.* Collegeville, MN: Liturgical Press, 1988.

——. *The Birth of the Messiah: A Commentary on the Infancy Narratives in the Gospels of Matthew and Luke.* New updated ed. Anchor Bible Reference Library. New York/London: Yale University Press, 1993.

——. *An Introduction to the New Testament.* New York: Doubleday, 1997.

——. *The Gospel According to John (XIII-XXI): Introduction, Translation, and Notes.* Anchor Yale Bible 29A. New Haven, CT/London: Yale University Press, 2008.

——. *Priest and Bishop: Biblical Reflections.* Eugene, OR: Wipf and Stock Publishers, 1999.

Bühner, J.-A. "ἀποστέλλω." In *Exegetical Dictionary of the New Testament.* Edited by Horst Robert Balz and Gerhard Schneider. Grand Rapids, MI: Eerdmans, 1990.

Butler, Sara. *The Catholic Priesthood and Women: A Guide to the Teaching of the Church.* Chicago: Hillenbrand Books, 2006.

Campbell, R. Alastair. *The Elders: Seniority within Earliest Christianity.* London/New York: T&T Clark, 2004.

Catholic Church. *Code of Canon Law, Latin-English Edition.* Washington, DC: Canon Law Society of America, 1998.

——. *The Roman Missal: Renewed by Decree of the Most Holy Second Ecumenical Council of the Vatican, Promulgated by Authority of Pope Paul VI and Revised at the Direction of Pope John Paul II.* 3rd typical ed. Washington, DC: United States Conference of Catholic Bishops, 2011.

Coenen, L. "Bishop, Presbyter, Elder." In *New International Dictionary of New Testament Theology.* Vol. 1, 188–200. Edited by Lothar Coenen, Erich Beyreuther, and Hans Bietenhard. Grand Rapids, MI: Zondervan Publishing House, 1986.

Collins, John J. *The Scepter and the Star: The Messiahs of the Dead Sea Scrolls and Other Ancient Literature.* Anchor Bible Reference Library. New York: Doubleday, 1995.

Coloe, Mary L. *God Dwells with Us: Temple Symbolism in the Fourth Gospel.* Collegeville, MN: Michael Glazier, 2001.

Colson, Jean. *Ministre de Jésus-Christ ou le Sacerdoce de l'Évangile, étude sur la condition sacerdotale des ministres chrétiens dans l'Église primitive.* Théologie historique 4. Paris: Beauchesne et ses fils, 1965.

Congregatio de Cultu Divino et Disciplina Sacramentorum, Vox Clara Committee. *The Roman Pontifical.* Vatican City: Vox Clara Committee, 2012.

Conti, Martino. *La Vocazione e le vocazione nella Bibbia.* Brescia, IT/Rome: La Scuola Editrice/Edizioni Antonianum, 1985.

Cullmann, Oscar. *The Christology of the New Testament.* Philadelphia, PA: Westminster Press, 1963.

de la Potterie, Ignace. *The Hour of Jesus: The Passion and Resurrection of Jesus According to John.* New York: Alba House, 1989.

de Vaux, Roland. *Ancient Israel: Its Life and Institutions.* New York: McGraw-Hill, 1961.

Dockx, S. "L'ordination de Barnabé et de Saul d'après Acts 13,1–3." *Nouvelle Revue Théologique* 98 (1976): 238–258.

Echlin, Edward P. *The Deacon in the Church: Past and Future.* Staten Island, NY: Alba House, 1971.

Eusebius of Caesaria. *Historia ecclesiastica.* In *Eusebius: Church History, Life of Constantine the Great, and Oration in Praise of Constantine.* Translated by Arthur Cushman McGiffert. Edited by Philip Schaff and Henry Wace. A Select Library of the Nicene and Post-Nicene Fathers of the Christian Church, 2nd ser., vol. 1. New York: Christian Literature Company, 1890.

Ferguson, Everett. "Ordain, Ordination." In *The Anchor Yale Bible Dictionary.* Vol. 5, 37–40. Edited by David Noel Freedman. New York: Doubleday, 1996.

Ferraro, Giuseppe. *Le preghiere di ordinazione al diaconato, al presbiterato, all'episcopato.* Naples, IT: Edizioni Dehoniane, 1977.

Feuillet, André. *The Priesthood of Christ and His Ministers.* Garden City, NY: Doubleday, 1975.

Fitzmyer, Joseph A. "Aramaic Kepha and Peter's Name in the New Testament." In *To Advance the Gospel: New Testament Studies,* 112–120. 2nd ed. Grand Rapids, MI: Eerdmans, 1981.

———. *The Gospel according to Luke I–IX: Introduction, Translation, and Notes.* Anchor Yale Bible 28. New Haven, CT/London: Yale University Press, 2008.

———. *Romans: A New Translation with Introduction and Commentary.* Anchor Yale Bible 33. New Haven, CT/London: Yale University Press, 2008.

Fletcher-Louis, Crispin H. T. "Jesus as the High Priestly Messiah: Part 1." *Journal for the Study of the Historical Jesus* 4 (2006): 155–175.

Forestell, J. Terence. *As Ministers of Christ: The Christological Dimension of Ministry in the New Testament: an Exegetical and Theological Study.* New York: Paulist Press, 1991.

Galot, Jean. *Theology of the Priesthood.* San Francisco: Ignatius Press, 1985.

Gams, Pius Bonifacius. *Series Episcoporum Ecclesiae Catholicae, quotquot innotuerant a beato Petro Apostolo.* Graz, AT: Akademische Druck- u. Verlagsanstalt, 1957.

Gese, Hartmut. *Essays on Biblical Theology.* Minneapolis, MN: Augsburg Publishing House, 1981.

Gesenius, Friedrich Wilhelm. *Gesenius' Hebrew Grammar.* Edited by E. Kautzsch and Sir Arthur Ernest Cowley. 2nd English ed. Oxford, UK: Oxford University Press, 1910.

Ginzberg, Louis, Henrietta Szold, and Paul Radin. *Legends of the Jews.* 2nd ed. Philadelphia, PA: Jewish Publication Society, 2003.

Grabbe, Lester L. "A Priest is without Honor in his Own Prophet: Priests and Other Religious Specialists in the Latter Prophets." In Lester L. Grabbe and Alice Ogden Bellis, *The Priests in the Prophets: The Portrayal of Priests, Prophets and Other Religious Specialists in the Latter Prophets,* 79–97. London: T&T Clark: 2004.

Greenfield, Jonas C., Michael E. Stone, and Ester Eshel. *The Aramaic Levi Document: Edition, Translation, Commentary.* Leiden: Brill, 2004.

Greshake, Gisbert. *The Meaning of Christian Priesthood.* Westminster, MD: Christian Classics, 1989.

Hahn, Scott W. *The Kingdom of God as Liturgical Empire: A Theological Commentary on 1–2 Chronicles.* Grand Rapids, MI: Baker Academic, 2012.

————. *Kinship by Covenant: A Canonical Approach to the Fulfill-ment of God's Saving Promises.* Anchor Yale Bible Reference Library. New Haven, CT/London: Yale University Press, 2009.

Hartley, John E. *Leviticus.* Word Biblical Commentary 4. Dallas, TX: Word, 2002.

Hawthorn, Gerald F. "Philippians, Letter to the." In *Dictionary of Paul and His Letters.* Edited by Gerald F. Hawthorne, Ralph P. Martin, and Daniel G. Reid. Downers Grove, IL: InterVarsity Press, 1993.

Hegesippus. "Fragments from His Five Books of Commentaries on the Acts of the Church." In *Fathers of the Third and Fourth Centuries: The Twelve Patriarchs, Excerpts and Epistles, the Clementina, Apocrypha, Decretals, Memoirs of Edessa and Syriac Documents, Remains of the First Ages,* 762–765. Translated by B. P. Pratten. Edited by Alexander Roberts, James Donaldson, and A. Cleveland Coxe. The Ante-Nicene Fathers 8. Buffalo, NY: Christian Literature Company, 1886.

Heil, John Paul. "Jesus as the Unique High Priest in John." *Catholic Biblical Quarterly* 57 (1995): 729–745.

Herron, Thomas J. *Clement and the Early Church of Rome: On the Dating of Clement's First Epistle to the Corinthians.* Edited by Scott Hahn. Steubenville, OH: Emmaus Road Publishing, 2008.

Hill, Joyce. "Carolingian Perspectives on the Authority of Bede." In Scott DeGregorio, *Innovation and Tradition in the Writings of the Venerable Bede,* 235–236. Morgantown: West Virginia University Press, 2006.

Hirsoh, Emil G. "High Priest." In *The Jewish Encyclopedia: A De-scriptive Record of the History, Religion, Literature, and Customs of the Jewish People from the Earliest Times to the Present Day.* Vol. 6, 389–393. Edited by Isidore Singer. New York/London: Funk & Wagnalls, 1906.

Holder, Arthur G. "Bede and the Tradition of Patristic Exegesis." *Anglican Theological Review* 72 (1990): 399–411.

Holmes, Michael William. *The Apostolic Fathers: Greek Texts and English Translations.* Updated ed. Grand Rapids, MI: Baker Books, 1999.

Holtz, T. "αἰών." In *Exegetical Dictionary of the New Testament.* Vol. 1, 44–46. Edited by Horst Robert Balz and Gerhard Schneider. Grand Rapids, MI: Eerdmans, 1990.

Horton, Fred L. *The Melchizedek Tradition*. Cambridge, UK/New York: Cambridge University Press, 1976.

Hoskins, Paul M. *Jesus as the Fulfillment of the Temple in the Gospel of John*. Eugene, OR: Wipf and Stock Publishers, 2007.

International Commission on English in the Liturgy. *Rite of Baptism for Children: Approved for Use in the Dioceses of the United States of America*. New York: Catholic Book Publishers, 1977.

Irenaeus of Lyons. *Adversus haereses*. In *The Apostolic Fathers with Justin Martyr and Irenaeus*. Edited by Alexander Roberts, James Donaldson, and A. Cleveland Coxe. The Ante-Nicene Fathers 1. Buffalo, NY: Christian Literature Company, 1885.

Jeffers, James S. *The Greco-Roman World of the New Testament Era: Exploring the Background of Early Christianity*. Downers Grove, IL: InterVarsity Press 1999.

Jenson, Philip Peter. *Graded Holiness: A Key to the Priestly Conception of the World*. Journal for the Study of the Old Testament Supplement Series 106. Sheffield, UK: Sheffield Academic Press, 1992.

Jeremias, Joachim. *The Eucharistic Words of Jesus*. Translated by John Bowden. London: SCM, 1966.

Jerome, *Adversus Helvidium*. In *St. Jerome: Letters and Select Works*. Translated by W. H. Fremantle, G. Lewis, and W. G. Martley. Edited by Philip Schaff and Henry Wace. A Select Library of the Nicene and Post-Nicene Fathers of the Christian Church, 2nd ser., vol. 6. New York: Christian Literature Company, 1893.

John Paul II, Pope. *Priesthood in the Third Millennium: Addresses of Pope John Paul II 1993*. Compiled by James P Socias. Princeton, NJ/Chicago: Scepter Publishers and Midwest Theological Forum, 1994.

Johnson, Luke Timothy. *The Acts of the Apostles*. Edited by Daniel J. Harrington. Sacra Pagina Series 5. Collegeville, MN: The Liturgical Press, 1992.

Johnson, Michael D. *The Purpose of Biblical Genealogies: With Special Reference to the Setting of the Genealogies of Jesus*. London: Cambridge University Press, 1969.

Josephus, Flavius. *Antiquitates Judaicae*. In *The Works of Josephus: Complete and Unabridged*. Translated by William Wiston. Peabody, MA: Hendrickson, 1987.

Just, Arthur A. *Luke*. Ancient Christian Commentary on Scripture, New Testament 3. Downers Grove, IL: InterVarsity Press, 2005.

Keener, Craig S. *Acts: An Exegetical Commentary.* Vol. 2, *3:1–14:28.* Grand Rapids, MI: Baker Academic, 2013.

———. *The Gospel of John: A Commentary.* Vol. 1. Grand Rapids, MI: Baker Academic, 2012.

———. *The Gospel of Matthew: A Socio-Rhetorical Commentary.* Grand Rapids, MI/Cambridge, UK: Eerdmans, 2009.

Kerr, Alan. *The Temple of Jesus' Body: The Temple Theme in the Gospel of John.* Journal for the Study of the New Testament Supplement Series 220. London/New York: Sheffield Academic Press, 2002.

Kistemaker, Simon J., and William Hendriksen. *Exposition of the Book of Revelation.* New Testament Commentary 20. Grand Rapids, MI: Baker Book House, 2001.

Kiuchi, N. *Purification Offering in the Priestly Literature: Its Meaning and Function.* Sheffield, UK: Sheffield Academic Press, 1987.

Kloppenburg, Bonaventure. *The Priest: Living Instrument and Minister of Christ, The Eternal Priest.* Chicago: Franciscan Herald Press, 1974.

Koester, Craig R. *Hebrews: a New Translation with Introduction and Commentary.* Anchor Yale Bible 36. New Haven, CT/London: Yale University Press, 2008.

Köstenberger, Andreas J. *John.* Baker Exegetical Commentary on the New Testament. Grand Rapids, MI: Baker Academic, 2004.

Lagrange, Marie-Joseph. Évangile selon Saint Jean. Paris: J. Gabalda, 1925.

Lane, Thomas J. "The Jewish Temple is Transfigured in Christ and the Temple Liturgies are Transfigured in the Sacraments." *Antiphon 19 (2015): 14–28.*

———. *Luke and the Gentile Mission: Gospel Anticipates Acts.* European University Studies Series XXIII/571. Frankfurt am Main: Peter Lang Press, 1996.

Lane, William L. *Hebrews 1–8.* Word Biblical Commentary 47A. Dallas, TX: Word, 1998.

Lauterbach, J. Z. "Ordination." In *The Jewish Encyclopedia: A Descriptive Record of the History, Religion, Literature, and Customs of the Jewish People from the Earliest Times to the Present Day.* Vol. 9, 428–430. Edited by Isidore Singer. 12 vols. New York/London: Funk & Wagnalls, 1901–1906.

Levine, Baruch A. *Leviticus.* The JPS Torah Commentary. Philadelphia, PA: Jewish Publication Society, 1989.

Limbeck, M. "Ἰσκαριώθ." In *Exegetical Dictionary of the New Testament*. Vol. 2, 200–201. Edited by Horst Robert Balz and Gerhard Schneider. Grand Rapids, MI: Eerdmans, 1990.

Lohse, Eduard. "χείρ." In *Theological Dictionary of the New Testament*. Vol. 9, 424–434. Edited by Gerhard Kittel, Geoffrey W. Bromiley, and Gerhard Friedrich. Grand Rapids, MI: Eerdmans, 1964.

Marcus, Joel. *Mark 1–8: A New Translation with Introduction and Commentary*. Anchor Yale Bible 27. New Haven, CT/London: Yale University Press, 2008.

Martínez, Florentino García, and Eibert J. C. Tigchelaar. *The Dead Sea Scrolls Study Edition (Translations)*. Leiden/New York: Brill, 1997–1998.

McHenry, Stephen P. "Three Significant Moments in the Theological Development of the Sacramental Character of Orders: Its Origin, Standardization, and New Direction in Augustine, Aquinas, and Congar." PhD diss., Fordham University, 1983.

Meier, John P. "The Circle of the Twelve: Did It Exist During Jesus' Public Ministry?" *Journal of Biblical Literature* 116 (1997): 635–672.

———. *A Marginal Jew, Rethinking the Historical Jesus.*Vol. 3, *Companions and Competitors*. New Haven, CT/London: Yale University Press, 2001.

Mekkattukunnel, Andrews G. *The Priestly Blessing of the Risen Christ: An Exegetico-Theological Analysis of Luke 24, 50–53*. European University Studies XXIII/714. Bern, CH: Peter Lang, 2001.

Merkle, Benjamin L. *The Elder and Overseer: One Office in the Early Church*. New York: Peter Lang, 2003.

Metzger, Bruce Manning. *A Textual Commentary on the Greek New Testament: Companion Volume to the United Bible Societies' Greek New Testament (4th Rev. Ed.)*. 2nd ed. London/New York: United Bible Societies, 1994.

Milgrom, Jacob. *Leviticus 1–16: A New Translation with Introduction and Commentary*. Anchor Yale Bible Commentary 3. New Haven, CT/London: Yale University Press, 2008.

———. *Leviticus 23–27: A New Translation with Introduction and Commentary*. Anchor Yale Bible 3B. New Haven, CT/London: Yale University Press, 2008.

———. *Numbers*. The JPS Torah Commentary. Philadelphia, PA: Jewish Publication Society, 1990.

Montague, George T. *First and Second Timothy, Titus*. Edited by Peter S. Williamson and Mary Healy. Catholic Commentary on Sacred Scripture. Grand Rapids, MI: Baker Academic, 2008.

———. *First Corinthians*. Catholic Commentary on Sacred Scripture. Grand Rapids, MI: Baker Academic, 2011.

Mounce, William D. *Pastoral Epistles*. Word Biblical Commentary 46. Dallas, TX: Word, 2000.

Munzer, K., and C. Brown. "Remain." In *New International Dictionary of New Testament Theology*. Vol. 3, 223–230. Edited by Lothar Coenen, Erich Beyreuther, and Hans Bietenhard. Grand Rapids, MI: Zondervan Publishing House, 1986.

Murphy-O'Connor, Jerome. "The Essenes and their History." *Revue Biblique* 81 (1974): 215–244.

Neusner, Jacob. *Judaism and Scripture: The Evidence of Leviticus Rabbah*. Chicago: University of Chicago, 1986.

———. *The Mishnah: A New Translation*. New Haven, CT: Yale University Press, 1988.

———. "Money-Changers in the Temple: the Mishnah's Explanation." *New Testament Studies* 35 (1989): 287–290.

———. *The Babylonian Talmud: A Translation and Commentary*. Peabody, MA: Hendrickson Publishers, 2011.

———. *The Jerusalem Talmud: A Translation and Commentary*. Peabody, MA: Hendrickson Publishers, 2008.

———. "Sacrifice and Temple in Rabbinic Judaism." In *The Encyclopedia of Judaism*. Edited by Alan J. Avery-Peck, and William Scott Green. Vol. 3, 1290–1302. Leiden/Boston/Köln: Brill, 2000.

Newman, John Henry. *Parochial and Plain Sermons*. Vol. 6. London/Oxford/Cambridge, UK: Rivingtons, 1868.

Nichols, Aidan. *Holy Order: The Apostolic Ministry from the New Testament to the Second Vatican Council*. Dublin: Veritas Publications, 1990.

Niederwimmer, Kurt and Harold W. Attridge. *The Didache: A Commentary*. Hermeneia—a Critical and Historical Commentary on the Bible. Minneapolis, MN: Fortress Press, 1998.

Noth, Martin. *A History of Pentateuchal Traditions*. Englewood Cliffs, NJ: Prentice-Hall, 1972.

O'Collins, Gerald and Michael Keenan Jones. *Jesus Our Priest: A Christian Approach to the Priesthood of Christ.* Oxford, UK: Oxford University Press, 2010.

Ó Fearghail, Fearghus. "Sir 50,5–21: Yom Kippur or The Daily Whole-Offering?" *Biblica* 59 (1978): 301–316.

Osborn, Noel D., and Howard Hatton. *A Handbook on Exodus.* UBS Handbook Series/Helps for Translators. New York: United Bible Societies, 1999.

Osborne, Grant R. *Matthew.* Zondervan Exegetical Commentary on the New Testament 1. Grand Rapids, MI: Zondervan, 2010.

Oswalt, John N. *The Book of Isaiah, Chapters 40–66.* The New International Commentary on the Old Testament. Grand Rapids, MI: Eerdmans, 1998.

Pedersen, Johannes. *Israel: Its Life and Culture.* London: Oxford University Press, 1926.

Pesch, Rudolf. *Die biblischen Grundlagen des Primats.* Freiburg: Herder, 2001.

———. "πέτρα." In *Exegetical Dictionary of the New Testament.* Edited by Horst Robert Balz and Gerhard Schneider. Vol. 3, 80–81. Grand Rapids, MI: Eerdmans, 1990.

Pitre, Brant. "Jesus, the New Temple, and the New Priesthood." *Letter & Spirit* 4, *Temple and Contemplation: God's Presence in the Cosmos, Church, and Human Heart* (2008): 47–83.

Porter, Stanley E. *The Paul of Acts.* Wissenschaftliche Untersuchungen zum Neuen Testament 115. Tübingen: Mohr Siebeck, 1999.

Prosperi, Paolo. "Novum in Vetere Latet. Vetus in Novo Patet: Towards a Renewal of Typological Exegesis." *Communio: International Catholic Review* 37 (2010): 389–424.

Ratzinger, Joseph. *Behold The Pierced One: An Approach to a Spiritual Christology.* Translated by Graham Harrison. San Francisco: Ignatius Press, 1986.

———. *Called to Communion: Understanding the Church Today.* Translated by Adrian Walker. San Francisco: Ignatius Press, 1996.

———. *Daughter Zion: Meditations on the Church's Marian Belief.* Translated by John M. McDermott. San Francisco: Ignatius Press, 1983.

———. "Primacy, Episcopacy, and Apostolic Succession." In Karl Rahner and Joseph Ratzinger, *The Episcopate and the Primacy,* 37–63. New York: Herder and Herder, 1962.

————. *The Feast of Faith: Approaches to a Theology of the Liturgy.* Translated by Graham Harrison. San Francisco: Ignatius Press, 1986.

————. *The God of Jesus Christ: Meditations on the Triune God.* Translated by Brian McNeil. San Francisco: Ignatius Press, 2008.

————. *Introduction to Christianity.* Translated by J. R. Foster. Revised ed. San Francisco: Ignatius Press, 2004

————. *Jesus of Nazareth: From the Baptism in the Jordan to the Transfiguration.* New York: Doubleday, 2007.

————. *Jesus of Nazareth. Holy Week: From the Entrance into Jerusalem to the Resurrection.* San Francisco: Ignatius Press, 2011.

————. *Many Religions—One Covenant: Israel, the Church, and the World.* Translated by Graham Harrison. San Francisco: Ignatius Press, 1999.

————. *Pilgrim Fellowship of Faith: The Church as Communion.* Translated by Henry Taylor. Edited by Stephan Otto Horn and Vinzenz Pfnür. San Francisco: Ignatius Press, 2005.

————. *Principles of Catholic Theology: Building Stones for a Fundamental Theology.* Translated by Mary Frances McCarthy. San Francisco: Ignatius Press, 1987.

Ritz, Hans-Joachim. "βούλομαι." In *Exegetical Dictionary of the New Testament.* Vol. 1, 225–226. Edited by Horst Robert Balz and Gerhard Schneider. Grand Rapids, MI: Eerdmans, 1990.

Sacchi, Paolo. *Jewish Apocalyptic and its History.* Translated by William J. Short. Journal for the Study of the Pseudigrapha Supplement Series 20. Sheffield, UK: Sheffield Academic Press, 1990.

Sarna, Nahum M. *Exodus,* The JPS Torah Commentary. Philadelphia, PA: Jewish Publication Society, 1991.

Sheehan, John F. X. "Melchisedech in Christian Consciousness." *Science Ecclésiastiques* 18 (1966): 127–138.

Spicq, Ceslas. *L'Épître aux Hébreux.* Études bibliques. Paris: Gabalda, 1952–1953.

Stewart-Sykes, Alistair. *The Original Bishops: Office and Order in the First Christian Communities.* Grand Rapids, MI: Baker Academic, 2014.

Srawley, J. H. *The Epistles of St. Ignatius, Bishop of Antioch.* Revised 2nd ed. Early Church Classics 2. London/Brighton, UK: SPCK, 1910.

Stein, Robert H. *Mark*. Baker Exegetical Commentary on the New Testament. Grand Rapids, MI: Baker Academic, 2008.

Strack, Hermann Leberecht, and Paul Billerbeck. *Kommentar zum Neuen Testament aus Talmud und Midrasch*. Vol. 3. Munich: C. H. Beck, 1978.

Stuart, Douglas K. *Exodus*. The New American Commentary 2. Nashville, TN: Broadman & Holman Publishers, 2007.

Tertullian. *De praescriptione haereticorum*. In *Latin Christianity: Its Founder, Tertullian*. Translated by Peter Holmes. Edited by Alexander Roberts, James Donaldson, and A. Cleveland Coxe. The Ante-Nicene Fathers 3. Buffalo, NY: Christian Literature Company, 1885.

Tigay, Jeffrey H. *Deuteronomy*. The JPS Torah Commentary. Philadelphia, PA: Jewish Publication Society, 1996.

Tipei, John Fleter. *The Laying on of Hands in the New Testament: Its Significance, Techniques, and Effects*. Lanham, MD: University Press of America, 2009.

Torrell, Jean-Pierre. *A Priestly People: Baptismal Priesthood and Priestly Ministry*. Mahwah, NJ: Paulist Press, 2013.

Turner, David L. *Matthew*. Baker Exegetical Commentary on the New Testament. Grand Rapids, MI: Baker Academic, 2008.

Universidad de Navarra. *Saint Paul's Letters to the Thessalonians, and Pastoral Letters*. The Navarre Bible. Dublin/New York: Four Courts Press/Scepter Publishing, 2005.

Van Dam, C. "Urim and Thummim." In *The International Standard Bible Encyclopedia*. Vol. 4, 957–959. Revised and edited by Geoffrey W. Bromiley. Grand Rapids, MI: Eerdmans, 1988.

Vanderkam, James C. "2 Maccabees 6, 7A and Calendrical Change in Jerusalem." *Journal for the Study of Judaism in the Persian, Hellenistic and Roman Period* 12 (1981): 52–74.

Vanhoye, Albert, Ugo Vanni, and Franco Manzi. *Il sacerdozio della nuova alleanza*. Milan, IT: Àncora, 1999.

Vanhoye, Albert. *Old Testament Priests and the New Priest according to the New Testament*. Persham, MA: St. Bedes' Publications, 1986.

Vanni, Ugo. *Il Sacerdozio nell'Apocalisse e nella Prima Lettera di Pietro: Un impegno che abbracia tutta la vita del Cristiano in vista del regno di Dio*. Rome: AdP, 2009.

Vermes, Geza. *Scrolls, Scriptures, and Early Christianity*. Library of Second Temple Studies 56. London/New York: T&T Clark, 2005.

Weinfeld, Moshe. *Deuteronomy 1–11: A New Translation With Introduction and Commentary.* Anchor Yale Bible 5, New Haven, CT/London: Yale University Press, 2008.

Westermann, Ernst Jenni and Claus. *Theological Lexicon of the Old Testament.* Peabody, MA: Hendrickson Publishers, 1997.

Westgaard, Joshua A. "Bede and the Continent in the Carolingian Age and Beyond." In Scott DeGregorio, *The Cambridge Companion to Bede,* 201–215. Cambridge, UK: Cambridge University Press, 2010.

Wicks, Jared. *Doing Theology.* Mahwah, NJ: Paulist Press, 2009.

Wigoder, Geoffrey, Fred Skolnik, and Shmuel Himelstein. *The New Encyclopedia of Judaism.* New York: New York University Press, 2002.

Wildberger, Hans. *Isaiah 13–27.* A Continental Commentary. Minneapolis, MN: Fortress Press, 1997.

Willamson, H. G. M. *Ezra-Nehemiah,* Word Biblical Commentary 16. Dallas, TX: Word, 2002.

Wrede, William. *Das Messiasgeheimnis in den Evangelien: zugleich ein Beitrag zum Verständnis des Markusevangeliums.* Göttingen: Vandenhoeck & Ruprecht, 1901.

Wuerl, Donald W. *The Catholic Priesthood Today.* Chicago: Franciscan Herald Press, 1976.

BIBLICAL INDEX

Genesis

2:7 115
3:19 205
4:4 4
5:32 57
8:20 4
9:26 . . . . 206n2
9:26–27 205
10. 102
11. 205
11:10–32 205
11:11 205
13:8 214
14:14 214
14:18 . . . . 56, 68, 205
14:18–20 56
14:19 . . . . 206n2
14:19–20 206
15:5 96
17:5 . . . . 148, 218
17:8 96
17:15 . . . . 148, 218
22:2 4
22:13 4
24:1 57
26:3–4 96
27:4 3
27:5–38 3
27:18–29 3
27:30–38 4
28. . . . . 4n6
28:13–14 96
29:11–15 214
29:33 217

31:54 4
32:28 . . . . 148, 218
35:10 . . . . 148, 218
46:1 4
48 205
48:1 56–57
48:17–20 . . . . 4n6
48:18 172
48–49 . . . . 81n10
49:3–4 . . . . 3, 4n6
49:5–7 . . . . 11n25

Exodus

1:2 217
13:2 . . . . 9, 110, 215
16:32–34 62
18:25 77
19:5–6 . . . . 12, 192
19:6 . . . . xvii, xx, 13,
                    13n27, 189–193, 196
19:22, 24 4
20:24 17
24:8 38
25–27 224
25–31. . . . . 5, 8
25:17–21 47
25:22 47
27:20 17
27:20–21 27
27:21 17
28. . . . . 6, 207
28:1 . . . . 5, 207
28:4, 39, 40 90
28:5–14 207

28:15–29 207
28:30 14
28:31–35 207
28:32 42
28:36 110
28:36–38 207
28:40 207
28:41 . . . . 110, 209
28:42 207
28–29 5
29. 58
29:4 109
29:5 90
29:5–6 207
29:7 . . . . 6, 27
29:8–9 208
29:9 . . . . 13, 23, 90 209
29:9, 29, 35 . . . . 55, 209
29:18 34
29:20 208
29:21 . . . . 6, 27, 110
29:22, 26, 27 58
29:35 208
29:36 208
29:38–42 17
29:42 34
30:7 . . . . 62n48
30:16 34
30:17–21 10
30:22–33 207
30:26–30 208
30:30 110
32:26 8
32:28 8
32:29 . . . . 8, 209
36–38 224
39:27 90
39:29 90
40 224
40:15 . . . . 13, 24

Leviticus
1:1–5 15
1:4 16
1:14–15 15
3:1–2, 7–8, 12–13 15
3:2, 8, 13 16
4:1–7 15
4:3 10
4:4, 15, 24, 29, 33 16
4:13–18, 22–25,
    27–30, 32–34 15
5:7–10 15
6:12 16
6–7 12
7:11–15 22
7:12 22
8 5
8:4 88
8:6 109
8:7 90
8:7–9 207
8:8 14
8:10–12 208
8:12 . . . . 6, 110
8:13 . . . . 90, 208
8:14, 18, 22 . . . . 16n32
8:23–24 208
8:30 . . . . 6, 110
8:33 209
8:33–36 208
9 208
9:22 . . . . 17, 43
10. 10
10:1–2 . . . . 7n15, 10
10:8–9 10
10:10 17
10:11 15
11. 17
11–15. 10
13–15. 17

15:16–18 10
16. 63
16:4 90
16:6 37
16:6–11 37
16:11–14 44
16:12–14 47
16:15–16 37
16:21 . . . . 16, 172
16:32 209
17:11 16
21:1–9 10
21:10 . . . . 6, 208–209
21:10–15 10
21:16–24 10
21–22. 10
22:4 10
22:4–9 10
22:15 19
23. 16
24:5–9. 62
24:14 172
27. 12

Numbers
3:3 209
3:5–10 9
3:11, 40–51 . . . . 5, 9
3:11–13 3
3:13 9
3:14–17 9
4. . . . . 9n23
4:3 9
4:5–15. 9
4:15 . . . . 11, 27
4:20 9
6:24–26 17
6:27 17
8:3, 13, 19 9
8:5–22 9

8:10 172
8:11, 13 172
8:16 . . . . 5, 9
11. . . . . 102, 105
11:14 102
11:16–17 . . . . . . 26, 102, 130, 187
11:16–25 174
11:24–25 . . . . 102, 130, 177
11:26 102
12:7 49
13:16 . . . . 148, 218
16. 13
16:8–10 13
17. 62
18:2–6 9
18:3 9
18:8–19 . . . . 12, 156
18:20 . . . . 11, 108
18:21 12
18:25–28 12
19. 65
20:25–29 7
25:6–13 221
25:10–13 24
27:15–23 138
27:18 172
27:19–20 173
27:21 14
27:23 172
28:6 34
35:1–8 11
35:25 6

Deuteronomy
7:6 12
10:6 7
10:8 . . . . 9, 17
10:8–9 . . . . 9, 11
10:9 108
12:12 108

14:2, 21 12
14:27, 29 108
15:19 110
18:1–2 . . . . 12, 108
18:1–8 11
18:3 156
18:3–5 12
18:4 12
18:18 211
19:15 168
21:5 17
26:18 12
31:9–11 15
31:25 9
33. 81n10
33:8 14
33:8–10 12
33:8–11 9
33:10 . . . . 15, 34
34:6 214
34:9 . . . . 130, 172, 173, 177,
                239–240, 245

Joshua
3. 11
3:3 11
6:4, 8, 9, 13, 16 11
8:33 11
13:14 11
15:25 221
18:7 11
21. 11
21:13–19 11
23–24 . . . . 83n10
24:33 7

Judges
17:10 3
20:28 7

1 Samuel
1–2. . . . . 103n48
2:35 . . . . 24n55
6:15 9
12:6 76
13:9 4
13:13 4
14:41 14
22:17–19 14
23:9–12 14
28:6 14
30:7–8 14

2 Samuel
6:6–7 11
6:17 4
6:18 . . . . 17n36
6:23 214
7. 25, 36
7:9, 13–16 25
7:12–14 52
15:24 9

1 Kings
2:35 7
4:6 95
8:14, 55 . . . . 17n36
9:25 4
11:29–33 40
12:31–32 77
12:32 14
13:34 14
16:9 95
17:21 116
18. 221
18:3 95

2 Kings
10:5 95
15:5 95

1 Chronicles

5:29–34 7
5:29–41 . . . . 7, 176
5:30 7
6:3–8 7
6:3–15 . . . . 7, 176
6:4 7
6:35–38 7
6:50–53 7
9:11 7
13:9–10 11
15:2, 12, 15 9
15:24 11
16:4 9
16:6 11
23:13 17
24:1–19 6

2 Chronicles

5:4 9
5:12 11
7:6 11
13:11 17
13:12, 14 11
15:3 15
29:15–16 11
29:26 11
35:3 9

Ezra

2:61–62 57
2:63 14
2:69 90
3:2 11
7:1–5 7

Nehemiah

7:63–64 57
7:65 14
7:69 90

7:70 90
11:10–11 7

1 Maccabees

2:17–28 221
4:52–59 33
13:42 49

2 Maccabees

2:17 . . . . 13, 189
3:4 . . . . 8n19
4:7 7
4:13–15 19
4:23–29 8
4:30–38 8

Psalms

2 51–52
2:6 51–52
2:7 51–52
16 11
16:5 11
20:3 34
40:6–7 66
51:19 34
108:8 136–137
109:8 136
110 . . . . 35–36, 52
110:1 . . . . 35–36, 43, 52, 66
110:4 . . . . 36, 52, 59, 61
115:14–15 18
118:22 190
121:7–8 18
128:5 18
134:3 18

Wisdom of Solomon

9:8 60
15:11 115

Sirach/Ecclesiasticus
33:3 14
45:7 24
45:15 24
45:23–24 24
50:1 27
50:20–21 43

Isaiah
1:6 100
11:2–3 . . . . 53n37
22. 89, 95
22:15–19 89
22:20–21 89
22:21 90–91
22:22 . . . . 89–90, 95
22:25 95
28:7 18
43:20 192
43:21 192
51:1–2 96
52:7 212
52:13–53:12. 39
53:11, 12 39
56. 32
56:6 32
56:6–7 . . . . 21, 32
60–62 13
61:6 . . . . 13, 13n27, 189–190
61:7 13

Jeremiah
1:1 19
2:3 12
2:8 19
4:9 19
5:31 19
6:13 19
7. 19
7:30 19

8:10 19
13:13 19
14:18 19
20:1–2 19
23:11 19
26:8, 11 19
31:31–34 . . . . 61, 70
31:33–34 67
32:32 19
32:40 61
33:17 24
33:18 24–25
34:19 19

Ezekiel
1:3 19
7:26 19
16:60 61
22:26 . . . . 15, 19
34:25 61
37:9 116
37:26 61
44:23 15
44:28 11

Daniel
7:13 36
9:26 8
11:22 8

Hosea
4:4–10 18

Amos
7:14–15 6

Micah
3:9–11 19

Zephaniah
3:1–4 19
3:4 19

Malachi

1:6–14 19
1:6–2:9 20
1:11 . . . . 20, 20n41
2:1–9 19
2:8 19
3:1 . . . . 20, 171
3:1–4 20
3:3–4 20

Matthew

1:1 30
1:25 214–215
2 . . . . 161n50
3:9 87
4:1, 3 46
4:20 75
4:18–22 74
4:22 75
7:24 87
9:9 74
9:17 131
9:37–38 104
10:1 . . . . 79–80, 83
10:1–2, 5 82
10:1–4 . . . . 79, 98
10:2 . . . . 79, 89
10:2–4 . . . . 80, 83, 217
10:4 119
10:5 117
10:5–6 100
10:5–15 . . . . 98, 100
10:14 101
10:15 101
10:40 . . . . 113, 85
10:40–42 84
11:1 82
11:10 . . . . 20, 171
11:19 10
12:6 31–32
13:11 77
13:55 . . . . 215, 220
15:1–2 108
16 94
16:16 86–87
16:16–19 . . . . 91n34
16:17–19 96
16:18 . . . . . 86–91, 90n31, 96, 218
16:18–19 . . . . 86, 90–91, 94
16:19 90
16:20 77
16:21 . . . . 38n18, 130
17:1 . . . . 89, 218
17:22–23 . . . . 38n18
18 91
18:17 88
19:28 . . . . 82, 119
20:17 82
20:18–19 . . . . 38n18
20:25–27 108
21:12 35
21:13 32
22:41–45 35
22:44 52
23:2 95
26:14, 20, 47 82
26:20 107
26:26–28 35
26:28 39
26:37 . . . . 89, 218
26:47 130
26:57 130
26:61 31
26:64 36
26:73 120
27:1 130
27:51 . . . . 42, 50
27:56 213
28:16–20 . . . . 117, 179

28:18–20 100
28:19 . . . . .115, 117, 118n77

Mark
1–8 . . . . .99n45
1:2 20
1:13 46
1:16–20 . . . . 74, 76
1:17 74
1:17, 20 76
1:18 74
1:20 75
1:25–26, 34, 39 99
2:13–14 74
2:14 219
2:22 131
3. 76
3:10 99
3:13 . . . . 75–76, 79–80
3:13–14 79
3:13–19 . . . . 75–76, 86
3:14 . . . . xviii, 76–79, 81–82, 109
3:14–19 85
3:15 . . . . 78, 80
3:16 218
3:16–18 217
3:16–19 . . . . 78, 83
3:17 219
3:19 119
3:21 215
3:22 99
3:31–32 213
4:10 82
4:11 77
5:34 99
5:37 . . . . 89, 218
6 98
6:3 . . . . 213, 215
6:5 99

6:7 . . . . 78, 82
6:7–13 98–99
6:8–9 99
6:11 99
6:13 99
6:14–29 98
6:30 . . . . 77, 79, 98
7:3 108
8:29 88
8:30 77
8:31 . . . . 38n18, 130
9:2 . . . . 89, 218
9:14–29 140
9:31 . . . . 38n18
9:35 82
9:37 99
9:38–40 140
9:41 85
10:32 82
10:33–34 . . . . 38n18
10:42–45 108
11:11 82
11:15 35
11:17 32
12:35–37 35
12:36 52
14:10, 17, 20, 43 82
14:17–18 107
14:22–24 35
14:24 39
14:33 . . . . 89, 218
14:40 92
14:43 130
14:53 130
14:58 31
14:62 36–37
15:1 130
15:38 . . . . 42, 50
15:40 . . . . 213, 219–220

16:7 117
16:8 117
16:9–20 116
16:14 117
16:14–16 . . . . 116, 179
16:15 . . . . 115, 117
16:16 . . . . .117, 118n77
16:17–18 117

Luke
1:9 6
1:23 148
1:32 30
1:32–33 24
2:3–4 30
2:7 214
2:11 161
4:1 139
4:2 46
5:17–26 121
5:27–28 74
5:29–6:11 121
5:38 131
6:10 . . . . 105n51
6:12 79
6:12–13 . . . . 79, 99, 103
6:12–16 78
6:13 . . . . .xviii, 76, 79, 81–82,
100, 107
6:14 218
6:14–16 . . . . 79, 83, 217
6:16 119
6:17–19 121
7:1–10 121
7:11–17 121
7:24 171
7:27 . . . . 20, 171
7:34 10
7:36–50 122
8:1 82

8:10 77
8:19–20 213
8:51 . . . . 89, 218
9 . . . . 98, 102
9:1–2 103
9:1–6 . . . . 98, 100–101
9:1, 12 82
9:7–9 . . . . 98, 101
9:10 . . . . 79, 98, 101
9:20 88
9:21 77
9:22 . . . . 38n18, 130
9:28 . . . . 89, 218
9:38 80
9:44 . . . . 38n18
9:48 85
9:49–50 140
9:51 92
9:52 171
9:54 219
10 . . . . .xix, 98, 102, 124, 132
10:1 . . . . 101, 103–104
10:1–12 101
10:1, 17 101
10:1–20 101
10:2 104
10:9 104
10:13–16 101
10:16 113
10:17 104
10:17–20 101
10:19 104
10:34 100
11:38 108
15:1 10
17:5 79
17:25 . . . . 38n18
18:31 82
18:32–33 . . . . 38n18

19:46 32
20:41–44 35
20:42–43 52
22 94
22:3 82
22:14 . . . . 79, 107
22:19 . . . . xix, 114–115, 200
22:19–20 39
22:25–27 108
22:30 . . . . 82, 119
22:31–32 . . . . 91–92, 96
22:32 . . . . 86, 91–94
22:47 82
22:52 130
22:54–62 92
22:67–69 36
23:2 139
23:34 139
23:45 50
23:46 139
24:1 120
24:10 . . . . 79, 120
24:13, 18 105
24:15–16 55
24:31, 36 55
24:33 117
24:36–49 117
24:46 118
24:47 118
24:48 118
24:49 118
24:50–51 43
24:50–53 . . . . 43n28

John
1:14 . . . . 111, 127
1:14, 17 127
1:17 111
1:35–51 74
1:41–42 218

1:42 218
1:43 219
1:45 105
1:45–51 219
2:12 213
2:15 35
2:19 31
2:19, 21 xviii
2:21 31
3:5 192
3:14–15 . . . . 38n18
3:31 42
4:21–23 33
4:23 . . . . xix, 74
4:23–24 . . . . 112, 115
4:38 113
6 114
6:13 81
6:15 192
6:51c 35
6:66 81
6:66–71 81
6:67 . . . . 81, 107
6:67, 70, 71 82
6:70 . . . . 79, 81, 107
6:71 81
7:1–10 213
7:3–4 215
7:14 33
7:37 33
8:12 33
9 171
9:1–7 33
9:5 33
9:28 95
10:11 . . . . 38n18, 113
10:15 94
10:17 108
10:22–39 33
10:36 . . . . 33, 110, 112–113

11:16 219
11:51 113
12-21. . . . . 108n58
12:24 . . . . 38n18
13. . . . . .35, 81, 107-108
13-17. 78
13:2, 26, 29 107
13:5, 22, 23, 35 107
13:6, 8, 9, 24, 36, 37 107
13:7 109
13:8 108
13:13-15 108
13:18 107
13:20 . . . . 85, 99
13:23-24 94
14:5 107
14:6 . . . . xv, 111
14:8, 9 107
14:22 107
15:4-7 81
15:8 107
15:13 113
15:15 . . . . 78, 109
15:16 . . . . 81, 111
15:16, 19 107
16:6 127
16:13 112
16:17, 29 107
17. . . .xviii, 30, 37-38, 38n15, 40,
42-43, 107, 109
17:1-5 37
17:6, 26 38
17:6-19 37
17:11 . . . . 38, 109
17:12 . . . . 38, 107
17:14 109
17:14, 16 110
17:17 . . . xv, xix, 74, 90, 109-113,
117, 127, 146, 152, 161, 200
17:17-19 . . 77, 109, 114-115, 200

17:18 . . . . 110, 113, 200
17:19 . . . . .113-114, 179, 200
17:20-26 37
18:16 94
18:18 93
18:33, 36 192
19:11 42
19:23 40-42
19:24 42
19:25 220
19:25-27 213
20 200
20:4-8. 94
20:14-15 55
20:19 115
20:19-23 . . . . 115, 179
20:19, 26 55
20:21 . . . . 115, 117
20:21-22 113
20:21-23 117
20:22 115
20:22-23 157
20:23 . . . . 90n31, 115-116
20:24 . . . . 81-82, 115, 219
20:25 219
20:28 219
20:30-31 . . . . 129n3
21. 94
21:2 . . . . 105, 219
21:7 94
21:9 93
21:15-17 . . . . . 86, 93-94, 96, 122
21:18 94
21:18-19 94

Acts
1. . . . . 118n77, 120
1:1 . . . . 121, 127
1:2, 24 81
1:4 . . . . 118n77

1:5 . . . . 118n77
1:8 . . . . 118n77
1:13 217
1:13–14 . . . . 83, 120
1:14 213
1:15 . . . . 105, 120
1:15–26 . . . . 92, 119
1:20 136
1:21 119
1:21–22 119
1:23 . . . . 105, 220
1:24 103
1:26 . . . . 115, 119–120
2. 120
2:1 120
2:4 120
2:7 120
2:14 120
2:14–36 120
2:17 . . . . 130n4
2:32–36 25,36
2:33 . . . . 50, 134
2:34–35 52
2:36 77
2:37 120
2:41 . . . . 118n77, 120
2:42 120
2:43 120
2:46 162
3–4 121
3:1 162
3:1–10 121
3:6 179
4:1–22 121
4:5, 8, 23 131
4:10 179
4:36 . . . . 105, 131, 150
5:12 121
5:12–16 121

5:17–18 121
5:19–42 121
6. . . . . 138, 140, 188
6–8 140
6:1 137
6:1–6 . . . . 121, 138
6:2 . . . . 82, 86, 138, 140
6:3 . . . . . . 103, 138, 150, 183–184
6:5 138
6:6 . . . . 138, 146, 150, 173
6:7 . . . . 45, 131
6:12 131
6:13 139
7. . . . . 118n77, 139
7:55 139
7:59 139
7:60 139
8–12. . . . . 118n77
8:1, 4 114
8:4–7 144
8:5–7 139
8:14–17 . . . . 144, 173
8:16 139
8:17 . . . . 139, 150
8:18 173
8:18–24 176
8:26–40. 139
8:39 . . . . 139n19
9:1–9 143
9:6. 149
9:17–18 173
9:18 . . . . 143, 146, 149
9:20, 22 143
9:23–24 143
9:26 . . . . 143, 148
9:26–28 146
9:26–30 143
9:27 143
9:28 143

9:29–30 143
9:30 143
9:36–43 121
10. 121
10:44–45 150
11:1–5 150
11:1–18 122
11:19–21 144
11:22–24 144
11:23 144
11:24 144
11:25–26 . . . . 143, 151
11:26 . . . . 149, 149n33
11:27–28 147
11:30 . . . . 132, 145, 149n33
12. 97
12:2 . . . . .119, 218
12:12–17 162
12:17 . . . . 97, 151, 220
13. . . . . 143–144, 146, 149,
            151–152, 173
13–14. 150
13–28 . . . . 118n77
13:1 . . . . 146–148, 206, 149n33
13:1–3 . . . . . xix, 128, 146, 146n31,
      147–148, 150–152 161, 173, 201
13:2 . . .105, 148, 150–151, 160, 173
13:3 . . . . .149–151, 174
13:4 . . . . 150, 173
13:9 . . . . .148, 150, 173, 218
13:33 52
13:46 101
14:4, 14 . . . . 79, 148
14:23 . . . . 133, 136–137, 143,
            151, 162, 173–175
15. . . . . 121, 145, 150, 220
15:1–4 . . . . 144, 150
15:2, 4, 6, 22, 23 132
15:12 150

15:13 . . . . 105, 113
15:19 150
15:22 142
16:4 132
16:10–17 174
16:11–40 163
16:12–40 138
17:1–9 163
18. 164
18:6 101
18:11 164
18:19–21 . . . . 165, 178
18:22 145
18:24–26 178
19. 134
19:1–6 173
19:1–20 178
19:1–20:1 165
19:10 165
20 . . . . 133–134, 136, 177–178
20:4 164
20:5–15 174
20:16 165
20:17 . . . . 133, 136, 162, 165
20:17, 28 167
20:18–35 177
20:28 . . . . . 133–134, 136, 151, 163,
            165, 177, 178
20:35 . . . . 129n3
20:38 177
21:1–18 174
21:8 139
21:8–14 145
21:15 145
22:17 162
21:18 . . . . 132, 220
21:26 162
23:14 131
24:1 131

25:15 131
27:1–28:16 174

Romans

1:1 . . . . 153, 160
1:3 30
1:3–4 36
1:13 165
1:16 101
3:25 47
5:8 43
6:23 205
8:32 43
11:13 153
12:1 . . . . 191, 196
13:4 141
15:8 141
15:16 . . . . 154, 156, 160
15:26 145
15:27 148
16. 165
16:1 141
16:5 162
16:7 . . . . 141, 165
16:23 162

1 Corinthians

1:1 153
1:10 160
1:16 164
1:17 153
2:1–5 164
3:2 164
3:5 . . . . 138, 158
3:6 164
3:7–9 158
3:9 160
3:10 164
3:11 88
4:1 . . . . 155–156, 160

4:14–15 164
4:15 163
4:16 164
4:17 177–178
5:7 43
7:25 47
9:1 153
9:13–14 . . . . 156, 160
9:14 156
9:16–17 155
11. 39
11:23 138
11:23–25 39
11:23–26 114
11:24 . . . . xix, 114
11:25 39
12:4–6 117
12:28 . . . . 147, 164–165
12:28–29 86
15:3 43
15:3–5 . . . . 117, 149, 153
15:5 . . . . 82, 86, 91
15:5–6 142
15:6 105
15:7 220
15:9 153
15:25 . . . . 192, 214
16:1–3 145
16:15 162
16:15–16 . . . . 141, 164
16:17–18 164
16:19 162

2 Corinthians

1:1 153
2:10 . . . . 157–158, 160
2:17 160
3:4–18 157
3:6 . . . . 138, 157–158
5:10 159

5:18 159
5:20 158–160
6:4 158
8–9 145
8:19 174
9:12 195
11:23 138
11:33 143
13:14 117

Galatians
1:1 153
1:3–4 43
1:12 . . . . 146, 153
1:15 160
1:17 153
1:18–19 143
1:18–24 143
1.19 219–220
1:21 143
2:1 145
2:7–8 160
2:9 149
2:10 145
2:11 151
2:11–14 91
2:20 43
4:21–31 157

Ephesians
1:1 153
2:20 . . . . 88, 147
3:2 155
3:5 147
3:7 158
4:11 . . . . .86, 141, 147, 165, 180
5:2 43
6:20 158–159

Philippians
1:1 . . . . . . 136, 138, 141, 157, 160,
162–163, 167, 181
1:7, 13, 14, 17 163
2:8 54
2:25 . . . . 142, 163
4:18 195

Colossians
1:1 153
1:7 . . . . 141, 165
1:23, 25 158
1:25 155
2:1 165
4:10 214
4:12 . . . . 141, 165
4:15 162
4:17 . . . . 141, 165

1 Thessalonians
1:8–2:12 163
2:6 153
2:7 163
2:11 163
5:12 . . . . 141, 163–164

1 Timothy
1:3 167
1:15 47
1:18 . . . . 151, 176
2:5 179
2:5–6 43
2:7 153
3:1 167
3:1–7 . . . . 134, 136, 167, 169
3:2 . . . . 136, 167
3:2–3 168
3:2–7 169
3:4–5 168
3:4–7 168

3:6 168

3:7 168

3:8 138

3:8–13 . . . . .138, 167, 169

3:10 169

4:6 138

4:14 . . . . .151, 174–176, 178

5:1 . . . . 130n4

5:17 . . . . 164, 167–168

5:17–22 . . . . 134, 167–168

5:19 167–168

5:22 . . . . .168–169, 176, 178

2 Timothy

1:1 153

1:6 . . . . .151, 174, 176, 178

1:11 153

2:8 30

Titus

1. 136

1:1 153

1:5 . . . . .167, 168, 176, 178

1:5–6 167

1:5–9 . . . . 134, 168

1:6 169

1:6–9 168

1:7 . . . . .136, 155, 167, 169

1:7–9 . . . . 136, 167

1:9 167

2:14 43

Philemon

2. 162

Hebrews

1–2. 45

1:4 46

1:5 52

1:13 52

2:1 44

2:2 46

2:10–16 46

2:11–12 46

2:14 . . . . 46, 54

2:17 . . . . 46–50, 62, 69

2:17–18 . . . . 46, 49

2:17–10:18 44

2:18 . . . . 46, 48, 50

3:1 . . . . 49, 69

3:1–6 49

3:1–4:14. 48

3:2 77

3:2, 5 49

3:3–6 49

3:6 49

3:12 44

4:14 . . . . 48–49, 69

4:15 . . . . 46, 49–50, 65, 69

4:16 . . . . 50, 67, 169

4:15–16 . . . . 48–49, 51

4:15–5:10. 48–49

5. 58

5:1 . . . . 51, 53, 55

5:1–4 51

5:1, 4 51

5:1–6 . . . . 52, 55

5:1–10 51

5:2 48

5:4 . . . . 51, 59

5:5 . . . . 51, 52, 54, 70

5:5–6 . . . . 51, 55

5:5–10 51

5:6 . . . . 52, 61, 70

5:7 53

5:7–8 54

5:7–10 53

5:8 53

5:9 . . . . 54–55, 58, 67, 114

5:9–10 63

5:10 . . . . 55, 70, 206

6:1–2 175

6:1–4 175

6:2 . . . . 173, 175

6:4 175

6:6 44

6:19–20 63

6:20 . . . . 67, 70, 206

7 . . . . 52, 55, 60, 68

7:1 56

7:1–3 57

7:1–10 56

7:1–28 206

7:2 56

7:3 56

7:4–10 57

7:11 . . . . 57–58, 70

7:11–19 56–57

7:12 . . . . 58, 61

7:13–14 58

7:14 30

7:15 70

7:16 . . . . 58, 70

7:17 . . . . 59, 70

7:18 59

7:19 59

7:20–21 59

7:20–22 53

7:20–28 . . . . 56, 59

7:21 . . . . 59, 70

7:22 59

7:23 59

7:24 . . . . 59, 70

7:25 59

7:26 70

7:26–27 59

7:26–28 59

7:28 59

8 . . . . 60–61, 65

8–9 60

8:1 . . . . 50, 60, 70

8:1–2 . . . . 47, 58

8:1–6 60

8:2 . . . . 60, 60n47, 64

8:2, 5 70

8:3 . . . . 61, 70, 191

8:4 . . . . 61, 70

8:5 . . . . 60, 64

8:6 . . . . 61, 148

8:7 61

8:7–13 . . . . 45, 60–61

8:8–13 70

8:10–12 . . . . 61, 67

8:13 62

9 47

9:1 62

9:1–5 . . . . 60, 62, 64

9:1–10 62

9:1–28 . . . . 60, 62

9:2 62

9:3 62

9:4 62

9:5 62

9:6 63

9:6–7 63

9:7 63

9:8 63

9:8–9a 63, 64

9:8–10 63

9:9b–10 63

9:10 63

9:11 70

9:11–12 63

9:11–14 65

9:11–28 63

9:12 . . . . 60n47, 64–66

9:13 65

9:14 65–66

9:15 65
9:15–22 65
9:15–28 66
9:16 65
9:16–17 66
9:18–22 65–66
9:21 148
9:23–28 66
9:24–28 61
10. 50, 66
10:1 70
10:1–4 66
10:1–18 . . . . 55, 66
10:5–7 66
10:5–10 66
10:9b–10 66
10:11 . . . . 113, 148
10:11–14 66
10:12b–13 66
10:14 66
10:15–18 66
10:16–17 67
10:19 . . . . 67, 104
10:19–20 63
10:19–25 67
10:20 67
10:21 . . . . 67, 70
10:22 67
10:25 . . . . 44, 67
12:12–13 44
13:7 142
13:7, 17, 24. 142
13:10 142
13:15 . . . . 142, 196
13:16 142
13:17 142
13:24 142

James
1:1 220
2:25 171
5:14 . . . . 100, 134

1 Peter
1:1 . . . . 97, 190
1:2 117
1:18–19 43
2:2 190
2:4 190
2:5 . . . . xx, 190–192, 196–197
2:7 192
2:7–8 192
2:9 . . . . xx, 190, 192–193, 196
2:25 . . . . 136, 179
3:18 43
5 179
5:1 . . . . 134, 136, 178
5:1–2 136
5:2 136
5:4 179

3 John
1. 171
9. 171
9–10. 171

Jude
1. 220

Revelation
1–3. 171
1–5. . . . . 171n64
1:4–6 . . . . xx, 190, 192
1:4b–6 196
1:5–6 196
1:6 193
1:9 194
1:9–10 170
1:20 170

2:1, 8, 12, 18 170

2:7, 11, 17, 29. 170

3:1, 7, 14 170

3:6, 13, 22 170

4:4 . . . . 135n14

5 194

5:5 . . . . 30, 194

5:9–10 . . . . xx, 190, 194, 196

5:10 194

20 194–195

20:2 194

20:4 194–195

20:5–6 195

20:6 . . . . xx, 190, 194–196

20:14 195

21:8 195

21:14 89

22:16 30